AN OUTLINE OF

AN OUTLINE OF
PLANNING LAW

BY

SIR DESMOND |HEAP, LL.M.

Comptroller and City Solicitor to the Corporation of London
President of the Law Society
Member of the Council of the Royal Institution of Chartered Surveyors
Member of the Council and Past President of the Royal Town Planning Institute
General Editor: Encyclopedia of Planning Law and Practice
General Editor: Encyclopedia of Betterment Levy and Land Commission
Member: Editorial Board of Journal of Planning and Environment Law

SIXTH EDITION

LONDON
SWEET & MAXWELL
1973

First Edition ..	..	..	1949
Second Edition	..	..	1955
Third Edition ..	..	..	1960
Fourth Edition	..	..	1963
Fifth Edition ..	..	..	1969
Second Impression	..	..	1971
Sixth Edition ..	..	..	1973

*Published in 1973 by
Sweet and Maxwell Limited of
11 New Fetter Lane, London and
printed in Great Britain by The
Eastern Press Limited of London
and Reading*

SBN   Hardback   17030 1
           Paperback   17040 9

PREFACE

Town Planning Law has been consolidated again—this time by the Town and Country Planning Act 1971 which functions as from April 1,1972, except section 21 and Part II of the Act (relating to the " new-style " development plans) which particular provisions are being brought into effect progressively, in different parts of the country, by successive commencement orders made by the Secretary of State.

But the law never stands still. Hardly was consolidation completed than a Bill amending the 1971 Act was introduced. It became, in due course, the Town and Country Planning (Amendment) Act 1972. It functions as from July 27, 1972 (except for sections 8 and 9 which function from August 27, 1972) and it makes important amendments to the 1971 Act particularly with respect to the conduct of public inquiries held in connection with the bringing into operation of the " new-style " development plans prepared under Part II of the 1971 Act.

This sixth edition of this *Outline* has been prepared in order to embrace the contents of the consolidating Act of 1971 (the new principal Act) *as it now stands*, that is to say, as recently amended by the short, but important, planning Act of 1972.

It is specially to be mentioned that as from April 1, 1974, important amendments to the principal Act of 1971 will be effected by the coming into operation on that day of the Local Government Act 1972. Those provisions of the Local Government Act 1972 which will affect the town planning scene as from April 1, 1974, are set out in full in the Appendix to this book. They should be read and noted with care by anyone seeking to rely on the contents of this book *after April* 1, 1974. Put very briefly, the changes will affect the naming of those local government authorities *outside Greater London* which will be local planning authorities—they will be called " county planning authorities " and " district planning authorities " respectively—and will also affect the discharge of planning functions under sections 6 to 10 of the 1971 Act (relating to structure plans) and under section 11 of the 1971 Act (relating to local plans).

There is never a good (or optimum) time for publishing a law book; whatever date is chosen it is bound to cause problems.

Accordingly, in the case of this Sixth Edition of this book, the reader's attention is most especially drawn to the fact that the Town and Country Planning General Development Order 1963 (together with its amendments of 1964, 1965, 1967, 1968 and 1969 respectively) is entirely repealed as from March 1, 1973 and replaced by the Town and Country Planning General Development Order 1973. This latter order consolidates, with amendments, the 1963 Order and its five subsequent amending orders. An explanatory note on the 1973 order is set out as an Addendum at page xliii and the new order must be borne in mind whenever in the book reference is made (as it is, very particularly, in Chapter 8) to the 1963 Order.

This edition does not purport to take any note of the Land Compensation Bill introduced into Parliament on November 9, 1972, but not yet enacted into law. Government " thinking " behind the Bill is well set out in the White Paper dated October 1972 entitled *Development and Compensation—Putting People First* (Cmnd. 5124). The Bill confers a new right to compensation for injurous affection to land caused, in certain circumstances, by the use of highways, aerodromes and other public works; provides for the acquisition of land and the execution of works by public authorities in order to mitigate the adverse effect of certain public works on their surroundings; makes provision for the benefit of persons displaced from land by public authorities; and amends the law relating to compulsory purchase of land and to planning blight. These are all intricate and important matters but they are not yet " the law." Accordingly, they must stand over—assuming they become " the law "—for treatment in some later edition of this book.

*   *   *   *

All previous editions of this *Outline* have emanated from Guildhall in the City of London. By way of a change, this edition comes from the President's Room (of which the author is, for the nonce, the incumbent) at the Law Society's Hall in London, West Central 2.

D. H.

THE PRESIDENT'S ROOM,
   THE LAW SOCIETY'S HALL,
      CHANCERY LANE,
         LONDON, W.C.2.
            March 1, 1973.

EXTRACT FROM
THE PREFACE TO THE FIRST EDITION 1949

THE Town and Country Planning Act, 1947, came into full force
and effect on July 1, 1948. Notwithstanding its monumental proportions—it comprises 120 sections and 11 Schedules and fills 206
pages of a King's Printer's copy—it tells but half the story of the
new planning law. The other half of that law is to be found in
the rules, regulations, orders and directions made by the Minister
of Town and Country Planning under powers conferred on him
by the Act itself. At the time of this writing the Minister has
exercised these powers of making subordinate legislation thirty-one
times, with the result that the regulations made under the Act now
run to some 170 closely printed pages.

A true understanding of the new planning law involves the
inter-reading of the Act with its multiplying brood of regulations,
and the object of this book is to draw together the various sections
of the Act with their relevant regulations and thereby provide a
concise and reasonably complete statement of the new planning
law in as readable a form as possible and freed from entanglement
with the actual sections of the Act—sections whose length and
terminological complexity may well dismay and abash the new-
comer to planning law.

It is felt that there is need at present for some such statement
of the new planning law as is referred to in the previous paragraph—some statement embracing at once both Act and regulations—for the simple reason that however carefully people may
have avoided the impact of planning law in the past, they are going
to find it increasingly difficult to do so in the future and, accordingly, ought to be warned and advised in advance about that with
which, sooner or later (and, it would now appear, sooner rather
than later), they are going to collide.

Notwithstanding the revolutionary nature and far-reaching
effects of the new planning law, ignorance of its provisions remains
widespread, and a rude awakening is undoubtedly in store for many
who today have not yet realised the short-term, let alone the long-
term, implications of the new Act.

*   *   *   *   *   *

vii

That there is need for the Act is unquestionable. To get the best possible use out of such land as is available in Great Britain to the very large number of people who have to dwell upon it (and England, it may be remembered, is the most densely populated country in the world) it is clearly necessary that land must not be wantonly nor irresponsibly used. It must, on the contrary, be used carefully; it must, in short, be subjected to planned control. This necessary control is provided by the new planning law, but the proof of the pudding is in the eating and the success of this enactment will depend largely upon the manner of its administration, which will be a matter requiring tact, patience and understanding of a high order. Anything in the nature of a dictatorial attitude towards the initiative and enterprise of any enthusiastic developer will have to be avoided at all costs because if this Act needs a large number of planners to make it work (and it does) it certainly needs a very much larger number of enthusiastic developers to make it the success which it ought to be.

       *   *   *   *   *   *

Planning at its best must, if it is to be effective, come very near to being a sort of benevolent despotism. At its worst it could, of course, develop into an objectionable dictatorship. The most energetic enthusiasts of the new Act are not likely to agree with this view, but whatever may be one's attitude to the disposition of planning powers under the new Act, it is indisputable that one of its outstanding features (as is shown by the arrangements made for the progressive reduction in the number of local planning authorities) is its concentration of an increasing number of powers in a decreasing number of persons. The ultimate implications of a policy of that kind are manifestly important. If the enhanced planning powers which the new Act creates ever got into unenlightened hands an unsatisfactory state of affairs would arise in which the private individual would find himself more planned against than planning. Planning should at all times be simply a means to an end and it is to be hoped that every care will be taken to ensure that the complex administrative machinery of the new Act is not worked in such a fashion that planning becomes not merely a means to an end but an end in itself.

With an imperfect understanding of what is happening the little man of this country is now setting out on a planning expedition into what are to him uncharted seas. For the welfare of his ship as a whole he has surrendered a great deal of his own individual freedom. His voyage is one of discovery and he will want to discover something really worth while (and this is where the enthusiastic developer joins hands with the administrative planner) or he will be profoundly dissatisfied. He is going to weigh critically the gains with the losses, and the gains must be substantial or the voyage will not be worth the price of the ticket.

*   *   *   *   *   *

After nearly forty years of growth and development the law of town and country planning has now become a highly specialised branch of the statute law of this country. The law, of course, has many highly specialised branches, but it is doubtful if any of them operates in so widespread a fashion as does planning law which, accordingly, is invested with a general importance quite beyond that normally accorded to a specialised subject. The fact is that planning law now has its bearing, and (as time progresses and development plans come into operation) will increasingly make its mark upon the lives and property of everyone; the great, the small; the planners and the planned; the landlord and the tenant; the vendor, the purchaser and the developer of land; the local authority and the private individual—in short, upon everyone and everybody at almost every turn everywhere.

Ultimately the only plan which people will enjoy is the one which, in effect, they make themselves, and that is why it is of first-rate importance that the private individual should understand as much as possible about the new planning law and its implications. It is hoped that this *Outline* may, in some degree, contribute to this end.

DESMOND HEAP.

GUILDHALL, E.C.2.
February 23, 1949.

CONTENTS

xi

*The General Development Order 1963, referred to in this chapter, is revoked and replaced as from March 1, 1973 by the Town and Country Planning General Development Order 1973 (S.I. 1973 No. 31). An explanatory note is set out as an Addendum at page xliii.

TABLE OF STATUTES

TABLE OF STATUTORY INSTRUMENTS

TABLE OF CASES

ADDENDUM

The Town and Country Planning General Development Order 1973

Coming into operation March 1, 1973

This Order consolidates, with amendments, the Town and Country Planning General Development Order 1963 and five subsequent amending orders, made under enactments now consolidated in the Town and Country Planning Act 1971.

The Order is the general Order, applicable to all land in England and Wales, providing for the grant of permission for the development of land under Part III of the Act of 1971, pursuant to the provisions of section 24 of the Act. Schedule 1 to the Order sets out in detail the classes of development for which the permission is granted by the Order itself (subject to articles 3 and 4 of the Order). Provision is made for the manner in which applications for planning permission (and certain other applications under Part III of the Act of 1971) are made and dealt with (articles 5 to 9), and for the procedure in relation to the making of appeals to the Secretary of State (article 16). Articles 10 to 14 provide for consultations and directions affecting the grant of planning permission; article 17 deals with planning registers, and article 18 with established use certificates.

The principal amendments made by this Order to the previous Order as amended, are as follows:

(*a*) article 4 is amended to provide for certain kinds of directions made by local planning authorities under that article to come into operation without the necessity for the approval of the Secretary of State to be obtained;

(*b*) in relation to outline planning permissions (article 5) the landscaping of the site has been added to the reserved matters in respect of which the subsequent approval of the local planning authority may be required by condition;

(*c*) the special period of 3 months within which the local planning authority are to give notice of their decision on an application affecting a trunk road has been abolished (article 5(3));

(*d*) the classes of development designated by article 8 for the purposes of section 26 of the Act (publication of notices of applications) have been extended and amended;

(*e*) the provisions of article 9 of the 1963 Order relating to development affecting trunk roads have been revised in what is now article 11 both to take account of the wider responsibilities of the Secretary of State, and to apply to the different kinds of highway likely to be affected;

(*f*) in article 13 (formerly article 11) the requirement to consult the Minister of Agriculture, Fisheries and Food has been dispensed with and a requirement to consult river authorities on certain applications has been added;

(*g*) the layout of Schedule 1 has been re-arranged so as to include in Column (1) a number of limitations on the permissions granted which were previously set out in Column (2). The Standard Conditions (formerly Part II of Schedule 1) have been removed, and their place has been taken by a general limitation which now appears as article 3(3).

(*h*) Class I of Schedule 1 is amended to grant permission additionally for porches, hardstandings, and oil tanks; and Class II permits the formation, laying out and construction of certain accesses.

(*i*) Class IV.1 (temporary buildings and plant) is amended to cover the situation where the main operations do not require planning permission *e.g.* they are being carried out by or on behalf of the Crown.

(*j*) Class IV.2. is amended to make it clear that permission for temporary uses is limited to a total of 28 days in the year for all purposes cumulatively, and does not allow 28 days each for a number of different uses. Motor car and motor-cycle racing and the holding of markets are each limited to a maximum of 14 days;

(*k*) in Class XII, XIX (formerly XVIII) and XX (formerly XIX) a provision that in certain cases detailed plans and specifications must be approved before the permission is exercisable, is substituted for the former requirement of a separate application for planning permission;

(*l*) the permissions for certain developments by drainage boards and river authorities have been placed in separate classes and the extent of the permission for river authorities has been enlarged (Class XVI);

(*m*) a number of amendments have been made to the Class relating to statutory undertakers (formerly XVII now XVIII), and a section granting permission for certain developments by the Post Office has been added;

(*n*) several of the forms prescribed in Schedules 2 to 6 have been amended in detail.

CHAPTER 1

HISTORICAL OUTLINE

1. The Public Health Code—1848 to 1972

THERE are three clear-cut yet interrelated codes of legislation on the Statute Book and these are (to quote them in chronological order of enactment) the public health code, the housing code and the town planning code. It is impossible to consider in detail any one of these codes without having at least a passing knowledge of the other two and, accordingly, in the historical outline given in this chapter reference is made to all of them. Each in its particular sphere is important, but there can be no doubt that the most important, the most comprehensive and the most far-reaching of all three is, since the passing of the Town and Country Planning Act 1947, the planning code. Indeed, public health and housing, though they still retain their separate legislative codes, are but two of the many facets of town planning, and the town planning code is, theoretically, large enough to embrace the other two.

The Industrial Revolution in England, the invention of machinery and the introduction of the factory system into methods of manufacture brought about a general exodus from the country into the town. The rural areas became more and more sparsely populated as the towns, or urban areas, filled to overflowing with the great influx of people seeking work in the new manufacturing centres. Congestion and overcrowding in the towns were rampant, and cheap, insanitary dwellings were hurriedly erected, sometimes in the shadow of the factories themselves, in an effort to provide shelter for all. The erection of the new buildings was not subjected to supervision or control by local authorities, for such things as building by-laws did not exist, and the new dwellings in consequence were built in close and unregulated proximity with little or no regard to the requirements of proper ventilation and sanitation.

This form of development with all its natural and deplorable consequences to the health of the public was allowed to continue for the most part unchecked until Parliament intervened with its first general enactment dealing with the subject of public health, the Public Health Act 1848. Such Acts as the Towns Improvement

1

Clauses Act, the Town Police Clauses Act, and the Waterworks, Gasworks, Cemeteries and Markets and Fairs Clauses Acts had been passed by Parliament in the previous year, 1847, with the object of bringing about developments and improvements in connection with the particular matters to which each of the Acts referred. But these Acts were not of general application. They formed ready-made codes of legislation lying dormant until incorporated by reference into local Acts of Parliament obtained as a result of local initiative, after which they came into operation within the particular area covered by the local Act.

The Public Health Act 1848, however, was the first of a series of general Acts dealing with the public health which culminated in that monumental enactment, the Public Health Act 1875, which repealed and consolidated former enactments on the subject and embodied further legislation for the protection and improvement of the public health. By-laws with respect to new streets and buildings could be made by local authorities and control could thereby be obtained over the erection of *future* buildings and the laying out of *future* streets. The powers conferred on local authorities with reference to sanitary matters, the making up of private streets, the construction of new buildings, infectious diseases, nuisances and other matters directly connected with the public health by the 1875 Act have since been augmented by the provisions of further Public Health Acts (largely adoptive) passed in 1890, 1907 and 1925. The Public Health Act 1936 is largely a consolidating enactment repealing and re-enacting most (but not all) of the earlier statutes dealing with the subject and is now the principal Act on this subject. The Act is amplified and amended by the Public Health Act 1961, the Health Services and Public Health Act 1968 and the Public Health (Recurring Nuisances) Act 1969.

The Public Health Acts could prevent a repetition of the building horrors which followed the rush to the towns during the Industrial Revolution, but they did not even pretend to deal with the problem of removing the slums which developed in the wake of that upheaval. Moreover, it was characteristic of public health law to cater for the particular and not the general; that is to say, each man's plot of land was regarded as an isolated entity entirely shut off from its neighbours and having no connection with them whatsoever. A man could develop his own plot in accordance, of course, with the requirements of local building by-laws, but otherwise in a fashion which paid not the slightest regard to the sort of development which was taking place, or which was likely to take place, on adjoining or neighbouring land. One could not be prevented from erecting dwelling-houses in unhealthy industrial districts and it was possible for industrial buildings to intrude upon the quietude of residential areas. This sort of thing was beyond the scope of the Public Health Acts and was left, as were the slums of the post-Industrial Revolution period, to be dealt with by a different type of legislation.

2. The Housing Code—1890 to 1972

There had been earlier statutes such as the Artisans' and Labourers' Dwellings Act 1868 and the Artisans' and Labourers' Dwellings Improvements Acts 1875 and 1879, dealing with housing accommodation, but the first real assault on the slums was made by the Housing of the Working Classes Act 1890, an Act which marks the first important stage in the new type of legislation known as housing law, and passed with a view to remedying the deficiencies of public health law regarding the housing of the working classes.

The Act of 1890 made provision for the removal of insanitary dwellings and for the supply of new houses for the working classes and began a series of enactments on the subject of housing which culminated in the Housing Act 1925, which repealed and replaced the 1890 Act as the principal Act dealing with the law of housing.

The Housing Act 1925 was amended several times before yielding place, in 1936, to a further consolidating measure, the Housing Act 1936, which thereupon became the principal Act on the subject. This Act was, in its turn and after much amendment between 1936 and 1956, during which all references to " the working classes " were eliminated from the legislation, repealed (with the exception of certain financial and ancillary provisions) and replaced by a new consolidating measure, namely, the Housing Act 1957.

Financial matters relating to housing have themselves since been consolidated and are now dealt with in the Housing (Financial Provisions) Act 1958 and the House Purchase and Housing Act 1959.

The Housing Act 1957 and the Housing (Financial Provisions) Act 1958 have been amended by the Housing (Underground Rooms) Act 1959, the Housing Act 1961, the Housing Act 1964, the Housing (Slum Clearance Compensation) Act 1965, the Housing Subsidies

Act 1967, the Housing Act 1969, the Housing Act 1971 and the Housing Finance Act 1972, all of which may be cited together as the Housing Acts 1957 to 1972 (1972 Act, s. 108 (2)). Notwithstanding all the foregoing statutory additions and amendments, the Housing Act 1957 remains the principal Act on housing. It is not limited in its scope to any particular class of persons or income groups but is of general application to all sorts of persons. Briefly its main purposes may be said to be seven in number, that is to say:

(1) to establish certain local authorities as housing authorities under the Act (Part I of the Act);

(2) to provide for the inspection and repair of individual insanitary houses (Part II of the Act);

(3) to provide for the removal or closure of unfit houses incapable of being made fit at reasonable expense (Part II of the Act);

(4) to provide for the general clearance of areas of unfit houses—slum clearance (Part III of the Act);

(5) to secure the abatement of overcrowded housing conditions (Part IV of the Act);

(6) to provide new housing accommodation for all sorts and classes of people (Part V of the Act); and

(7) to legislate for the expenses of, and borrowing by, local authorities in connection with the discharge of their duties under the Act (Part VI of the Act).

3. The Town Planning Code—1909 to 1972

If public health law and also, to a more limited extent, housing law were the product of the nineteenth century, town planning law is the creature of the twentieth. The Housing Acts, remedying one defect of the Public Health Acts, might deal with the slums and with the provision of new dwellings, but there was still (to put the matter quite shortly) the problem of the dwelling-house built in the shadow of the factory and of the factory erected in the midst of the garden suburb. Housing law did not cater for them any more than did public health law, but it was felt that the matter was associated more with the subject of housing than with that of public health, and accordingly in 1909 it was housing law which introduced town planning law into the parliamentary arena in the Housing, Town Planning, etc., Act of that year, Part I of which dealt with the " Housing of the Working Classes " and Part II with " Town Planning."

The Housing, Town Planning, etc., Act 1909

The Act of 1909 is, in fact, the first enactment in Great Britain to deal with the subject of town planning. By section 54 of the Act local authorities were empowered to make a " town planning scheme . . . as respects any land which is in course of development or appears likely to be used for building purposes, with the general object of securing proper sanitary conditions, amenity and convenience in connection with the laying out and use of the land and of any neighbouring lands."

Here at last was an opportunity of controlling not merely the construction of individual buildings (that was possible under the Public Health Acts) but of building development *as a whole*, regarding the land of individual owners not as so many isolated plots but as parts of a greater whole and providing for the development of each plot not only in accordance with the requirements of local building by-laws but, in the words of section 54, with due regard to " amenity and convenience in connection with the laying out and use of the land and of any neighbouring lands." Thus residential districts could be safeguarded against the undesirable intrusion of industrial buildings (even though they *did* comply in all respects with the local building by-laws), and industrial areas could be set apart for the purpose of industrial development only.

These are some of the things which could be achieved by a local authority through the medium of a town planning scheme made under the 1909 Act. It was necessary for a local authority desirous of making a scheme first to obtain the approval of the Local Government Board to such course (1909 Act, s. 54 (2)), and the scheme itself, when made by the local authority, could not take effect until approved by the Board, which approval could not be given in certain circumstances until the scheme had been laid before Parliament (1909 Act, s. 54 (4)).

The Housing, Town Planning, etc., Act 1919

The planning machinery created by the Act of 1909 proved to be cumbersome and difficult of operation, and improvements which it was hoped would facilitate the making of schemes were sought to be provided ten years later by the Housing, Town

Planning, etc., Act 1919, whereby the necessity of first obtaining
the consent of the Local Government Board to the making of a
scheme was in most cases removed (1919 Act, s. 42), as was also
removed the necessity of laying schemes before Parliament (1919
Act, s. 44). Henceforth schemes were to come into force immediately upon being approved by the Board under section 54 (4) of
the 1909 Act.

Section 45 of the 1919 Act first introduced the subject of
interim development whereby, during the preparation of a scheme,
development of land might continue and the developer yet remain
certain (assuming he followed the instructions of section 45) of
obtaining compensation in respect of his development if it was
later injuriously affected by the making of the scheme.

Section 46 of the 1919 Act attempted to stimulate the making
of schemes by rendering it obligatory for certain local authorities
with a population of 20,000 to prepare and submit planning schemes
for approval within a specified period, and by section 47 it was open
to the Local Government Board to *require* a local authority to
prepare a scheme if satisfied that in the circumstances a scheme
ought to be made. Voluntary planning was thus replaced in
certain cases by compulsory planning, and the first hint of regional
planning appeared in a provision in section 42 to the effect that
two or more authorities might agree to act together in the making
of a town planning scheme and appoint a joint committee for that
purpose.

The Ministry of Health Act 1919

In 1919 the Local Government Board was succeeded by the
Ministry of Health established under the provisions of the Ministry
of Health Act 1919 and all town planning matters which previously were referred by local authorities to the Local Government
Board came under the control of the Ministry of Health, which
remained the central authority for all matters appertaining to town
planning until the establishment in 1943 of the Ministry of Town
and Country Planning.

The Housing, etc., Act 1923

By the Housing, etc., Act 1923, Part II of which dealt with
town planning, further slight amendments were made in planning
law, the most important of which was the power given (1923 Act,

s. 20) to an authority responsible for the administration of a town planning scheme to withdraw or modify any provisions in the scheme which had given rise to an award of compensation in respect of injurious affection being made against the authority.

Until 1925 housing and town planning had gone hand in hand onto the Statute Book, but each of the subjects had assumed such large proportions and importance in 1925 that, when the law on the two matters was consolidated, a divorce was effected, housing being diverted into the Housing Act 1925 and town planning into the Town Planning Act 1925.

The Town Planning Act 1925

The 1925 Act consolidated the former planning enactments without introducing any remarkable new features, but further provisions of importance were enacted in the Local Government Act 1929.

The Local Government Act 1929

County councils had not so far been able to take any active part in the preparation of schemes except in a case where under section 47 (3) of the 1919 Act the Local Government Board empowered a county council to act in place of a county district council which had failed to prepare a town planning scheme on being ordered so to do by the Local Government Board. But by the Local Government Act 1929, power was first given to county councils (1929 Act, s. 40) to act jointly with other local authorities in the preparation of planning schemes and (1929 Act, s. 42) to play the part of an authority responsible for enforcing and carrying into effect the provision of a scheme. Moreover county district councils were entitled to relinquish to a county council their planning powers and functions under the 1925 Act (1929 Act, s. 43).

Town and Country Planning Act 1932

Such was the state of affairs when the Town and Country Planning Act 1932 was passed. This Act repealed the whole of the former enactments dealing with town planning (including those sections of the Local Government Act 1929 previously mentioned) and re-enacted the law in consolidated form and with many important changes. It came into force on April 1, 1933.

The most remarkable feature of the 1932 Act was that it permitted the town planning of built-up areas and also of land not likely to be developed at all, whereas only unbuilt land actually being, or likely to be, developed was formerly within the scope of the Town Planning Acts. This was a sweeping extension of the town planning powers of local authorities. The 1932 Act reintroduced the necessity, abolished in 1919, of obtaining the consent of the Minister of Health (formerly the Local Government Board) to the making of a planning scheme, and once more schemes had to be laid before Parliament before they could come into operation. The statutory obligation imposed on certain local authorities by the 1919 Act of preparing planning schemes within a limited period was repealed.

The 1932 Act secured control of development through the medium of town planning schemes (or planning schemes as they came to be called after 1932) made by local authorities and confirmed by the Minister of Health. When in operation the letter of a planning scheme was binding equally upon the authority who made it and upon those who sought to undertake development within the area to which it related. A planning scheme was by nature rigid and if, by effluxion of time, it became out of touch with what were for the time being the best ideas in planning, it could only be amended by some further planning scheme made in accordance with the involved machinery established by the 1932 Act for that purpose.

Prior to the coming into operation of a planning scheme developers could develop under the protection of Interim Development Orders made under the 1932 Act. Interim development control was not, however, enforceable until the Town and Country Planning (Interim Development) Act 1943 came into force but if a developer developed in accordance with interim development control he could claim compensation when the relevant planning scheme ultimately came into operation if it was *then* found that his development contravened any provisions of the scheme and accordingly had to be removed or stopped.

Any person who sustained injurious affection by reason of the coming into operation of a planning scheme could claim compensation therefor from the local authority responsible for carrying out the scheme and, conversely, such authority could claim 75 per cent. of the increase in value (or betterment, as it was popularly called) of property resulting from the provisions of the scheme. In fact few planning schemes ever came into operation at all with the result that, on the one hand, little compensation ever came to be paid by responsible authorities (though the potential liability for it often led them to give decisions based not so much on the dictates of good planning as upon those associated with financial considerations) and, on the other hand, little betterment was ever recovered by them.

The extended scope of the 1932 Act, especially the application of its provisions to built-up areas, was responsible for the increased complexity of many of its sections. It was symbolic of the change which had taken place that the 1932 Act contained fifty-eight sections and six schedules as compared with the twenty-two sections and four schedules of the Town Planning Act 1925. The 1932 Act remained the principal Act relating to planning until the coming into force on July 1, 1948, of the Town and Country Planning Act 1947, which, with its one hundred and twenty sections and eleven schedules, made the 1932 Act a small thing indeed.

The Minister of Town and Country Planning Act 1943

Under the Town and Country Planning Act 1932 the central authority for all planning matters remained the Minister of Health, and throughout the Act of 1932 references to " the Minister " meant the Minister of Health. This continued to be the position until, by virtue of the Minister of Works and Planning Act 1942, the powers and duties of the Minister of Health in connection with planning assigned to him by the Town and Country Planning Act 1932 were, with slight exceptions, transferred to the newly appointed Minister of Works and Planning. This state of affairs was, however, altered by the Minister of Town and Country Planning Act 1943, whereby provision was made for the transfer of the powers and duties exercisable under the Town and Country Planning Act 1932 by the Minister of Works and Planning to the newly established Minister of Town and Country Planning, the Minister of Works and Planning being renamed " the Minister of Works " and the Minister of Works and Planning Act 1942 being retitled " the Minister of Works Act 1942." The central authority for planning matters became the Ministry of Town and Country Planning and references throughout the Town and Country Planning Act 1932 to "the Minister" had to be construed as references to the Minister of Town and Country Planning, except in the amended sections 32 and 51 (3) of the 1932 Act, in each of which "the Minister" remained the Minister of Health.

Thus did planning, after thirty-four years as the slightly irregular offspring of the Ministry of Health, ultimately achieve legitimacy by being graced with a Minister whose interests were not divided but were concerned entirely with matters of town and country planning. This arrangement was, however, short-lived, for in 1951 the style and title of the Minister of Town and Country Planning were changed to the "Minister of Local Government and Planning" by the Transfer of Functions (Minister of Health and Minister of Local Government and Planning) (No. 1) Order 1951,[1] and were later, in the same year, further changed to the "Minister of Housing and Local Government" by the Minister of Local Government and Planning (Change of Style and Title) Order 1951.[2]

The general function of the Minister of Housing and Local Government was set out in section 1 of the Act of 1943 whereby he was charged with the duty of "securing consistency and continuity in the framing and execution of a national policy with respect to the use and development of land throughout England and Wales." In pursuance of this policy the Minister had conferred upon himself by subsequent planning legislation an increasing number of powers until his control over the use of land in town and country is now very strong indeed.

The Town and Country Planning (Interim Development) Act 1943

The first enactment to be steered to the Statute Book by the new Minister was the Town and Country Planning (Interim Development) Act 1943. This Act brought all land in England and Wales not already subject to an operative planning scheme under interim development control and gave, for the first time, power to all interim development authorities to enforce such control.

The Town and Country Planning Act 1944

Notwithstanding its title, the major portion of this Act dealt not so much with planning but with land acquisition and new

---

[1] S.I. 1951 No. 142.
[2] S.I. 1951 No. 1900. See also, at p. 25, the Secretary of State for the Environment Order 1970, S.I. 1970 No. 1681.

powers of acquiring land compulsorily (and, in exceptional cases, very speedily) for a variety of purposes in areas of extensive war damage (blitzed areas) and their associated overspill areas and also in areas of bad layout and obsolete development (blighted areas) and their associated overspill areas.

This Act introduced the important new concept of positive town planning by empowering local planning authorities to undertake themselves (subject to certain restrictions) the actual development of their own areas. It also introduced the " 1939 standard " for compensation payable on the compulsory purchase of land, a standard later abolished by the Town and Country Planning Act 1947 and replaced by the principle of compensation based on the value of land for its existing use only. This latter principle, after modification under the Town and Country Planning Act 1954, was itself abolished under the Town and Country Planning Act 1959 and replaced (by provisions now to be found in the Land Compensation Act 1961) by the market value principle of compensation payable on the compulsory purchase of land.[3]

The Town and Country Planning Act 1947

The 1947 Act made an entirely new beginning by repealing all previous town planning legislation (re-enacting, however, in its own Eleventh Schedule some important provisions of the 1944 Act) and enacting principles entirely new to planning law. It was, on enactment, the principal Act relating to the control of land use in England and Wales.

It came into force on " the appointed day " which was July 1, 1948 (Town and Country Planning Act 1947 (Appointed Day) Order 1948).[4] It was amended by four subsequent Acts relating to town planning passed, respectively, in 1951, 1953, 1954 and 1959, and also by the Land Compensation Act 1961 on the particular matter of compensation payable on the compulsory purchase of land.

The 1947 Act and its four town planning amending enactments were repealed and such of their provisions as had not become spent by lapse of time were consolidated in the Town and Country Planning Act 1962 which came into operation on " the commencement date," April 1, 1963 (1962 Act, s. 225 (1)). The 1962 Act

[3] See Chap. 19.
[4] S.I. 1948 No. 213.

thus became the principal Act relating to town and country planning
in England and Wales until the further consolidating Act of 1971
(as to which more is said later in this Chapter) but it is the object of
this historical review of town planning legislation, before reaching
the 1962 Act, to trace, briefly, through the town planning Acts of
1951, 1953, 1954 and 1959, the development of town planning law
from the principal Act of 1947 to its replacement by the principal
Act of 1962.

It is impossible to exaggerate the importance of July 1, 1948,
from the point of view of the local planning authority, the landowner or the building developer, for the 1947 Act (which, as stated,
came into effect on that date) contained some of the most drastic
and far-reaching provisions ever enacted affecting the ownership of
land (which for this purpose includes buildings) and the liberty of
an owner to develop and use his land as he thinks fit.   Indeed, after
July 1, 1948, ownership of land, generally speaking, carries with it
nothing more than the bare right to go on using it for its existing
purposes.   The owner has no *right* to develop it, that is to say, he
has no *right* to build upon it and no *right* even to change its use.
Until the 1947 Act was amended by the Town and Country Planning
Act 1954 a landowner selling his land could expect to obtain (in
theory, at least) only its existing use value, because whatever
development value the land had was expropriated by the state under
the 1947 Act.   The 1947 Act did not nationalise the land; what it
did do was to nationalise the development value in land—a state of
affairs which was reversed by the 1954 Act under which development
value in land was returned to the landowner though, as will be seen
later,[5] it is only development value which had accrued to land before
January 7, 1947, which is compensated under the 1954 Act on the
imposition of planning restrictions or on the compulsory purchase
of land under a notice to treat served before October 30, 1958.

The objects of the 1947 Act may be grouped under seven headings
and summarised as follows:
  (1) to replace the former system of planning control through
      the medium of rigid planning schemes by a new system of
      control through the medium of flexible development plans
      prepared by a greatly reduced number of planning authorities
      and subjected to constant review (Part II of the Act) [6];

[5] See Chaps. 16 and 19.
[6] See Chap. 3.

(2) to prohibit (with exceptions) the carrying out of any kind of development whatsoever, and whether before or after the coming into operation of a development plan, without the consent of a local planning authority (Part III of the Act) [7];

(3) to provide for the levying by a new body, the Central Land Board, of development charges payable (with exceptions) on the carrying out of any kind of development (Part VII of the Act);

(4) to expropriate for the state the development value in all land and, in consequence, to enable landowners to make claims on a £300m. Fund for loss of the development value of their land (Part VI of the Act);

(5) to confer upon local authorities wider powers for undertaking development themselves than they have ever previously held and, as a corollary to this, to confer upon such authorities wider powers for the compulsory acquisition of land (Part IV of the Act) [8];

(6) to provide increased financial assistance to local authorities to enable them to discharge their functions under the Act, including especially the acquisition of land and its development or redevelopment by the local authorities themselves (Part IX of the Act); and

(7) to amend the law relating to compensation for compulsory acquisition of land by abolishing the 1939 standard and substituting compensation based on existing use value only (Part V of the Act).

Objects numbered (3), (4) and (7) above have been substantially amended (as is shown below) by later legislation relating to town and country planning.

The Town and Country Planning (Amendment) Act 1951

This Act corrected certain drafting errors in the 1947 Act (particularly in relation to section 23 thereof) but did not disturb the main principles of the 1947 Act.

The Town and Country Planning Act 1953

The financial portions of the 1947 Act relating respectively to the making of claims on the £300m. Fund for loss of development

---

[7] See Chaps. 7 and 8.
[8] See Chaps. 20 and 18 respectively.

value (Part VI of the 1947 Act) and to the payment of development charge before undertaking development (Part VII of the 1947 Act) were the subject of criticism between 1948 and 1952 with the result that the Government of the day produced the White Paper of November 1952 entitled " Proposals for amending the Financial Provisions of the 1947 Act." [9]

The new financial structure for town planning, as outlined in the White Paper, was brought into being first by the Town and Country Planning Act 1953, under which development charges were abolished for all development commenced on or after November 18, 1952 (the date of the introduction into Parliament of the Bill for the 1953 Act), and the distribution of the £300m. Fund to successful claimants (a distribution due, under the 1947 Act, to take place in 1954) was suspended. The making of payments to those who suffered as a result of planning restrictions or requirements imposed in the public interest was left by the 1953 Act to be dealt with by subsequent legislation which followed in 1954.

The Town and Country Planning Act 1954

This Act, which came into force on January 1, 1955, completed the implementation, begun under the 1953 Act, of the provisions of the White Paper of 1952 by replacing the financial provisions of the 1947 Act with a new code of compensation payments. These payments were limited to the amount of the claims made under the 1947 Act on the £300m. Fund but were to be paid not at one given time (as was the arrangement under the 1947 Act) but only if and when a landowner was prevented from reaping the development value in his land by either—

  (a) suffering the imposition of planning restrictions (subject to exceptions) which prevent or limit the development of his land; or
  (b) having his land compulsorily acquired at its existing use value under a notice to treat served before October 30, 1958. (If the notice to treat is served after October 29, 1958, then the market value provisions of Part I of the 1959 Act will apply.)

The objects of the 1954 Act may be grouped under five headings and summarised as follows:

9 Cmd. 8699.

(1) to provide for the making of payments by the Central Land
    Board in respect of *past* matters and events (other than
    planning decisions) occurring *before* the commencement of
    the Act (Part I of the Act);
(2) to provide for the payment of compensation by the Minister
    of Housing and Local Government in respect of *past*
    planning decisions occurring *before* the commencement of
    the Act (Part V of the Act);
(3) to provide for the payment of compensation by the Minister
    in respect of planning decisions occurring *after* the com-
    mencement of the Act (Part II of the Act) [10];
(4) to provide for the payment of compensation by public and
    local authorities in respect of *any* compulsory purchase of
    land under a notice to treat served *after* the commencement
    of the Act but *before* October 30, 1958 (Part III of the
    Act); and
(5) to provide for the payment of compensation by local plan-
    ning authorities in respect of revocations or modifications
    of planning decisions occurring *after* the commencement of
    the Act (Part IV of the Act).

The Town and Country Planning Act 1959

After the coming into operation of the 1954 Act on January 1,
1955, there were two codes of compensation payable in respect of
the acquisition of land. Development value in land having been,
in effect, returned to the landowner by the operation of the 1953
Act in abolishing development charges, it followed that on a sale
of his land a landowner had, after the commencement of the 1953
Act, clearly the right to sell not only the existing use rights in his
land but also the development rights. Thus on a sale of land by
private treaty the vendor could demand the current market value
of the land. But on a sale of land to a public body purchasing
under compulsory purchase powers the acquiring authority were
precluded by the joint effect of the 1947 Act and the 1954 Act
from paying more than the existing use value plus the 1947 development value of the land—in short, nothing was paid for post-1947
development values.

As time went on the discrepancy between the price payable

[10] See Chap. 16.

under these two codes of compensation—the code applicable on a sale by private treaty and the code applicable on a sale under compulsory purchase powers—tended to get greater. This caused dissatisfaction which was commented upon in the Report of the Committee on Administrative Tribunals and Inquiries 1957 (the Franks Report),[11] which declared (in paragraph 278):

" One final point of great importance needs to be made. The evidence which we have received shows that much of the dissatisfaction with the procedures relating to land arises from the basis of compensation. It is clear that objections to compulsory purchase would be far fewer if compensation were always assessed at not less than market value. It is not part of our terms of reference to consider and make recommendations upon the basis of compensation. But we cannot emphasise too strongly the extent to which these financial considerations affect the matters with which we have to deal. Whatever changes in procedure are made dissatisfaction is, because of this, bound to remain."

Accordingly, the Government of the day decided in 1958 to bring to an end the double code of compensation payable on the acquisition of land and the result was the enactment of the Town and Country Planning Act 1959.

This Act came into force on August 16, 1959. Its objects may be grouped under six heads and summarised as follows:

(1) to provide for market value compensation (in lieu of compensation at the rate, under the 1954 Act, of existing use value plus 1947 development value) in the case of any compulsory purchase of land under a notice to treat served after October 29, 1958 (Part I of the Act) [12];

(2) to give local authorities and other public bodies greater freedom from Ministerial control in the acquisition, appropriation and disposal of land (Part II of the Act);

(3) to provide further opportunity for challenging in the courts certain orders made under the 1947 Act and certain decisions and directions of the Minister of Housing and Local Government under the Town Planning Acts 1947 to 1959 (Part III of the Act);

[11] Cmnd. 218.
[12] See Chap. 19.

(4) to secure greater publicity for planning applications and to ensure that owners and agricultural tenants are informed of any planning applications affecting land owned or occupied by them (Part III of the Act) [13];
(5) to provide for the obligatory purchase by a local authority of an owner-occupier's interest in land detrimentally affected by town planning proposals—planning blight (Part IV of the Act) [14]; and
(6) to give local authorities additional powers to buy land in advance of their requirements (Part V of the Act).[14]

The Town and Country Planning Act 1962

As already mentioned the town planning Acts of 1947, 1951, 1953, 1954 and 1959 were repealed (except as to one or two details of minor importance) and the whole of their provisions (except those already spent) collected into one enactment as the Town and Country Planning Act 1962. The repeal of former legislation was, of course, without prejudice to anything done under it including the making of many orders, rules and regulations.

The Town and Country Planning Act 1962 came into operation on April 1, 1963 (1962 Act, s. 225 (1)) and thereupon became the principal Act relating to town and country planning in England and Wales. It continued so to be (although amended in 1963, 1965, 1966 and, quite substantially, in 1968) until the coming into operation of the further consolidating Act, namely, the Town and Country Planning Act 1971, on April 1, 1972. In the meantime, this historical review continues by making reference to the four amending Acts of 1963, 1965, 1966 and 1968 respectively.

The Town and Country Planning Act 1963

This Act modified the effect of Schedule 3 to the Town and Country Planning Act 1962. That schedule specified eight classes of development which were regarded as falling within the notion of the " existing use " of land.

If planning permission for development falling within Part II of the aforesaid Schedule 3 was refused (or granted subject to conditions) then compensation might have to be paid, under section 123 of the 1962 Act, by the local planning authority.

---

[13] See Chap. 8.   [14] See Chap. 18.

Schedule 3 to the 1962 Act made reference (in paragraphs 3 and 7 respectively) to the enlargement of buildings by not more than one-tenth of their cubic content. It was this matter of enlargement up to one-tenth of cubic content which was modified by the 1963 Act.

The reason for this modification of Schedule 3 to the 1962 Act lay in the acceptance by the Government of the possibility that local planning authorities might be inclined to grant planning permission for office development (in cases where it ought, on planning grounds, to have been refused) owing to their fear of the burden of compensation to which refusal would render them liable. Such fear had been much increased in recent years since " Modern building methods . . . have made it possible for developers to get more floor space within a given building cube. With a 10 per cent. addition to the cube, the increase in floor space may well be of 40 per cent. in some cases." [15] This had produced a corresponding increase in the value of an existing office building where there was the right to rebuild or alter it with a 10 per cent. addition to the cubic content—and that was the measure of compensation for which the local authority might be liable if they refused planning permission for such development.

Accordingly, the Act of 1963 limited the increase by reference to *floor space* as well as *cubic content* and, in the case of buildings erected or rebuilt since July 1, 1948, removed altogether, from development which was to be taken into account, the right to enlarge the building.

The Control of Office and Industrial Development Act 1965

Part I of this Act imposed further restrictions on office development, whereby an office development permit (O.D.P.) from the Board of Trade needed to be obtained (in addition to the customary grant of planning permission from the local planning authority) before development involving the provision of office space of 3,000 square feet or more was commenced. Part I of this Act was to cease to function on August 4, 1972, unless Parliament otherwise determined. The provisions were extended until August 5, 1977, by section 5 of the Town and Country Planning (Amendment) Act 1972.

[15] See Government White Paper, " London-Employment: Housing: Land," Appendix 2, para. 4 (Cmnd. 1952, February 1963).

Part II of this Act enabled the exemption limit for industrial development *not* requiring an industrial development certificate (I.D.C.) under the Town and Country Planning Act 1962 to be varied.

The Industrial Development Act 1966 (Part III)

This Part of this Act enacted further provisions relating to industrial development certificates granted under the Town and Country Planning Act 1962 and extended the meaning of " industrial building " (as used in the 1962 Act) by providing that an industrial development certificate should be required for a building used, or designed for use, for scientific research in the course of trade or business.

The Town and Country Planning Act 1968

The administrative processes associated with town planning control over the development of land originally laid down in the 1947 Act came of age on July 1, 1969. The 1947 Act itself may be said to have been forced upon the country by the imperative need to do something about post-war redevelopment, for the aftermath of the Second World War, 1939 to 1945, had rendered it inescapable that something of this nature *should* be done. The 1947 Act was the answer.

But planning control of land development is a constantly evolving process. No sooner was the consolidating Act of 1962 on the Statute Book than recurrent voices prophesying (or demanding) change became increasingly noisy and the wind of change in the town planning world began to blow with increasing force. In 1965 a Group, specially appointed by the Minister of Housing and Local Government and known as " The Minister's Planning and Advisory Group " (PAG), published their Report on a new styling for Town and Country Planning Control. Thereafter came the White Paper entitled " Town and Country Planning," published in June 1967 (Cmnd. 3333), in which the case for change was advocated in the following terms:

" Britain is fortunate in having had, for many years, the planning system established by the Town and Country Planning Act of 1947 (now consolidated in the Town and Country Planning Act 1962) and the Town and Country Planning

(Scotland) Act of the same year. It was then, thanks to the care and foresight of Lord Silkin, the most advanced and complete system of land use planning in the world. It did much to help in the reconstruction of our war-damaged cities and it protected the countryside from a resumption of the uncontrolled urban sprawl of the thirties. But the time has now come to profit from twenty years' experience and to make the changes required by new circumstances, new policies and new advances in planning techniques.

"Three major defects have now appeared in the present system. *First*, it has become overloaded and subject to delays and cumbersome procedures. *Second*, there has been inadequate participation by the individual citizen in the planning process, and insufficient regard to his interests. *Third*, the system has been better as a negative control on undesirable development than as a positive stimulus to the creation of a good environment.

"These are the main defects which the revision of the system must tackle and the Government propose to remedy them. To combine the safeguarding of individual interests with quicker decisions means streamlining; to emphasise the positive environmental approach requires a concentration of effort on what is vital, and less central control over detail; and, in considering the changes necessary, we must recognise that planning now is operating in a very different context from that immediately after the war.

"When the Acts were being prepared, planning was based on the belief that our population was likely to remain stable and there was little appreciation at that time of the likely growth in the volume of motor traffic—and still less of the impact that this would have on the structure of our towns and on the countryside. Now, the best working assumption on population is that we may have to provide homes for perhaps $17\frac{1}{2}$ million extra people in Great Britain by the end of the century—an increase of nearly a third. As well as building homes for a growing population, we must replace those houses which have come to the end of their useful life. While this is a continuing process, there already exists a need for about three million houses to replace slums and other old houses which are not worth rehabilitating. Not only must the occupiers be given new homes, but the cleared sites should be put to good use.

" Meanwhile, traffic problems will be mounting. The number of motor-cars on the road (already 9½ million in 1966) is expected to exceed 18 million in 1975, with even bigger increases to follow. The revised planning system must be able to cope justly, flexibly and swiftly with all this.

" A new factor has been introduced into planning by the Government's regional policies and by the setting up of the Economic Planning Councils in the regions and in Scotland and Wales. Some of these Councils have been publishing regional studies which should help to shape physical and economic development in the regions. The new planning process must take account of these evolving regional policies.

" The plans drawn up must also be realistic in financial terms and the demands they make on the main capital expenditure programmes must be reasonable in amount and in timing. However admirable they may be, plans which cannot be realised are positively harmful. They stand in the way of more realistic plans, and cause needless worries to people who fear that their interests may be affected.

" People must be able to participate fully in the planning process, and their rights must be safeguarded. Many changes have already been made in planning procedures following the Report (Cmnd. 218) of the Committee on Administrative Tribunals in 1957 (the Franks Committee) and the subsequent setting up of the Council on Tribunals. One of the Government's main aims in the present review of planning legislation is to ensure that there are greater opportunities for the discussion of important changes while they are still at the formative stage and can be influenced by the people whose lives they will affect. They intend also to maintain the rights of objectors— whether they are individuals or organisations—to argue their case at the formal stages.

" The problem is that safeguards built into the planning procedure automatically slow it up. Procedural safeguards, vital though they are, slow the progress towards decision, and there is growing impatience at present delays. These delays may hold up development that matters greatly to the people concerned and may be of economic importance for the country

as a whole. While the preservation of proper rights of representation is of overriding importance, some streamlining of
the system is essential if unfairness to those who wish to
develop is to be avoided.

" There are therefore conflicting but basic requirements to
be reconciled. On the one hand there is the desire for more
consultation and wider association of the public with planning;
on the other, there is the need for quicker decisions. The
Government believe that the way to satisfy these requirements
lies in devolution of responsibility for some planning decisions,
and in simplification of procedures. With these aims in mind,
the Government have decided to introduce legislation to
improve and modernise the town and country planning
system . . . "

The promise of the White Paper was fulfilled in the Town and
Country Planning Act 1968 which was divided into seven Parts as
follows:

Part I provided for the overriding structure plan and the consequential local plan (or plans) which, under the 1968 Act were to
constitute together the development plan (to use the old expression)
for any area. Accordingly, Part II of the Town and Country
Planning Act 1962 (relating to the making, approval and coming
into operation of development plans) was totally repealed and
replaced by Part I of the 1968 Act.

Part II of the Act made alterations in the method of enforcement
of planning control.

Part III of the Act provided for certain planning appeals to the
Minister to be determined, not by the Minister as heretofore, but
by an Inspector appointed by the Minister to hear the appeal and
this was to be the position whether the appeal was by way of a
private hearing or by way of a public local inquiry.

Part IV of the Act dealt with the acquisition and disposal of
land. Its main purpose was to adapt the powers of compulsory
acquisition as contained in the Town and Country Planning Act
1962 to the new development plan provisions which no longer
provided for the designation of land in development plans as being

subject to compulsory acquisition. This Part also contained new provisions relating to planning blight.

Part V of the Act was intended to make more effective provision for the preservation of buildings of special architectural or historic interest.

Part VI of the Act contained a variety of changes in planning law, some of them being quite novel and of great importance.

Part VII of the Act was supplemental to the foregoing six Parts.

The Town and Country Planning Act 1971

As to England and Wales all the provisions of the Town and Country Planning Acts 1962 to 1968 are now repealed (with a few exceptions) and re-enacted in consolidated form in the Town and Country Planning Act 1971 which received the Royal Assent on October 28, 1971. Its provisions came into operation, in general, on April 1, 1972—" the commencement date " (s. 294 (1)) except as to Part II of the Act (relating to the " new-style " development plans comprising structure plans and local plans) and this Part will come into operation from time to time and from place to place as is appointed by order made by the Secretary of State under section 21 of the 1971 Act (*ibid.*). The provisions as to " old-style " development plans, which continue to apply in any area until such time as Part II of the 1971 Act is applied thereto, are relegated to Schedule 5 to the Act. Certain provisions of the 1971 Act are modified by Schedule 6 pending the repeal of Schedule 5 in any area. Schedule 7 to the 1971 Act provides for the transition from Schedule 5 to Part II of the Act.

The Town and Country Planning Act 1971 is now the principal Act relating to town and country planning in England and Wales.

The Town and Country Planning (Amendment) Act 1972

Town planning law never stops! Within days of the consolidating Act of 1971 receiving the Royal Assent on October 28, 1971, a short amending Bill was introduced into Parliament on November 3 1971. This Bill later became the Town and Country Planning (Amendment) Act 1972. This Act inserts certain new provisions into the Act of 1971 and also makes certain amendments to that Act, the purpose of the 1972 Act being:

(1) to provide for joint structure plans;
(2) to amend the procedure relating to structure plan inquiries;
(3) to dispense with structure plans in London boroughs;
(4) to control demolition in conservation areas; and
(5) to extend for a further five years the special powers of control of office development.

The Town and Country Planning Act 1971 (as amended 1972), when conjoined with the host of Orders, rules and regulations made under it (and under earlier legislation now replaced by the 1971 Act), together comprise the town and country planning code under which the use of all land in England and Wales is now controlled.

It may be added that a comparable control is available in Scotland under the Town and Country Planning (Scotland) Act 1972.

CHAPTER 2

CENTRAL AND LOCAL ADMINISTRATION

1. The Secretary of State for the Environment

THE Minister of Housing and Local Government was, under the Town and Country Planning Act 1962, the central authority for the administration of planning throughout England and Wales. The Minister's style and title has had the habit, over the years, of changing [1] but by whatever name he was called he has still remained charged, by virtue of section 1 of the Act which created his office, namely, the Minister of Town and Country Planning Act 1943, " with the duty of securing consistency and continuity in the framing and execution of a national policy with respect to the use and development of land throughout England and Wales." These words are of the greatest importance because they gave the Minister the last word (subject only to Parliament itself) in all matters of policy relating to the control of land use in England and Wales.

Under the Secretary of State for the Environment Order 1970 [2] all the functions and property of the Minister of Housing and Local Government were (inter alia) transferred to the Secretary of State (art. 2) and the Ministry of Housing and Local Government was dissolved (ibid.). Thus, central control over all matters relating to town and country planning in England and Wales is now handled by the Secretary of State who heads the Department of the Environment.

The 1971 Act confers upon the Secretary of State discretionary powers of a wide nature. The exercise of such powers under the Town and Country Planning Act 1947 and the New Towns Act 1946 has been under judicial review in a number of cases to which reference may usefully be made when the exercise of similar powers under the Town and Country Planning Act 1971 is under consideration. The cases are as follows:

A. Decisions under the Town and Country Planning Act 1947:

[1] See p. 9.
[2] S.I. 1970 No. 1681.

25

(1) *Phoenix Assurance Company* v. *Minister of Town and Country Planning* [3];

(2) *Robinson* v. *Minister of Town and Country Planning* [4] (overruling the *Phoenix* decision, *supra*);

B. Decisions under the New Towns Act 1946:

(1) *Fletcher* v. *Minister of Town and Country Planning* [5];

(2) *Rollo* v. *Minister of Town and Country Planning* [6];

(3) *Franklin* v. *Minister of Town and Country Planning.* [7]

Further authority on the attitude of the courts in a case where a Minister of the Crown has power to act (as the Secretary of State frequently has under various sections of the 1971 Act) if he " is satisfied " as to something or other, may be found in *Thorneloe & Clarkson Ltd. and Others* v. *Board of Trade.* [8]

2. Local Planning Authorities and Local Authorities [8a]

The 1971 Act draws a distinction, which needs to be carefully watched, between local planning authorities and local authorities.

Local planning authorities are the councils of counties and of county boroughs (s. 1 (1)) together with the Greater London Council so far as Greater London *as a whole* is concerned (s. 5 and Sched. 3, para. 1).

Local authorities are the councils of counties, of county boroughs, of London boroughs, of non-county boroughs, of urban districts and of rural districts, together with the Greater London Council and the Common Council of the City of London (s. 290 (1)).

The Secretary of State may constitute, as a local planning authority, *a joint planning board* representing a united district comprising two or more counties or county boroughs (s. 1 (2) (3) and Sched. 1). A joint planning board has been constituted for the Lake District by the Lake District Planning Board Order 1951 [9] and for the Peak District by the Peak Park Planning Board Order 1951. [10]

---

[3] [1947] 1 All E.R. 454.
[4] [1947] K.B. 702.
[5] [1947] 2 All E.R. 496.
[6] [1948] 1 All E.R. 13.
[7] [1948] A.C. 87.
[8] [1950] 2 All E.R. 245.
[8a] When the Local Government Act 1972 comes into operation on April 1, 1974, the new local Government areas for England and Wales (outside Greater London) will be called " counties " and " districts " respectively. The contents of this heading must be read, after April 1, 1974, in the light of this important change. See further hereon, the Preface, *ante*. See also p. 29.
[9] 1951 S.I. No. 1491.
[10] S.I. 1951 No. 1533.

It will be seen that whilst every local planning authority is also a local authority under the planning Acts, the converse is not always true. Speaking generally, it may be said that whilst all *local authorities* have powers with respect to the acquisition of land,[11] the actual development of land and the making of land available to other parties for planning purposes,[12] it is only those authorities who are *local planning authorities* who may deal with the making of development plans under Part II of the 1971 Act,[13] with the day to day control of town planning through the grant or refusal of planning permission for development under Parts III and IV of the 1971 Act,[14] and with the enforcement of planning control under Part V of the 1971 Act.[15]

So far, however, as concerns matters under Parts III, IV and V, sections 171 to 173, 175, 177 and 246 of, and Schedules 11 and 14 to, the 1971 Act, the Secretary of State is empowered (s. 3 (1) (2)) by regulations to authorise, or even to require, a local planning authority (other than a county borough) to delegate their powers to any county district council within their area.

Formerly, county councils were authorised under the Town and Country Planning (Authorisation of Delegation) Regulations 1947 [16] to delegate to any county district council within their area any of their functions under Part III of the 1947 Act relating to the control of development and the enforcement of planning control, and many county councils did so in accordance with Schemes of Delegation which varied from place to place. The Town and Country Planning (Authorisation of Delegation) Regulations 1947 were later revoked. They are now replaced by Part II of the Town and Country Planning General Regulations 1969,[17] but this is without prejudice to any delegation agreement made under the earlier regulations (reg. 9). Any such agreement continues in force until superseded by a delegation made under the 1969 Regulations (*ibid.*).

The Town and Country Planning General Regulations 1969, Part II, entitle a council of a county district having a population of sixty thousand or more to claim *as of right* a wide measure of delegation of powers under the 1971 Act (reg. 6). The regulations also authorise the Secretary of State, if satisfied that there are special

[11] See Chap. 18.
[12] See Chap. 20.
[13] See Chaps. 4 and 5.
[14] See Chap. 8.

[15] See Chap. 14.
[16] S.R. & O. 1947 No. 2499.
[17] S.I. 1969 No. 286.

circumstances justifying such a course, to *require* similar delegation to the council of a county district with a population of less than sixty thousand (reg. 6 (6)).

When a joint planning board has been constituted a local planning authority under section 1 of the 1971 Act, the joint planning board may, under the General Regulations 1969, delegate such functions as are referred to in the preceding paragraph to any county district council, county council or county borough council within their united district (s. 3 (3) and reg. 7).

It is to be noted that the functions of a local planning authority relating to the making of development plans (dealt with in Part II of the 1971 Act) cannot be delegated at all.

Within the administrative area of Greater London (defined in section 2 (1) of the London Government Act 1963) there are special and exceptional provisions, contained in section 5 of, and Schedule 3 to, the 1971 Act and in the Town and Country Planning (Local Planning Authorities in Greater London) Regulations 1965 [18] (as slightly amended in 1967), for applying the provisions of the 1971 Act to Greater London and for establishing local planning authorities for that area.

The Greater London Council is the local planning authority for Greater London *as a whole* (s. 5 and Sched. 3, para. 1) with further provision that the council of a London borough (as defined in s. 1 and Sched. I, Part I of the London Government Act 1963) shall also be a local planning authority for certain purposes (s. 5 and Sched. 3, para. 2). The City of London, acting through the Common Council of the City, has the same planning powers as a London borough by virtue of the definition of " London borough " in section 290 (1) of the 1971 Act.

A local planning authority may establish such planning committees as it thinks expedient for the efficient discharge of their functions under the 1971 Act (s. 2 and Sched. 2) whilst a joint advisory committee may, with the approval of the Secretary of State, be established by two or more local planning authorities for the purpose of advising such authorities as to the discharge of their functions under the 1971 Act (*ibid.*). The Secretary of State himself has power, by order, to establish a joint advisory committee if he thinks it expedient to do so but must consult, before doing so, with any affected local planning authority (*ibid.*).

[18] S.I. 1965 No. 679.

Any planning committee of a local planning authority may appoint such sub-committees as they may determine (s. 2 and Sched. 2).

A local planning authority may, if they so wish, delegate certain planning functions to any officer of the authority (s. 4) in which event the decision of the officer becomes automatically the decision of the authority. This matter is more fully discussed in Chapter 8 to which reference should be made.[19]

3. The Lands Tribunal

The Lands Tribunal is an authority which figures so much in connection with the settlement of disputes about compensation for planning restrictions and for the compulsory purchase of land, that it is felt that a brief mention of the Tribunal may usefully be made here although the Tribunal is not, strictly speaking, part or parcel of either the central or local administration of matters relating to town and country planning.

The Lands Tribunal is the creation of the Lands Tribunal Act 1949 and was established on January 1, 1950, as a piece of machinery for settling disputes involving the valuation of interests in land. Prior to 1950 such disputes had been settled by Official Arbitrators appointed under the Acquisition of Land (Assessment of Compensation) Act 1919.

The jurisdiction of the Tribunal is specified in section 1 of the 1949 Act. The Tribunal consists of a president and such number of other members being lawyers or surveyors, as the Lord Chancellor may determine and appoint (1949 Act, s. 2).

The procedure of the Tribunal and the matter of costs and fees associated with it are governed by section 3 of the 1949 Act and the Lands Tribunal Rules 1963.[20] The jurisdiction of the Tribunal may be exercised by any one or more of its members (1949 Act, s. 3). The decision of the Tribunal is final, but there is an appeal by way of case stated on a point of law direct to the Court of Appeal (1949 Act, s. 3 (4) (11) (a)).

---

[19] It is to be noted that, as from April 1, 1974, ss. 1 (1) (2). 3 and 4 of, and Sched. 2 to, the 1971 Act (all referred to above) are repealed or substituted (Local Government Act 1972, ss. 272 (1), 273 (1) (2) (3) and Sched. 30) and replaced, in effect, by by the provisions of ss. 101, 102, 103, 182, 183 of, and Part 1 of Sched. 16 to, the Local Government Act 1972. These provisions of the 1972 Act are presented *in extenso* in the Appendix, *post*.

[20] S.I. 1963 No. 483.

CHAPTER 3

DEVELOPMENT PLANS—MAKING AND PROCEDURE (OLD STYLE)

1. Preparation of Development Plans

THIS Chapter deals with the making and bringing into operation of a development plan in accordance with the procedure first enacted in the 1947 Act and now contained in section 21 (2), Schedule 5, Part I, and Schedule 6 to the 1971 Act. This procedure may conveniently be called the " old style procedure."

Part II of the 1971 Act contains what may be called a " new style procedure " for the making and bringing into operation of a development plan *in those areas to which Part II of the 1971 Act has been made applicable.* This new style procedure, which splits a development plan into two distinct parts, known respectively as the " structure plan " and the " local plan " (or " plans "), is fully discussed in Chapters 4 and 5.

It is necessary, however, to include a discussion of the old style procedure for development plans because this old style will continue to apply (subject to one qualification) in all areas unless and until the new style procedure is brought into operation. Thus the old style procedure and the new style procedure are mutually exclusive procedures. The qualification just mentioned is to be found in the 1971 Act (s. 21 (3) and Sched. 7, para. 1) whereby proposals for alterations or additions to a development plan shall not be made under the old style procedure without the approval of the Secretary of State being first obtained.

* * *

The town planning schemes of former planning enactments were replaced under the 1947 Act by development plans and every local planning authority had to carry out, as soon as may be after July 1, 1948, a survey of their area, and within three years of July 1, 1948, had to prepare a development plan based on the survey.

Schedule 5, paragraph 1 (1), to the 1971 Act, now requires any local planning authority who have not already submitted to the Secretary of State a development plan for their area to do so within such period as the Secretary of State may allow.

A development plan is a plan indicating:

(a) *the manner* in which the land covered by the plan is to be used (whether by the carrying out of development or not) and

(b) *the stages* by which the development is to be carried out (Sched. 5, para. 1 (2)).

A development plan may be prepared for part only of a local planning authority's area (Sched. 5, para. 1 (5)) in anticipation of the making of a development plan for the whole of the area.

Details as to the form and content of development plans are given in Part II of the Town and Country Planning (Development Plans) Regulations 1965 [1] and in Ministry Circular No. 54/59.

Generally speaking, a development plan will consist of a basic map and a written statement (both of which are obligatory in all cases) together with such other map or maps as may be appropriate to the proposals contained in the aforesaid maps and statement. Such other maps may, for example, include a town map, an inset map, a comprehensive development area map, a street authorisation map, and a programme map (showing the stages by which the proposals contained in the written statement should be carried out).

A development plan must include such maps and such descriptive matter as is necessary to illustrate, with such particularity as may be appropriate, whatever proposals it contains for the future development of the land to which it relates (Sched. 5, para. 1 (3)). In particular a development plan may:

(1) *define the sites* of proposed roads, buildings, airfields, parks, pleasure grounds, nature reserves and other open spaces (*ibid.*);

(2) *allocate areas* for agricultural, residential, industrial or other purposes (*ibid.*); and

(3) *define as an area of comprehensive development* any area which should be developed or redeveloped as a whole (Sched. 5, para. (1) (4)).

[1] S.I. 1965 No. 1453.

If a development plan covers land across which is to be constructed a trunk road by virtue of an order of the Secretary of State (under the Highways Act 1959) or on which a new town is to be developed by order of the Secretary of State (under the New Towns Act 1965), the development plan is to have effect as if the provisions of the foregoing orders were included in the development plan itself (Sched. 5, para. 5).

2. Objections to, and Approval of, Development Plans

Before a development plan can come into operation it must be approved under the 1971 Act by the Secretary of State (Sched. 5, para. 2) and details as to the procedure for the submission to, and approval of plans by, the Secretary of State are contained (Sched. 5, para. 6 (2)) in Part III of the Town and Country Planning (Development Plans) Regulations 1965.[2]

Under the foregoing Regulations it is provided, *inter alia*, that notice of the submission of a development plan to the Secretary of State must be given (art. 17) in the *London Gazette* and in each of two successive weeks in at least one local newspaper circulating in the locality in which the land to which the development plan relates is situated (art. 2 (1)). Persons who object to the plan may send their objections in writing to the Secretary of State within whatever period is specified in the advertisement (Sched. 2, Part I). This period may not be less than six weeks from the date of the first local advertisement (*ibid.*) and whilst the Secretary of State must consider all objections duly made he is not obliged to hold any public local inquiry (art. 18). If he dispenses with such an inquiry he must afford a private hearing before one of his inspectors to any person who has made an objection and at any such private hearing the local planning authority is entitled to be heard (*ibid.*).

The Secretary of State may approve the development plan with or without modifications (Sched. 5, para. 2). In doing so he will be acting administratively and not judicially or quasi-judicially and, accordingly, can permit himself, notwithstanding objections which have been duly made to him and duly considered by him, to be influenced by matters of policy. He is expressly authorised (Sched. 5, para. 6 (3)) to hold discussions with the local planning authority or any other authority or person " behind the backs " (as it were)

2 S.I. 1965 No. 1453.

of objectors to the development plan. He may thus do under the 1971 Act what was held to be improper in *Errington* v. *Minister of Health*.[3] Provision is made as to the date of operation (Sched. 5, para. 7) and the right of an aggrieved party to challenge the legal validity of a development plan in the High Court (s. 244, as applied by Sched. 6, para. 3).

3. Review of Development Plans

A development plan *must* be reviewed by the carrying out of a new survey by the local planning authority at least once in every five years after the date of its approval by the Secretary of State (Sched. 5, para. 3 (1)) though it *may* be reviewed at any time (Sched. 5, para. 3 (2)). Thus a development plan never really achieves finality. The plan is under constant review and in this way is the better calculated to represent what, at any given moment, are the latest concepts of good planning.

Whenever a review has taken place the local planning authority must submit to the Secretary of State a report of the new survey together with proposals for such alterations or additions to the development plan as the new survey calls for (Sched. 5, para. 3 (1)).

The procedure which follows upon the review of a development plan is similar to that (described above) which applies on the first making, and submission to the Secretary of State for approval, of a development plan (Sched. 5, para. 6 (2)). Thus the provisions of the Town and Country Planning (Development Plans) Regulations 1965 [4] apply and Ministry Circulars Nos. 9/55, 51/58, 37/60 and 58/65, relating to the review of development plans, may usefully be consulted.

Reviews of development plans tend increasingly to relate to the redevelopment of city or town centres (" urban renewal " as this particular aspect of town planning is called). Thus the matter of comprehensive development proposals (and of drawings, plans, sections and written material to illustrate such proposals) is one which is assuming increasing importance on the occasion of public inquiries held by the Secretary of State in connection with proposals for amendment of development plans. Compulsory purchase of

[3] [1935] 1 K.B. 249.
[4] S.I. 1965 No. 1453.

land is a matter inescapably associated with the problems of urban renewal. In this connection reference can, with advantage, be made to Ministry Circular No. 38/62 and to the first of a series of planning bulletins [5] issued from time to time by the Ministry. This first bulletin—Planning Bulletin No. 1, issued jointly by the Ministry of Housing and Local Government and the Ministry of Transport— is entitled " Town Centres—Approach to Renewal " and includes advice on the techniques of preparing a new kind of map, called a Town Centre Map, which may be used in connection with any development plan review proposals which relate to the regeneration of town centres.

Further bulletins in the series include " 3. Town Centres— Cost and Control of Redevelopment," " 4. Town Centres—Current Practice," " 5. Planning for Daylight and Sunlight," " 7. Parking in Town Centres " and " 8. Settlement in the Countryside."

4. Designation of Land in Development Plans

It will be seen that many things may be provided for in a development plan. One of its most important features, formerly, was the designation of land as being liable to compulsory purchase by local authorities and other public bodies. By virtue, however, of the Town and Country Planning Act 1968 designation of land in a development plan as being subject to compulsory purchase ceased (1968 Act, s. 27 (b)). Any local authority needing land for town planning purposes can now, without any prior designation of the land, resort to the powers of section 112 of the 1971 Act to obtain the land. This is a matter more fully discussed in Chapter 18.

5. Default Powers of the Secretary of State with respect to Development Plans

If a local planning authority fail in their duty under the 1971 Act to prepare and submit to the Secretary of State for approval a development plan, or an amendment to a development plan, the Secretary of State may himself take the requisite action to make the development plan, or, as the case may be, to amend the existing development plan (Sched. 5, para. 4 (1)). Alternatively, the Secretary of State may authorise some neighbouring or other local

[5] Published by H.M.S.O.

planning authority to act in the place of the authority who are in default (Sched. 5, para. 4 (2)). In either case the Secretary of State may recover any expenses incurred by him from the authority in default (Sched. 5, para. 4 (5)). Similarly, a local planning authority acting in the place of an authority who are in default may recover their expenses from the latter authority (Sched. 5, para. 4 (6)).

6. Modification of Provisions in their Application to London

The foregoing provisions of this chapter relating to the preparation and bringing into operation of a development plan (or any amendment thereof) are made applicable to the administrative area of Greater London subject to modifications set out in Part II of Schedule 5 to the 1971 Act, and the Town and Country Planning (Development Plans for Greater London) Regulations 1966.[6]

---

[6] S.I. 1966 No. 48.

CHAPTER 4

DEVELOPMENT PLANS—MAKING AND PROCEDURE
(NEW STYLE)—STRUCTURE PLANS

1. Instituting the Survey

PART II of the Town and Country Planning Act 1971 relates to structure plans and local plans. Part II of the Town and Country Planning Act 1962 will continue to apply in all those areas of England and Wales to which the provisions of Part II of the 1971 Act are not for the time being made applicable. Thus for some time two systems of development plan procedure will be in operation. (On this the transitional provisions relating to development plans set out in Schedule 7 to the 1971 Act should be noted (s. 21 (3)).

Under Part II of the 1971 Act every local planning authority must *institute* a survey of their area (s. 6 (1)) or, maybe, part of their area (s. 6 (5)), if they have not already done so. In so doing, their duty is to examine those matters which may be expected to affect the development of their area or the planning of its development (s. 6 (1)). Such matters must be kept under constant review (*ibid.*).

The five-year obligation under the 1962 Act to *carry out* a re-survey of the local planning authority's area disappears under the 1971 Act. In place of it the authority *may*, if they wish, *institute* a fresh survey of their area at any time and they *must* do this if the Secretary of State so directs them (s. 6 (2)).

It will be noted that the 1971 Act refers to the duty to *institute* a survey as distinct from to *carry out* a survey, the verb " to carry out " being the one used in the 1962 Act. This change is deliberate. The new idea is that it may be helpful for a local planning authority occasionally to employ the services of outside consultants to undertake surveys. Thus, while the local planning authority would be responsible for instituting a survey (*i.e.* for setting one in motion) they would not actually be carrying it out.

In making one of the foregoing surveys what are the particular points to which the local planning authority should give attention? A good deal of instruction on this very important matter is given in

36

the 1971 Act (s. 6 (3)) which provides that the matters to be examined and kept under review by the local planning authority must include the following, namely:

(a) the principal physical and economic characteristics of the area of the authority (including the principal purposes for which land is used) and, so far as they may be expected to affect that area, of any neighbouring areas;

(b) the size, composition and distribution of the population of that area (whether resident or otherwise);

(c) without prejudice to paragraph (a) above, the communications, transport system and traffic of that area and, so far as they may be expected to affect that area, of any neighbouring areas;

(d) any considerations not mentioned in any of the foregoing paragraphs which may be expected to affect any matters so mentioned;

(e) such other matters as may be prescribed or as the Secretary of State may in a particular case direct;

(f) any changes already projected in any of the matters mentioned in any of the foregoing paragraphs and the effect which those changes are likely to have on the development of that area or the planning of such development.

If, in connection with a survey, a local planning authority needs to examine matters relating to the area of another such authority, the local planning authority must do such examination only in consultation with the other authority (s. 6 (4)).

2. Preparing a Structure Plan

Having made a survey of their area, the next duty of the local planning authority is to prepare and send to the Secretary of State a report of such survey together with a structure plan for their area, which plan is submitted to the Secretary of State for his approval (s. 7 (1)). This submission of the structure plan must be done within such period as the Secretary of State may direct in any particular case (*ibid.*). A structure plan may be submitted for a part of the area of a local planning authority (s. 7 (7)).

The expression " structure plan " is not defined in the 1971 Act. The structure plan is, however, a most important instrument because it is from the structure plan that the whole styling of future development control will stem.

The structure plan must be in the form of—

    (a) a *written statement* (s. 7 (3)), and

    (b) must contain, or be accompanied by, such *diagrams, illustrations* and *descriptive matter* as the local planning authority think appropriate for the purpose of explaining or illustrating the proposals in the plan, all such diagrams, illustrations and descriptive matter being treated as part of the plan itself (s. 7 (6)).

That part of the structure plan which forms the aforementioned written statement must do at least three things (s. 7 (3)), that is to say:

    (a) *it must* formulate the local planning authority's policy and general proposals in respect of the development and other use of land in their area (including measures for the improvement of the physical environment and the management of traffic);

    (b) *it must* state the relationship of those proposals to general proposals for the development and other use of land in neighbouring areas which may be expected to affect that area; and

    (c) *it must* contain such other matters as may be prescribed or as the Secretary of State may in any particular case direct.

An expression new to planning enactments since 1968 is the expression " the physical environment " (s. 7 (3) (*a*) above) which is not defined in the 1971 Act. A straightforward meaning of the expression is—the surroundings in which one lives, moves, works and generally has one's being. These surroundings are coming to be regarded as of increasing importance in the last decades of the twentieth century and their improvement is now declared by statute, for the first time, to be something to which planning control *must* give attention. It is perhaps significant that the 1971 Act speaks of " the improvement of the physical environment and the management of traffic " (s. 7 (3) (*a*)) in (as it were) the same breath because the assault on the physical environment by traffic of all kinds is relentless and increasing. Accordingly, with Treasury consent, the Secretary of State may make grants to promote research and education about the planning and design of the physical environment (s. 253).

A joint structure plan may be made by a combination of two or more local planning authorities in respect of their combined area (s. 10A—added by the Town and Country Planning (Amendment) Act 1972, s. 1 (1)).

Provision is made for the withdrawal of a structure plan by the local planning authority after it has been submitted to the Secretary of State for his approval and for the consequences of any such withdrawal (s. 10B—added by the Town and Country Planning (Amendment) Act 1972, s. 2).

It will be seen that the structure plan is very much in the nature of a statement of general policy showing trends and tendencies and illustrating a broad basic pattern for future development. It will comprise two distinct elements, namely, a " written statement " and such " diagrams, illustrations and descriptive matter " as the local planning authority think appropriate. In other words, there will be no *map* (ordnance survey or otherwise) associated with a structure plan.

" A structure plan is almost a misnomer because it is not a plan in the way that people think of a plan, namely, a map. It is a written statement "—Mr. Niall MacDermot, Minister of State, Ministry of Housing and Local Government, *Hansard*, Standing Committee G, February 20, 1968, col. 86.

In preparing their structure plan a local planning authority may well be imbued with high ideals and grand concepts. Nevertheless, with their heads, maybe, well up in the air, the 1971 Act expressly requires them to keep their feet firmly on the ground. The Act requires that both *the policy* and *the general proposals* of the planning authority must:

(a) *be justified by* the survey carried out under section 6 of the Act and by any other information which they may obtain; and

(b) *have regard to* current regional economic planning policies, to the resources likely to be available for the carrying out of the proposals of the structure plan and to such other matters as the Secretary of State may direct shall be taken into account (s. 7 (4)).

Thus, whatever may have been the situation in the past, in the future local planning authorities will find themselves, under the procedures of the 1971 Act, injuncted by Act of Parliament *not* to provide for more town planning control than they can afford.

3. Action Areas

A particularly important aspect (and one about which a good deal is going to be heard in the future) of a local planning authority's general proposals as set out in the structure plan is the requirement (s. 7 (5)) that the structure plan *must* indicate any part of the local planning authority's area which they may have selected for comprehensive treatment in accordance with a local plan (about which see Chap. 5) later to be prepared for that part of the authority's area. An area so indicated in a structure plan is known in the 1971 Act as an " action area " (s. 7 (5)) and the local plan later to be prepared for the action area will be known as an " action area plan," although this latter expression is not itself used in the Act.

The comprehensive treatment to be visited upon an action area will need to be commenced within a period of time to be prescribed by regulations made under the 1971 Act by the Secretary of State in any particular case (s. 7 (5)).   The object of the Act is clearly to provide that action areas shall be those areas where action in the planning field is required *not only on a comprehensive basis but also at an early date.*

As to the period of time to which action areas could relate the Minister of State, Ministry of Housing and Local Government, said on February 20, 1968, during the Committee stage of the Bill for the 1968 Act (*Hansard,* Standing Committee G, col. 80 *et seq.*):

> " With regard to the span of time to which action areas could relate, to be prescribed by the Minister, we have in mind, as a sort of outside limit, a ten-year period.   The period relates to the period from the time when the structure plan is approved, but I think that that would be the outside limit. As I have said, these are meant to be the areas which are envisaged for early treatment, early development, redevelopment and improvement.   Nevertheless, there will be different types of action area plans and they will themselves have to be phased if there are several action areas indicated in one plan.   As we have had occasion to make clear earlier, some action area plans will themselves be very detailed.   Other action area plans will

give general indications of the kind of development that is to take place. That will be so particularly where it is envisaged that the development will be by a private developer and one wants to leave scope for him to put forward his own detailed plans.

" Even when one gets to the stage of publication of the action area plan itself, its precise effect and the degree to which it would indicate to property owners how their property would be affected will vary according to the nature of the action area plan."

As earlier mentioned in this chapter, a structure plan will comprise a written statement together with diagrams, illustrations and descriptive matter; *but it will not contain a map*. How then is an action area to be indicated on a structure plan? What will be the relationship between any such indication and the local plan (the action area plan) later to be prepared by the local planning authority? The Minister of State, during the committee stage of the Bill for the 1968 Act, had the following comments on these two important questions (*Hansard*, Standing Committee G, col. 81 *et seq.*):

" Let me return to the main point, which is the amount of detail which should be given in the structure plan of what is envisaged by way of action in the action area and why we do not want that to be put on an Ordnance Survey map.

" Having regard to some of the things that have been said about the action areas being indicated only in a diagrammatic way, I think that perhaps insufficient regard is being paid to the fact that the structure plan is primarily a written statement, and it will be to the written statement that people will look to find the indication of what is intended in the action area. The structure plan, in the written statement, will discuss and consider the problems which give rise to the need for action and assess the extent of that need and the nature of the development that will be required in order to deal with it. It will indicate the nature of the development, redevelopment or improvement and, as the Bill makes clear, may indicate whether that action should be partly by one method or partly by another and the nature of the treatment to be selected. It would indicate the extent of the effort which is anticipated and foreseen.

It would involve assessment of the costs and a fairly detailed costing of the kind of action that is to take place. The Minister would, of course, be required to be satisfied—we have already discussed this point—that those costings were realistic and that early action on those matters was something that could be anticipated within the levels of anticipated future investment programmes. In this way, as far as the nature of the development is concerned, people will get a fairly good general indication from the written statement of the structure plan.

" But why do we not want the areas defined? There are two reasons. First, if the boundaries of an action area are to be defined precisely in the structure plan and this requires approval by the Minister, it immediately means that the Minister and his staff will get involved again in the kind of detail which we are seeking to avoid. That is the first and basic reason. Secondly, it is, we think, likely, at least in many cases, to intensify rather than reduce the problem of planning blight and it may actually be misleading. It will not be until one gets down to actual detailed planning that one will be able to have any confidence in any boundaries that might have been drawn in the structure plan. If we sought to draw boundaries in the structure plan, it is almost certain that they would have to be amended at later stages of the formulation of those plans and that then people who had thought that they were caught, as it were, might find that they escaped; and people who thought that they would escape might find that they were brought within the area of the redevelopment.

" It would again raise the problem to which I referred earlier. It would mean that people would start raising objection to structure plans not on the basis of the general nature of the proposals and their rightness, their wisdom and their practicality, but would be putting forward objections on the basis of individual property interests, which, again, is something we want to avoid if we are to achieve the division which is implicit in the separation of structure plans and of local plans. . . .

" Those are the reasons which have guided us. I hope that the explanations which I have given may go some way to reassure hon. Members who have thought that the only indication of an action area that will be given on a structure plan will be a star or other symbol on a diagram. It will not. There will be a great deal more by way of explanation in the written statement itself, but it is with the most deliberate intent, for the reasons which I have given, that we have omitted reference to maps in relation to structure plans and suggested instead that they should be illustrated by diagrams or other illustrative or descriptive matter "

4. Approval of Structure Plan by Secretary of State —Procedure

A structure plan having been prepared by a local planning authority requires submission to, and approval by, the Secretary of State before it comes into operation. However, before formally preparing a structure plan the local planning authority must give " adequate publicity " in their area to the report of their planning survey under section 6 of the 1971 Act and also of all the matters which they *propose to include* in their structure plan and any person who may be expected to have an interest in those matters is entitled to an " adequate opportunity " to make *representations to the local planning authority* about them and if such representations are made then the authority must consider them (s. 8 (1)).

What constitutes an " adequate opportunity " of making representations is not defined in the Act and when it comes to the matter of the local planning authority considering such representations the Act is again silent as to the *modus operandi*. Provision, however, is made (s. 18 (1) (*c*)) whereby the Secretary of State, by regulations, may do some filling-in of these important gaps by making provision with respect to the making of, and the consideration of, representations relating to any matter to be included in a structure plan.

Not later than the submission of the structure plan to the Secretary of State for approval, the local planning authority must make copies of the plan available for public inspection and each copy must be accompanied by a statement of the time within which *objections to the Secretary of State may be made* (s. 8 (2)).

In connection with a structure plan the local planning authority and the Secretary of State are entitled to disregard (s. 16) representations or objections with respect to certain development authorised by or under certain other enactments, namely, the Highways Act

1959, the Highways (Miscellaneous Provisions) Act 1961, the Highways Act 1971 and the New Towns Act 1965.

The local planning authority must inform the Secretary of State
  (a) of the steps they have taken to give publicity to the report of their survey and their actions in preparing a structure plan;
  (b) of the consultations which they have had with persons making representations about the plan; and
  (c) of their consideration of any such representations (s. 8 (3)).

If not satisfied with the local authority's information about these matters the Secretary of State may decline to consider the structure plan and return it to the local authority with suitable directions about further publicity and resubmission of the plan (s. 8 (4) (5)).

In considering whether to approve a structure plan the Secretary of State has a fairly free hand. He may take into account any matters which he thinks relevant whether or not these were taken into account in the preparation of the plan as submitted to him (s. 9 (2)).

After consideration, the Secretary of State may reject a structure plan or he may approve it in whole or in part and with or without modifications or reservations (s. 9 (1)). The Secretary of State must give such statement as *he* considers appropriate of the reasons governing his decision (s. 9 (8)).

If the Secretary of State decides that he will reject a structure plan outright he may do so without further ado and without considering any objections which have been made to it. If, however, he does *not* decide to reject it outright then, before determining whether or not to approve it, he must (s. 9 (3)):
  (a) consider any objections made in accordance with regulations under Part II of the 1971 Act;
  (b) cause a person (or persons) appointed by him to hold an *examination in public* of such matters affecting his consideration of the plan as *he* considers ought to be so examined.

Thus not *all* objections will be the subject of an examination in public, but only those selected for such examination by the Secretary of State. This is an important qualification.

Any such examination in public as is here mentioned will

constitute a statutory inquiry for the purposes of section 1 (1) (c) of the Tribunals and Inquiries Act 1971 but not for any other purpose of that Act (s. 9 (6)).

The Secretary of State, after consultation with the Lord Chancellor, may make regulations as to procedure at any such examination in public as is referred to above (s. 9 (4)).

No local planning authority nor anybody else can *demand a right* to appear at any such examination in public; appearance is by invitation only of the Secretary of State (s. 9 (5)). But if any such authority or person is *not* accorded, by the Secretary of State, an opportunity to appear, then in such a case the person (or persons) appointed by the Secretary of State to hold the examination may nevertheless allow any such authority or person the opportunity to be heard (*ibid.*). This discretion may be exercised at any time before or during the examination (*ibid.*).

In considering a structure plan the Secretary of State *may* consult with, and consider the views of, *any* local planning authority or other person but he is not obliged to do so (s. 9 (7)).

5. Regulations and Directions as to Details and Procedure

Further details

    (a) as to the form and content of a structure plan and

    (b) as to the procedure to be followed in connection with its preparation, submission, withdrawal, approval, adoption, making, alteration, repeal and replacement

are forthcoming through the medium of regulations made by the Secretary of State under the provisions of the 1971 Act (s. 18 (1)). In particular, and if the Secretary of State so wishes, such regulations may (s. 18 (1) (2)):

    (a) provide for publicity to be given to the report of any survey carried out by a local planning authority under section 6 of the Act;

    (b) provide for the notice to be given of, or the publicity to be given to, matters included or proposed to be included in a structure plan and the approval, adoption or making of any such plan or any alteration, repeal or replacement thereof or to any other prescribed procedural step, and for publicity to be given to the procedure to be followed as aforesaid;

(c) make provision with respect to the making and consideration of representations with respect to matters to be included in, or objections to, a structure plan or proposals for its alteration, repeal or replacement;

(d) without prejudice to paragraph (b) above, provide for notice to be given to particular persons of the approval or alteration of a structure plan, if they have objected to the plan and have notified the local planning authority of their wish to receive notice, subject (if the regulations so provide) to the payment of a reasonable charge for receiving it;

(e) require or authorise a local planning authority to consult with or consider the views of other persons before taking any prescribed procedural step;

(f) require a local planning authority to provide persons making a request in that behalf with copies of any structure plan or document which has been made public under section 8 (1) (a) of the Act or made available for inspection under section 8 (2) of the Act, subject (if the regulations so provide) to the payment of a reasonable charge;

(g) provide for the publication and inspection of a structure plan which has been approved or made or any document approved or made altering, repealing or replacing any such plan and for copies of any such plan or document to be made available for sale.

Clearly regulations touching *all* the above matters will be needed for the better and more effective working of the Act.[1]

But if there are to be *regulations* there are also to be *directions* because the 1971 Act provides that, subject to any regulations made as mentioned above, the Secretary of State may give directions (s. 18 (3)) either to local planning authorities in general, or to any one authority in particular,

(a) for formulating the procedure to be carried out by them in connection with the preparation and approval of a structure plan; and

(b) for requiring them to give him such information as he may need to help him to discharge his functions relating to structure plans.

[1] See now the Town and Country Planning (Structure and Local Plans) Regulations 1972; S.I. 1972 No. 1154. See also p. 49

6. Operation, Validity and Alteration of a Structure Plan

Subject to the provisions of section 242 of the 1971 Act (relating to the validity of development plans) a structure plan will become operative on a date appointed for the purpose in the relevant notice of approval by the Secretary of State (s. 18 (4)).

At any time after a structure plan has come into operation the local planning authority may submit to the Secretary of State proposals for alterations to the plan and they *must* submit such proposals if required to do so by the Secretary of State (s. 10 (1)).

The procedure for the submission and approval of structure plans as discussed above applies also to the alteration of a structure plan (s. 10 (2)).

7. Nature and Effect of a Structure Plan

Structure plans (as has already been mentioned) are by nature statements of broad policy illustrated by diagrams and descriptive matter. The preparation and bringing into operation of a structure plan will bring a local planning authority face to face with the Secretary of State. Thus, central control over all structure plans is always on hand. To put the matter another way would be to say that in every instance (*i.e.* without exception) it is the Secretary of State who will have the last say in the form and content of a structure plan.

The question for the man in the street, of course, is: *What will he be able to learn from a structure plan*? He will certainly not be able to learn as much as he has been able to learn from the development plan in the form in which it has been known for the last twenty-five years. Indeed, it is not the intention that he should do. Structure plans (which always need the Secretary of State's approval) are not to be cluttered with the detail to be found in current development plans or amendments thereof.

It may be repeated that the object of a structure plan will be to sketch out trends and tendencies, to lay down general lines and to show broadly and without detail how development is going to shape-up within the area of the structure plan.

Any person (landowner or developer) seeking further and better particulars about the shape of development yet to come in the future and on his own particular plot will need to move on from the structure plan to an investigation of what is known under the Act as a local plan (see Chap. 5).

The broad picture of the new structure plan system was highlighted by Mr. Niall MacDermot, Ministry of Housing and Local Government (*Hansard*, Standing Committee G, February 22, 1968, col. 107), when he said:

"The broad picture of the new structure plan system, compared with present development plans, has now emerged fairly clearly. We envisage it as a system which will broaden the spectrum of the development plans; which will give first expression to the concept of two levels of responsibility for the approval of the development plan; and which will change the nature of the development plan—in that the structure plan will be a written statement supported by a diagram and not a map—and which will introduce the concept of the action area designated in the structure plan.

"What we have done is to spell out in much more detail than was done in the previous Act what shall be the matters to be covered by the Survey on which the structure plan is to be based. Clause 2 (3) and clause 1 (3) (now ss. 7 (3) and 6 (3) respectively of the 1971 Act) combined give an indication of the contents of the structure plan. Their effect is to indicate that, although a structure plan will be basically about land use, *it will deal with the subject in terms of the policies applicable to the major uses* ... such as housing, education, recreation, industry and commerce and relating the broad intentions about the land use represented by those policies to the traffic policies, and to policies for the movement of people and of goods— the whole plan being framed with regard to its relationship to neighbouring areas."

8. The Structure Plan becomes " the Development Plan " of the Future

Finally, the question may be asked: How does a structure plan (as discussed above) ever become " the development plan " (as the old expression goes) for any particular area? The answer is to be found in section 20 of the 1971 Act whereby " the development plan " for the purposes of the 1971 Act, or any other Act relating to town and country planning, the Land Compensation Act 1961 and the

Highways Act 1959, is to be the structure plan (plus any alterations thereto) together with any local plan or plans (plus any alterations thereto) for the time being in force, together with the Secretary of State's notice of approval of the structure plan and the local planning authority's resolution adopting any local plan.

Thus "the development plan" of the future—the outcome of the procedures under Part II of the 1971 Act—is a conglomeration of all the aforementioned documents.

9. The Secretary of State's Default Powers

The Secretary of State has certain default powers with respect to structure plans whereby he himself or, where he so appoints, some other local planning authority may perform any of the duties and functions imposed on a local planning authority under Part II of the 1971 Act (s. 17).

10. Modification of Provisions in their Application to London

All the provisions of Part II of the 1971 Act relating to structure plans are made applicable to Greater London subject to the provisions of Schedule 4 to the 1971 Act (s. 19; and see Chap. 6).

11. Regulations

Under the provisions of the Town and Country Planning Acts 1962 to 1968 the Secretary of State made the Town and Country Planning (Structure and Local Plans) Regulations 1971 [2] which came into operation on August 6, 1971.

These regulations have been repealed and replaced by the Town and Country Planning (Structure and Local Plans) Regulations 1972,[3] made under the Town and Country Planning Act 1971 (as amended 1972) which came into operation on August 22, 1972. These regulations make provision with respect to the form and content of structure and local plans prepared under Part II of the 1971 Act, and with respect to the procedure to be followed in connection with the preparation, submission, withdrawal, approval, adoption, making, alteration, repeal and replacement of such plans.

The 1972 Regulations do not apply to Greater London which remains yet to be dealt with by separate Regulations.

[2] S.I. 1971 No. 1109.   [3] S.I. 1972 No. 1154.

CHAPTER 5

DEVELOPMENT PLANS—MAKING AND PROCEDURE (NEW STYLE)—LOCAL PLANS

1. What is a Local Plan?

A LOCAL plan is a plan prepared by a local planning authority under the aegis of an overriding structure plan. The prime distinguishing feature of a local plan is that at no time in its preparation and its being brought into operation does the local planning authority necessarily come face to face with the Secretary of State. This is one of the outstanding departures from former practice.

It is only exceptionally that the Secretary of State will come into the picture at all in connection with the preparation and bringing into force of a local plan. Nevertheless it is from the local plan rather than from the structure plan that the private individual will really be able to learn what the local planning authority's planning proposals for the future mean to him and his property.

When a structure plan is in course of preparation, or when it has actually been prepared (but not yet approved by the Secretary of State), the local planning authority for the area of the structure plan *may*, if they think it desirable, prepare a local plan for any part of their area (s. 11 (1)).

When a structure plan has been approved by the Secretary of State, the local planning authority *must*, as soon as practicable, consider (and from time to time thereafter must reconsider) the desirability of preparing a local plan for any part of their area (s. 11 (2)). If the authority conclude it is desirable to have a local plan, then they *must* prepare one (*ibid.*).

This general freedom whether or not to prepare a local plan is curtailed in respect of action areas (s. 11 (6)) *or* where the Secretary of State directs the preparation and adoption by the planning authority of a local plan of any such nature as he may specify (s. 11 (7) (8)). Before issuing any such direction the Secretary of State must consult the local planning authority (s. 11 (10)).

Where under the foregoing provisions a local planning authority are *required* to prepare a local plan, they are also *required* to take steps for the adoption of the plan by the local planning authority (s. 11 (11)).

A local authority whose area (or part thereof) is included in a combined area under section 10A of the 1971 Act—for the purpose of preparing and submitting to the Secretary of State a joint structure plan (s. 10A (1))—is not obliged, under section 11 of the Act, thereafter to prepare a local plan for any part of the combined area which is *outside* their own area (s. 11 (12)).

Like the expression " structure plan " the expression " local plan " is not defined in the 1971 Act, but such a plan may apply to any part of the area of the local planning authority and the Act clearly envisages that there may be a number of different local plans for different purposes covering the same part of the area (s. 11 (4)) and all stemming from the same overriding structure plan.

A local plan will consist of *a map* and *a written statement* (s. 11 (3)):

(a) formulating in such detail as the local planning authority think appropriate their proposals for the development and other use of land in that part of the area to which the plan applies, or for any description of development or other use of such land (including in either case such measures as the authority think fit for the improvement of the physical environment and the management of traffic); and

(b) containing such matters as may be prescribed or as the Secretary of State may in any particular case direct.

This specification for the contents of a local plan set out in section 11 (3) (*a*) and (*b*) of the 1971 Act may usefully be compared with the specification for the contents of a structure plan as given in section 7 (3) (*a*), (*b*) and (*c*) of the Act and referred to in the previous chapter (see page 38).

In addition to *the map* and *the written statement* already mentioned, a local plan must contain, or be accompanied by, such *diagrams, illustrations* and *descriptive matter* as the local planning authority think appropriate for the purpose of explaining or illustrating the proposals in the plan, or as may be prescribed or specified in directions given by the Secretary of State, any such diagrams, illustrations and descriptive matter being treated as forming part of the plan (s. 11 (5)).

In formulating proposals for a local plan, a local planning authority must have regard to the contents of the structure plan and to any other information and considerations which appear to them to be relevant or which may be prescribed by the Secretary of State or, in a particular case, directed by him to be taken into account (s. 11 (9)).

Thus a local plan, whatever its nature may be, will always be a plan made under the general aegis of some overriding structure plan and may be regarded as a statement of further and better particulars demonstrating a more detailed working-out of some particular aspect of town planning which, in the structure plan, is merely sketched as a matter of policy and not worked out in any detail. Regulations will be made by the Secretary of State giving details as to the form and content of local plans (s. 18 (1)).

2. Action Area Plans

If a structure plan indicates an area as an action area, then the local planning authority *must prepare a local plan* for that area (s. 11 (6)). Such a plan will be known as an action area plan. It is but one of the many types of local plan which could be prepared and adopted by a local planning authority under the overriding aegis of a structure plan. An action area plan will, it is felt, turn out to be one of the most important (perhaps *the* most important) of all the local plans which come to be prepared by a local planning authority.

3. Structure Plans and Local Plans—Relationship and Inter-play

The relationship of a structure plan to a local plan and the inter-play between these two kinds of vastly different plans was discussed at length in the Committee stage of the Bill for the Town and Country Planning Act 1968. Some very informative statements about all this were made on behalf of the Government by the Minister of State, Ministry of Housing and Local Government, who put the matter in the following terms on February 29, 1968 (*Hansard*, Standing Committee G, col. 186 *et seq.*):

" These amendments raise an important question, involving, as they do, the nature of local plans and the amount of detail which should appear in them. It is, of course, one of the main purposes of separating structure plans from local plans to rid the central Government of the responsibility for a mass of detail which is better dealt with and decided at local level. Of necessity, therefore, one expects local plans to be more detailed in their nature. That, indeed, follows from a number of provisions in the Bill, including the fact that the local plan, unlike the structure plan, will be primarily a map. There will be written explanatory material but it will primarily be a map or series of maps—maps drawn on ordnance survey maps.

" We then come to the question which the amendments raise, which is whether we should try to write into the Bill a requirement or definition of the amount of detail that should appear in the maps. Here again I wish to make a plea to the Committee for flexibility, and for very good reasons, I think. Local plans, as we envisage them, will vary considerably in their type and scope, and we should be losing some of the benefits of the change that we are making if we tried to prescribe too rigidly the requirements that would apply to all local plans, particularly in this matter of detail.

" Some local plans—in particular, for example, a local plan setting out a development which it is proposed should be carried out by a local authority—should set out and specify in considerable detail what it is in mind to do. That might be so whether the plan was for a comprehensive redevelopment of an area or perhaps for an improvement for an old area. People should know precisely what it is that the authority intends to be done.

" Another class of local plan, and a very important one in my view, would be of a much more general nature, and in these the planning authority would indicate the kind of development or redevelopment which it had in mind but where the intention was that it should be done by private developers. The authority would want to leave some scope and freedom to the private developer and his architects to make proposals about the detail of the plan.

" I think we are agreed that one of the defects of the present system is its negative nature and that planning authorities are not able to play the useful and constructive role in positive planning which we would like to see them play. We believe that some of the local plans of the kind that I have been indicating —that would give general broad indications for the developer

—would take the form, as it were, of a brief for the developer and his architect. It might, for example, state the general objectives of the plan and the broad outlines of the way in which the planning authority envisaged that they would be achieved. The proper grouping of usages within the area, the density and height of buildings on the site, provision for proper circulation of vehicles and foot passengers—matters of this kind will be indicated in the plan. It does not follow by any means that in such a case the planning authority would need to, or would want to, lay down at the plan-making stage the details of the buildings that it wants to see on the site to achieve the objectives of good design and satisfactory treatment of the environment. I think it will generally be considered advantageous to leave scope within the main framework for the imagination and initiative of private developers.

" If we were to insist on full detail in every case we should be forfeiting one of the main improvements which the Bill seeks to introduce. Also, there would be a certain inconsistency if the local planning authority were to be charged with the responsibility, in the general run of cases, of considering objections to a plan and deciding whether to adopt it formally or not, and we then denied the planning authority the right to judge what is appropriate as to its content and form. The authority will, of course, exercise its judgment in this matter in the light of the regulations made by the Minister and any directions or guidance given by him.

" But there is a remedy if the position were reached where a planning authority put forward a plan which was really wholly inadequate as to its detail and attracted objections on that ground—the remedy is the power of the Minister to intervene, either by requiring that an inquiry be held by a person of his choice or by calling in the plan for his own decision.

" All these plans will be sent to the Minister, and, naturally, we shall want to examine them, not in all their detail but generally, to be satisfied that, first, they conform with the structure plan, and, secondly, that they contain sufficient detail to be meaningful, having regard to the nature of the local plan."

4. How Many Local Plans will there Be?

Under the new procedures one structure plan (stating broad planning policy in outline) could be the progenitor of a litter of local plans (each dealing in greater detail with its own pet aspect of planning control). Here again it is wise to pay attention to the Government's own view of the matter as explained by the Minister of State on February 29, 1968 (*Hansard*, Standing Committee G, col. 190 *et seq.*) in the following way:

" I had expected that this was in the nature of a probing amendment. It gives me an opportunity to explain a little further the variety and flexibility of local plans which we envisage. Local plans will be either plans with a varying degree of detail about a particular part of the area of the planning authority or plans which have a particular function or cover a particular aspect of planning for a rather wider area. It is because of this that one may get more than one local plan relating to and bearing upon the same piece of land.

" First of all, area plans; there will be action area plans designated in the structure plan. These will be the plans of areas for early and intensive development or redevelopment. . . .

" Then we envisage that there may be district plans covering a larger part of the area of the planning authority. The basic purposes of these will be to state more fully the working features of the locality within the structure plan area and to show the principal land uses as a guide for development control. But, having made the district plans for a district, there is no reason why at a later stage one should not have a much smaller local plan dealing with a particular problem of some area within the district. I have mentioned before the possibility of a local plan for a village, dealing with, say, a scheme for the expansion of a village. There would be no need to repeal or amend the original district plan because one proceeded to elaborate in more detail plans for a village falling within that district.

" Again, one might have a different kind of local plan which would be in the nature of a special policy or project plan. It might be a plan to deal with opportunities for access to the countryside or facilities for recreation. This plan also could overlap areas covered by other local plans. One might have a plan for the progressive and phased working of minerals within an area. This, again, could go on in more detail than was done in the district plans or other local plans.

" It will, of course, be important and necessary to ensure that these different types of local plan are mutually compatible and do not conflict with each other. This is another argument for retaining for the planning authority the power to make and approve local plans and not to delegate its powers. One local planning authority will be responsible for all the local plans within its area. It will be primarily its responsibility, subject to supervision by the Ministry, to ensure that the local plans are mutually compatible. It would be a ground for rejection of any local plan if it appeared to be inconsistent with and to conflict with another plan. I think that if we were not to have the power which the subsection points to and if we were to compel local authorities to combine all possible different matters in a single local plan, it would lead to a considerable loss of simplicity, clarity and flexibility.

" Again, on the point of clarity, I think that an advantage of separating local plans in this way is that they will be much clearer to people than the present plans. We know the confusion that arises from trying to overload a plan with too much detail on different matters. For these reasons we think that the system will work and not cause confusion. On the contrary, it will facilitate planning."

5. Making Representations about a Local Plan

A local planning authority who *propose to prepare* a local plan must take such steps as will ensure " adequate publicity " of the matters which *it is proposed* to include in the plan and that persons who may be expected to have an interest in such matters are afforded an " adequate opportunity " of making representations to the authority in respect of them (s. 12 (1)).

This right to make representations *before* the ideas of the local planning authority have fully crystallised is an instance of that citizen participation of which so much has been heard in connection with the 1971 Act. By making representations the local citizen is enabled to " put in his oar " at a time when the local plan is at a formative stage and before the local planning authority have completely made up their mind about the plan.

The putting in of *representations* about a local plan to the local planning authority must not be confused with the right (which comes later) to put in *objections* to a local plan when the plan *has been prepared* by the local planning authority but not yet *adopted* by them. Representations must be made *before* the local plan is prepared by the local planning authority. Objections must be made *after* the plan has been *prepared* by the authority but *before* the plan has been *adopted* by the authority. (It is helpful to note the distinctive use of the two different verbs: *to prepare* and *to adopt.*)

If representations about a local plan are in fact made to the local planning authority, then the authority must consider them (s. 12 (1)). The question, of course, is: What will be the manner of such consideration? As the 1971 Act itself stands such consideration may be carried out in private by a committee of the local planning authority, the person making the representation having no right of audience either for himself or his representative before the committee.

However, something may yet be done about this because provision is made (s. 18 (1) (c)) whereby the Secretary of State, through the medium of regulations, can make provision with respect to the making of, and the consideration of, representations relating to matters to be included in a local plan.

6. Making Objections to a Local Plan

Once a local plan *has been prepared* by the local planning authority (and before it is *adopted* by the authority) the authority must, if the overriding structure plan has by then been approved by the Secretary of State, have copies of the local plan made available for public inspection and each copy must be accompanied by a statement of the time within which *objections* to the plan may be made to the authority (s. 12 (2)). *Objections, it will be noted, to a local plan must be sent to the local planning authority who prepared it and not to the Secretary of State as is the case with a structure plan.*

The local planning authority are entitled to disregard (s. 16) representations or objections to a local plan if they relate to certain development authorised under the Highways Act 1959, the Highways

(Miscellaneous Provisions) Act 1961, the Highways Act 1971 or the New Towns Act 1965.

The local planning authority must send a copy of the local plan as prepared by them to the Secretary of State (s. 12 (2)) and must send with the plan a statement containing such particulars, if any, as may be prescribed by the Secretary of State (s. 12 (3)):

(a) of the steps which the authority have taken to secure the giving of publicity to any relevant matter in the report of their survey under section 12 of the Act and the matters proposed to be included in the local plan; and

(b) of the authority's consultations with, and their consideration of the views of, other persons.

If the Secretary of State is *not* satisfied with the statement as sent to him by the authority he may intervene (s. 12 (4) and (5)).

The sending of the foregoing matters to the Secretary of State is primarily for information because a local plan *prepared* by a local planning authority and later formally *adopted* by them does not normally (*i.e.* in the general run of things) need any approval from the Secretary of State. Objections to the local plan, it will be remembered, are to be sent to the local planning authority themselves and not to the Secretary of State (s. 12 (2)). Accordingly, the next question is: How does the local planning authority handle the objections to their local plan when they have received them?

7. How does the Local Planning Authority deal with Objections?

This is a very important matter and the 1971 Act goes on to provide that in such a case a local planning authority may, if they wish, cause a public local inquiry or a private hearing to be held into any objection (s. 13 (1)). The authority are not, in general, and subject to regulations to be made by the Secretary of State (*ibid.*), obliged to afford either a public inquiry or a private hearing and if they choose to do neither of these things then, presumably, they will give due (but private) consideration in committee to any objection, in which event the objector will never meet the authority, nor their representatives, face to face. More, however, may yet be heard about this because the Act provides (s. 18 (1) (*c*)) for regulations to be made by the Secretary of State with respect to the consideration of objections to local plans.

It may be repeated that, generally speaking, a local planning authority has an option whether or not to afford a local inquiry or a private hearing in connection with any objection which is made to a local plan. Regulations, however, may provide that in the case of certain objections (that is to say, objections made in accordance with the regulations), the local planning authority *shall* be obliged to afford the objector either a local inquiry or a private hearing in connection with his objection.

If the local planning authority choose, or if, by regulations, they are obliged, to afford an objector to their local plan either a public inquiry or a private hearing, then the person holding the inquiry or hearing will be a person (an Inspector) appointed by the Secretary of State or, in such cases as may be prescribed by regulations, by the local planning authority themselves (s. 13 (1)).

If the Secretary of State *does* make regulations for the purposes of section 13 (1) of the 1971 Act either requiring a public inquiry or a private hearing to be held in connection with specified objections to a local plan, or allowing a local planning authority to appoint an Inspector of their own choice, then such regulations may make provision (s. 13 (2)):

(a) as to the appointment and the qualifications for appointment of persons to hold a public inquiry or private hearing into objections to a local plan, and enabling the Secretary of State to direct a local planning authority to appoint a particular person or one of a specified list or class of persons; and

(b) as to remuneration for a person so appointed.

Thus a local planning authority may be precluded from appointing one of their own officers (or indeed one of their own members) to hear an objection to their local plan and may be driven into selecting their Inspector from some panel of persons (local or otherwise) approved by the Secretary of State.

8. Adoption of a Local Plan by the Local Planning Authority

If no objections to an advertised local plan are received within the appropriate time the local planning authority may then proceed to the next step which is formally to adopt the plan by resolution of the authority (s. 14 (1)).

If objections to a local plan are made in due time, then " after considering the objections "—(*i.e.* after considering them with, or without, the holding of a public local inquiry or a private hearing as discussed above)—the local planning authority may proceed formally, by resolution, to adopt the plan either as originally prepared or as modified in the light of any objections that have been made and considered by the authority (s. 14 (1)).

A local planning authority may in no circumstances adopt a local plan unless it conforms generally to the antecedent structure plan as approved by the Secretary of State (s. 14 (2)).

The Secretary of State will make regulations under section 18 (1) of the Act giving details as to the procedure to be followed in connection with the adoption of a local plan.

If the Secretary of State so desires he can always take out of the hands of the local planning authority responsibility for approving a local plan which they have prepared (s. 14 (3) (4)). As previously mentioned, the Secretary of State must always receive from the local planning authority a copy of any local plan which they have prepared (s. 12 (2)). Thus advised about the contents of the local planning authority's local plan, the Secretary of State can, at any time before the plan has been formally adopted by the local planning authority, issue a direction that the plan shall not have effect unless it is approved by him (s. 14 (3)), in which case the procedure whereby the Secretary of State is to consider the plan and any objections which may have been made thereto, will follow the procedure applicable in the case of the submission to, and the approval by, the Secretary of State of a structure plan (s. 14 (4)).

This matter of the Secretary of State's power to " call in " a local plan for final approval (or rejection) by him is bound up with the right of a local planning authority to reject a recommendation made to them in his report by the Inspector appointed to hold a public inquiry or a private hearing. A local planning authority is no more bound to accept such a recommendation than is the Secretary of State in the case of a recommendation made to *him* by an Inspector. There could conceivably be a disagreement between what the Inspector recommends and what the local planning authority think is right. What is the position then?

This was the subject of debate on March 7, 1968, during the Committee stage of the Bill for the Town and Country Planning Act 1968, when the Minister of State said (*Hansard*, Standing Committee G, col. 299 *et seq.*):

" A difficult position could arise if, even after an inquiry, even after a recommendation by the inspector, the local authority still says, that the matter raises what is, for them, [sic] and that they, the locally elected planning authority, are the people to decide policy for this area, within the overall policy of the approved structure plan, and that their decision is so-and-so.

" The Ministry could not consider the issue in isolation. It would have to consider it in relation to the whole of that local plan, considering all the policy underlying it in relation to the rest of the detail of that local plan; that would require very detailed consideration by the Ministry. We shall have our power of ' call in ' and there will be cases where we think it right to use it. An issue of this kind might be a case in which the power would be used. And we still have the power of ' call in ' even after the provisional resolution by the local authority rejecting a recommendation of the inspector has been made. But the discretion whether the issue should be decided at Ministry level ought to rest with the Minister, not with the objector. To give the objector the right to impose upon the Ministry the duty of going into all that detail is too heavy. The Minister should be left to decide. There will be time, even after a local authority has rejected the inspector's recommendation and given its reasons for doing so, for the Minister to decide whether to call it in if he is asked to do so at that stage.

" It has been suggested that I might argue that there is always the remedy of the courts. I have never suggested that remedy. I do not recall using that argument on this kind of issue. It was certainly a slip if I did, because this kind of issue could not go to the courts. The appeal to the courts is on whether the proper procedure has been followed. But on the matter of substance, which would be an issue of policy, there would be no appeal to the courts.

" It is easy to say with horror in one's voice that a local authority is not bound to accept and can even reject the recommendation of the inspector. We all have the greatest respect for inspectors, but they are not democratically elected planning authorities. They are a very good vehicle for ensuring that objections are properly heard, that an independent, qualified and expert mind is brought to bear and to express an opinion, but when that has been done the decision should rest with the democratically elected authority which may be either the Minister or the local authority.

" Essentially, what we are considering here are local issues and local policies. If a matter raises more than local policy, it is an issue which will come up in the structure plans and will, therefore, be decided by the Minister, but what we are dealing with here is, *ex hypothesi*, a local matter raising a local question of policy. It is said—and again I quote one of my hon. Friend's phrases—that the local authority may be hell-bent to get its plans through. It may be hell-bent, but it will be subjected to some rigorous procedures as the Bill stands. I do not want to go over them again—hon. Members will remember the provisions for publicity and consultation in the formative stages and so on. What a local authority does and its reasons for doing so at every stage will be exposed to publicity—and local publicity—and it will have to answer for its actions at the end of the day.

" The amendment raises the basic issue of whether we want to delegate to local planning authorities the power to determine local plans, subject to the supervision and the power of ' call in ' of the Minister. If the attitude of mind about which hon. Members are worried really exists, that fact will become patent if, unreasonably and through sheer obstinacy and with no valid policy, a local authority rejects substantial objections and recommendations of the inspector, without giving convincing reasons for doing so. That is the kind of case in which the Minister would exercise his power of ' call in.' But the decision on that must rest with the Minister and not with the objector, and it would not be right, therefore, to give the objector the right of appeal which the Amendment suggests."

9. Operation, Validity and Alteration of a Local Plan

Subject to the provisions of section 242 of the 1971 Act (relating to the validity of development plans) a local plan will become operative on a date appointed for the purpose in the relevant resolution of the local planning authority adopting the plan (s. 18 (4)).

A local plan having been finally adopted by the local planning authority (or having been approved by the Secretary of State, in a case where he has taken over responsibility therefor) and having thereby come into operation, the local planning authority may, from time to time, make proposals for altering, repealing or replacing such local plan, provided that in a case where the local plan has been the subject of approval by the Secretary of State, such proposals for alteration, repeal or replacement receive the prior consent of the Secretary of State (s. 15 (1) and (2)).

The procedure for altering, repealing and replacing a local plan is similar to that discussed above relating to the preparation and approval for such a plan (s. 15 (3)).

10. The Local Plan becomes " the Development Plan " of the Future

The manner in which an operative local plan becomes " the development plan " (as the old expression goes) for any particular area is dealt with in section 20 of the 1971 Act about which reference may be made to Chapter 4, page 48.

11. The Secretary of State's Default Powers

In connection with local plans the Secretary of State has certain default powers enabling the Secretary of State himself or, where he so appoints, some other local planning authority to perform any of the duties or functions imposed upon a local planning authority with respect to local plans (s. 17).

12. Modification of Provisions in their Application to London

All the provisions of Part II of the 1971 Act relating to local plans are made applicable to Greater London subject to the provisions of Schedule 4 to the Act (s. 19; and see Chap. 6).

13. Regulations

Under the 1971 Act the Secretary of State has made the Town and Country Planning (Structure and Local Plans) Regulations 1972 [1] repealing and replacing (with amendments) the Town and

[1] S.I. 1972 No. 1154.

Country Planning (Structure and Local Plans) Regulations 1971.[2] The 1972 Regulations came into operation on August 22, 1972, and relate to the form and content of structure and local plans prepared under Part II of the 1971 Act, and to the procedure to be followed in connection with the preparation, submission, withdrawal, approval, adoption, making, alteration, repeal and replacement of such plans.

The 1972 Regulations do not apply to Greater London which remains yet to be dealt with by separate Regulations.

[2] S.I. 1971 No. 1109.

CHAPTER 6

DEVELOPMENT PLANS FOR GREATER LONDON— SPECIAL ARRANGEMENTS

THE whole of Part II of the 1971 Act relating to planning surveys, structure plans and local plans, when it comes to be applied to Greater London, is to be applied subject to the modifications set out in Schedule 4 to the Act (s. 19).

These modifications are enacted in order to fit the new procedures of Part II of the Act into the intricately intertwined relationship which exists between the Greater London Council and the thirty-two London boroughs, a relationship created by the London Government Act 1963.

For the purposes of the 1971 Act any reference in that Act to a " London borough " includes a reference to the City of London (s. 290 (1)), the City not being classed as a London borough by the 1963 Act.

1. Survey of Planning Areas

The matters to be examined and kept under review when a survey of a planning area is being prepared are set out in detail in section 6 (1) and (3) of the 1971 Act (see Chap. 4).

When the *Greater London Council* are doing such a survey their duty will be to keep in mind:

(1) such of the matters mentioned in section 6 of the 1971 Act *as they think fit*; or

(2) in the case of a fresh survey carried out under section 6 (2) of the Act by direction of the Secretary of State, such matters as the Secretary of State may direct (Sched. 4, para. 1).

When it is *a London borough council* who are doing the survey (and such a council can do it only " on such lines " as the Greater London Council directs (Sched. 4, para. 4)), then the matters which they must examine are (Sched. 4, para. 2):

(1) such of the matters mentioned in section 6 of the 1971 Act as have *not* been examined by the Greater London Council;

(2) such *other* matters as the Greater London Council may require them to examine; *and*

(3) in the case of a fresh survey carried out under section 6 (2) of the Act by direction of the Secretary of State, such matters as the Secretary of State may direct (Sched. 4, para. 2).

Section 10A of the 1971 Act relating to joint surveys, reports and plans, does not apply to the Greater London Council (Sched. 4, para. 3). Nevertheless, any two or more London borough councils may institute a joint survey for any combined area consisting of those boroughs or any part thereof (*ibid.*).

2. Structure Plans

The Greater London Development Plan is to be regarded as a structure plan for Greater London approved under section 9 and susceptible of alteration under section 10 of the 1971 Act (Sched. 4, para. 5 (1)). The Secretary of State may approve the Greater London Development Plan by stages (Sched. 4, para. 5 (2)).

If in the plan any area is shown as an area of comprehensive development, redevelopment or improvement, then the Secretary of State may direct that such an area shall be treated as an " action area " under the Act (Sched. 4, para. 5 (3)).

The Greater London Development Plan may be altered on the proposal of any London borough council (made with the approval of the Secretary of State) so as to indicate any area in the plan as an action area (Sched. 4, para. 6).

All London boroughs are relieved of the responsibility (laid on them by the Town and Country Planning Act 1968) of preparing structure plans (Sched. 4, para. 7), sections 7 to 10 of the 1971 Act not applying to any such council (*ibid.*).

Moreover, section 10B of the 1971 Act (as to withdrawal of structure plans) applies neither to the London boroughs nor to the Greater London Council (Sched. 4, para. 7).

3. Local Plans

Sections 11 and 12 (relating to the preparation of local plans and publicity in connection therewith) of the 1971 Act do not apply to the Greater London Council nor to any London borough council (Sched. 4, para. 7).

In lieu thereof the preparation of local plans and publicity for them is dealt with in paragraphs 8 to 13 of Schedule 4 to the 1971 Act.

A local plan will, generally, be made by the London borough for the area to which the plan applies (Sched. 4, para. 8 (3)) but in the case of an action area the local plan for such an area may be prepared sometimes by the Greater London Council (for any " G.L.C. action area ") (Sched. 4, paras. 8 (1) (2), 9 (1) (*a*)) and sometimes by the council of the London borough (Sched. 4, paras. 8 (3), 9 (1) (*b*)).

The contents of a local plan, whether prepared by the Greater London Council or by a London borough council, are dealt with in Schedule 4, paragraph 11, and publicity for such plan in Schedule 4, paragraphs 12 and 13.

Schedule 4 to the 1971 Act contains further provisions relating;
(1) to the power of the Secretary of State to suspend adoption of a local plan relating to a London borough (Sched. 4, para. 14);
(2) to the alteration of such a local plan (Sched. 4, para. 16); and
(3) to consultation between London borough councils and the Greater London Council before preparation of such a local plan (Sched. 4, para. 17).

4. Development Plan for a London Borough

What is to constitute the development plan for a London borough? The answer is (s. 20 (2) as amended by s. 4 (2) of the Town and Country Planning Act 1972) an amalgam of the following matters, namely:
(a) the provisions of the Greater London Development Plan as in force for the time being, together with the notices given from time to time by the Secretary of State indicating his approval of any feature or element of the plan;
(b) any alterations to that plan, together with the Secretary of State's notices of approval thereof;
(c) any provisions of a local plan for the time being applicable to the district, together with a copy of the resolution of adoption of the relevant council or, as the case may be, the Secretary of State's notice of approval of the local plan; and
(d) any alterations to that local plan, together with a copy of the

resolutions of adoption of the relevant council or, as the case may be, the Secretary of State's notices of approval thereof.

5. Regulations

The Secretary of State, acting under the 1971 Act, has not yet made any Regulations relating to structure and local plans in Greater London.

CHAPTER 7

THE MEANING OF " DEVELOPMENT "

1. Meaning of " Development " Summarised

Iт may be said that *development* (*i.e.* the development of land which here includes buildings, structures and erections) is the very essence of the Town and Country Planning Act 1971—the centre on which the whole of the Act turns and depends. Accordingly, an understanding of the meaning of " development," as that expression is used in the 1971 Act, is of prime importance for a full appreciation of the comprehensive and extensive scope of the law relating to town and country planning.

It is from section 22 of the 1971 Act (as read in the light of the definitions contained in section 290 (1)) that a knowledge of " development " and all that it means for the purposes of the Act is to be gleaned. Indeed, with this Act it is especially advisable to consider at length the interpretation section (s. 290) before turning to the rest of the Act, because this section provides special, and sometimes remarkably extended, meanings for no less than seventy-five expressions repeatedly used throughout the Act.

The far-reaching effect of the interpretation section on the scope and extent of the 1971 Act will be realised when it is mentioned that each of the expressions set in heavy type in the following paragraphs dealing with the meaning of " development " is given specialised definition (to which reference should be made) in section 290 (1) of the Act.

" Development " is defined (ss. 290 (1) and 22 (1)) as:
  (a) the carrying out of **building operations, engineering operations,** mining operations or other operations [1] in, on, over or under **land,** or
  (b) the making of any material change in the **use** of any **buildings** or other **land.**

---

[1] In *Cheshire C.C.* v. *Woodward* [1962] 2 Q.B. 126, it was held that there is no one test to find out what physical characteristics constitute development of land—it depends on all the circumstances and on the degree of permanency of the " building, engineering, mining or other operations."

69

It is provided by the 1971 Act that the following matters *shall constitute development*:

  (i) the use of a single dwelling-house for the purpose of two or more separate dwellings (s. 22 (3) (*a*));

  (ii) the deposit of refuse or waste materials on an existing dump if *either* (a) the superficial area of the dump is extended or (b) the height of the dump is extended and exceeds the level of the **land** adjoining the dump (s. 22 (3) (*b*));

  (iii) the display of **advertisements** on the external part of a **building** not normally used for such display (ss. 22 (4) and 64).

It is provided by the 1971 Act that the following matters *shall not constitute development*:

  (i) internal or external improvements, alterations, or maintenance works (not constituting the making good of **war-damage**) none of which materially affects the external appearance of the **building** so treated, provided that any works, begun [2] after December 5, 1968, for the alteration of a building by providing additional space in the building below ground level *will* constitute development (s. 290 (2) (*a*));

  (ii) maintenance or **improvement** works carried out by a **local highway authority** to, and within the boundaries of, a road (s. 22 (2) (*b*));

  (iii) the breaking open of streets, etc., for the inspection, repair or renewal of sewers, mains, pipes, cables, etc., by a **local authority** or a **statutory undertaker** (s. 22 (2) (*c*));

  (iv) the **use** of any **buildings** or other **land** within the curtilage of a dwelling-house for any purpose incidental to the enjoyment of the dwelling-house as a dwelling-house (s. 22 (2) (*d*));

  (v) the **use** of **land** for **agriculture** or forestry and the **use** for such purposes of any **building** occupied with land so used (s. 22 (2) (*e*));

  (vi) in the case of **buildings** or other **land** used for a purpose of any class specified in an Order made by the Secretary of State, the use thereof for any purpose in the same class

---

[2] As to when works are begun, see s. 43 of the 1971 Act.

(s. 22 (2) (f) and the Town and Country Planning (Use Classes) Order 1972.) [3]

Thus, as any building operation or change of use which falls under one or other of the items numbered (i) to (vi) respectively in the previous paragraph is declared by the Act *not* to constitute development, it follows that the need to obtain planning permission in respect of it cannot arise. It is also to be noted that in the case of sub-paragraphs (iv) and (v), by virtue of the definition of " use " in section 290 (1) of the Act, the erection of *new* buildings for any of the purposes mentioned in those sub-paragraphs *will* constitute development.

It is provided by the 1971 Act that the following six matters, though they may constitute development, *shall not require planning permission*:

   (i) the resumption—provided the resumption was *before* December 6, 1968—of the normal **use** of **land** which, on July 1, 1948 (the date when the Town and Country Planning Act 1947 came into operation), was being used temporarily for some different **use** (s. 23 (2));

  (ii) the **use**, *before* December 6, 1968, for an occasional purpose of **land** which, on July 1, 1948, was normally used for one purpose but which was also used (whether at regular intervals or not) for the said occasional purpose, provided (in the case of any resumption of the occasional use taking place on or after December 6, 1968) that there has been at least one such resumption *since* July 1, 1948, and *before* January 1, 1968 (s. 23 (3));

 (iii) the **use** of **land** unoccupied on July 1, 1948 (provided it had been occupied at some time on or after January 7, 1937), for the purpose for which it was last used before July 1, 1948 (s. 23 (4))[4];

 (iv) the resumption, on the expiration of a **planning permission** to develop **land** granted for a limited period, of the **use** of the **land** for the purpose for which it was normally used before the limited planning permission was granted, provided that such normal use does not contravene Part III of the 1971 Act or previous planning control (s. 23 (5) (6) (10));

[3] S.I. 1972 No. 1385.
[4] See *Cubitt Estates* v. *Westminster Corporation* (1952) 2 P. & C.R. 316 (L.T.).

(v) the resumption, where **planning permission** to develop **land** subject to limitations has been granted by a **development order,** of the normal **use** of the **land,** provided that such normal **use** does not contravene Part III of the 1971 Act or previous planning control (s. 23 (8) (10));

(vi) the resumption, after the service of an enforcement notice in respect of any unauthorised **development of land,** of the **use** of the **land** for the purpose for which, under Part III of the 1971 Act, it could lawfully be used if the unauthorised development had not been carried out (s. 23 **(9)**).

However, as to the **use** of **land** for a caravan site, it is to be noted that the freedom conferred under items (i), (ii) and (iii) in the previous paragraph from the need to obtain planning permission for such **use** does not apply unless the **land** has been used as a caravan site on at least one occasion during the period of two years ending on March 9, 1960 (s. 23 (7)).

It is provided by the 1971 Act that whilst the following matters *do* constitute development, planning permission in respect of them *shall be deemed to be granted*:

(i) the display of **advertisements** in accordance with regulations (s. 64 and the Town and Country Planning (Control of Advertisements) Regulations 1969 [5] as amended by the Town and Country Planning (Control of Advertisements) (Amendment) Regulations 1972 [6]);

(ii) certain development by a local authority or by a statutory undertaker which has been authorised by a government department (s. 40).

An effort will now be made to break down the definition of " development " into its various components and to examine each of these in turn to see what it amounts to having regard to provisions of the interpretation section of the 1971 Act.

2. Building Operations

The expression " building operations " includes (s. 290 (1)):

(a) rebuilding operations;

(b) structural alterations of buildings;

(c) structural additions to buildings; and

---

[5] S.I. 1969 No. 1532.
[6] S.I. 1972 No. 489.

(d) other operations normally undertaken by a person carrying on business as a builder.

The special definition of "building operations" leads in turn to the special definition of "building" which includes (s. 290 (1)) any structure or erection, and any part of a building, structure or erection, but does not include plant or machinery comprised in a building, structure or erection. A model village (Bekonscot) is a "structure or erection"[7] but swingboats are not a "building."[8]

Apart from the building and the rebuilding of buildings, structures or erections and the making of structural alterations or additions to buildings, structures or erections, other operations normally undertaken by a builder would include ancillary demolitions in connection with rebuilding and in connection with alterations. This and similar operations will be caught by the expression "building operations" and will accordingly constitute development under the Act.[9] Demolition of part of a building may amount to development and the removal of embankments surrounding ammunition magazines has been held to be development.[10]

3. Engineering Operations

"Engineering operations" includes (s. 290 (1)) the formation or laying out of means of access to highways and "means of access" includes (again s. 290 (1)) any means of access, whether private or public, for vehicles or for foot passengers, and includes a street. Thus it follows that engineering operations would include such a modest matter as the making of a gateway in the rear wall of a factory giving egress for pedestrians only from the factory yard into the back street.

4. Land

"Land" means (s. 290 (1)) any corporeal hereditament including a building, a structure or an erection.

5. Material Change of Use

All the foregoing matters relate to development as dealt with

[7] *Bucks C.C.* v. *Callingham* [1952] 2 Q.B. 515 (C.A.).
[8] *James* v. *Brecon C.C.* (1963) 15 P. & C.R. 20.
[9] *L.C.C.* v. *Marks and Spencer* [1953] A.C. 535 (H.L.).
[10] *Coleshill and District Investment Co. Ltd.* v. *Minister of Housing and Local Government* [1968] 1 W.L.R. 600; (1967) 19 P. & C.R. 157, C.A.

in sub-paragraph (a) of the definition of " development " as given on p. 69, which sub-paragraph envisages the carrying out of some positive operation in, on, over or under any land, building, structure or erection.

But it is not essential that land, buildings, structures or erections should themselves be subjected to any such positive operation at all before their development may be said to have occurred for the purposes of the 1971 Act, for, under sub-paragraph (b) of the definition as given on p. 69, development may take place when any material change occurs, not in the land or the building, structure or erection itself but in *the use* to which the land, building, structure or erection is for the time being put. The 1971 Act contains no definition of the expression " material change " as here used, although for the avoidance of doubt two examples of what may be said to constitute a material change are quoted in section 22 (3) and will be referred to later.

The Town and Country Planning Act 1932 employed the expression " change in the use." The 1962 Act (following the precedent of the 1947 Act) employs the same expression but qualifies it with the word " material." It is clear from this that no slight or trivial change of use will amount to development but it is difficult to draw any hard and fast line. It may well be that whilst material change of use is difficult to define theoretically it will be readily recognisable when in practice it occurs. If there is doubt in any particular case provision is made in section 53 of the 1971 Act for resolving this (see p. 86, and Ministry Circular 67/49).

The Secretary of State takes the view that for a change of use to be a *material* change of use the new use must be *substantially* different from the old use. In *Palser* v. *Grinling*,[11] " substantial " was accepted as meaning " considerable, solid or big," the other meaning of the word (which is " not unsubstantial," *i.e.* just enough to avoid the *de minimis* principle) not being accepted in that case.

If a house, formerly occupied by a *single* family, is let out in flats to a *number* of families, there may be a material change, as a matter of degree and fact, notwithstanding that the use of the house remains residential throughout.[12]

---

[11] [1948] A.C. 291 (H.L.).
[12] *Birmingham Corporation* v. *Minister of Housing and Local Government and Habib Ullah* [1964] 1 Q.B. 178; 15 P. & C.R. 404 (D.C.). See also *Borg* v. *Khan* (1965) 63 L.G.R. 309 (D.C.); *Clarke* v. *Caterham and Warlingham U.D.C.* (1966) 18 P. & C.R. 82 (D.C.); and Ministry Circular 67/49.

Difficulties arise when there has been an interruption in the use of land. It is a question of fact whether a particular use has been continuous or whether there has been a discontinuance of the use followed by a resumption or repetition of the use for the same purpose. Factors to be taken into consideration are the length of the interruption, and whether the land was put to any other use during the interruption.

Thus in *Postill* v. *East Riding County Council*,[13] land used as a riding school and for grazing was used, under a planning permission, for a circus, subject to a condition that the circus user should cease in September. The circus user ceased in accordance with the condition. It was held (a) that the resumption *ten months later* of the circus user was not a continuance of the same user and did not amount to a breach of the condition; and (b) that discontinuance did not necessarily mean permanent discontinuance.

On the other hand in *Fyson* v. *Bucks County Council*,[14] resumption in 1956 of a use for storage to which premises had last been put prior to 1949 was held not to be a material change of use. *Postill* v. *East Riding County Council, supra*, was distinguished on the ground that in the *Fyson* case the plaintiff had owned the land since 1951 and there had never been any use of the land since 1943 except for the storage of materials.

In *Klein* v. *Whitstable Urban District Council*,[15] there was held to be no discontinuance where caravans which had been removed from agricultural land in compliance with an enforcement notice were brought back onto the land six weeks later.

Difficulties also arise where there has been an intensification of a use. In *Guildford Rural District Council* v. *Fortescue, Same* v. *Penny*,[16] the court declined to accept as a general proposition that mere intensity of user or occupation could never be relevant. Without deciding the point, the court indicated that whether an intensification of user amounted to a material change of use would depend on the particular circumstances of the particular case. The justices having found that the increase in the number of caravans using a one-and-a-half-acre site from eight to twenty-

13 [1956] 2 Q.B. 386 (D.C.).
14 [1958] 1 W.L.R. 634 (D.C.).
15 (1958) 10 P. & C.R. 6 (D.C.).
16 [1959] 2 Q.B. 112 (C.A.).

seven did not amount to a material change of use, the Court of Appeal refused to disturb their finding.[17]

Where a group of buildings is used together for a single purpose, it may be that the use of any particular building should be disregarded, the use being that of the group as a whole.[18] So also where a building on a nursery garden hitherto used for sales of produce grown on the nursery becomes used also for sales of produce *not grown thereon*, this may amount to development since the former use was ancillary to the agricultural use of the land and the building, which were one unit.[19]

The question whether there is a material change of the use to which part of a house has been put when that use is extended to another part of the house, is a question of fact and degree. The proper unit for consideration may be the house as a whole.[20]

There is clearly a material change in the use when the nature of the use is changed, as when a residential user is converted to a business user by turning a private dwelling-house into a shop. The position is not so clear when the nature of the use remains constant but its type is changed, *e.g.* when the type of business user is changed and the change does not fall squarely within one of the classes in the Schedule to the Town and Country Planning (Use Classes) Order 1972 [21] (referred to later in this chapter). The fact that it does not fall within the Order does not preclude consideration of the question whether or not there is a material change of use. The important matter is the character of the use, rather than the purpose of the particular occupier: *East Barnet Urban District Council* v. *British Transport Commission.*[22]

Many changes of use are excepted from the definition of development by the Town and Country Planning (Use Classes) Order

---

[17] See also *Brookes* v. *Flintshire C.C.* (1956) 6 P. & C.R. 140; *Washington U.D.C.* v. *Gray* (1958) 10 P. & C.R. 264 (D.C.); *Marshall* v. *Nottingham Corporation* [1960] 1 W.L.R. 707; *Finch* v. *Leatherhead U.D.C.* (1961) 13 P. & C.R. 97; *Horwitz* v. *Rowson* [1960] 1 W.L.R. 803; *George Cohen 600 Group* v. *Minister of Housing and Local Government* [1961] 1 W.L.R. 944 (D.C.); *Devon C.C.* v. *Allen's Caravans (Estates) Ltd.* (1962) 14 P. & C.R. 440.

[18] *Vickers-Armstrong* v. *Central Land Board* (1957) 9 P. & C.R. 33 (C.A.); *Trentham (G. Percy) Ltd.* v. *Gloucester C.C.* [1966] 1 W.L.R. 506; *Brazil (Concrete) Ltd.* v. *Amersham R.D.C.* (1967) 18 P. & C.R. 396 (C.A.).

[19] *Williams* v. *Minister of Housing and Local Government* (1967) 18 P. & C.R. 514 (D.C.).

[20] *Brooks* v. *Gloucestershire C.C.* (1967) 19 P. & C.R. 90.

[21] S.I. 1972 No. 1385.

[22] [1962] 2 Q.B. 484 (D.C.).

1972.[21] Thus the changing of a butcher's shop into a baker's shop, a greengrocer's shop or a hairdresser's shop (but not, be it noted, into a shop for the sale of hot food, a tripe shop or a cat's-meat shop) does *not* constitute development; nor does the changing of a solicitor's office into an accountant's office or into a bank.

It is to be noted, however, that even though such changes do not in themselves constitute development it is now clear (since the decision in *Corporation of City of London* v. *Secretary of State for the Environment and Another* [23] that, on granting planning permission, the local planning authority can, at that time, impose conditions which preclude the use of the land for which planning permission is granted being changed (except of course, with further planning permission) from the use stated in the planning permission to any other use even though such other use is within the same use class as is the use covered by the planning permission. Interesting advice on this situation will be found in Ministry Circular No. 5/68, para. 23.

6. Section 22, subss. (3) and (4)

After the definition of development has been dealt with generally in subsection (1) of section 22, subsections (3) and (4) of section 22 proceed to give examples of three uses of land which are declared to involve a material change of use and which accordingly constitute development under the Act. These three uses are summarised as follows:

(1) The use as two or more separate dwelling-houses of any building previously used as a single dwelling-house (s. 22 (3) (*a*)).

As to what constitutes " two or more separate dwelling-houses " reference may usefully be made to cases decided under the " Rent Acts," [24] in which it was held that the letting of two rooms with the use jointly of other rooms and amenities was, in effect, a sharing of the house and not a letting of a " separate dwelling." [25]

The rooms shared must be essential living rooms such as a kitchen,[26] or even a " kitchenette." [27] A sharing of

---

[23] (1971) 23 P. & C.R. 169.
[24] See *Neale* v. *Del Soto* [1945] K.B. 144 (C.A.).
[25] See also *Sharpe* v. *Nicholls* [1945] K.B. 382 (C.A.); *Krauss* v. *Boyne* [1946] 1 All E.R. 543; *Stevenson* v. *Kenyon* [1946] 2 All E.R. 595 (C.A.).
[26] *Neale* v. *Del Soto, supra.*   [27] *Winters* v. *Dance* [1949] L.J.R. 165 (C.A.).

accommodation other than living accommodation, such as a bathroom and water-closet, which are essential by modern standards, does not involve a sharing of the house.[28] But the rule applies whether the sharing is between tenant and landlord or between tenant and tenant.[29] Two self-contained flats, capable of being let as separate flats, were held to be capable of being let as a single " dwelling-house " within the meaning of the Rent and Mortgage Interest (Restrictions) Act 1933, s. 16 (1).[30] Many of these cases were reviewed in *Baker* v. *Turner*.[31]

(2) The deposit of refuse or waste materials, even though they are deposited on a site which is already used for the purpose, provided that either, (a) the superficial area of the deposit is thereby extended, or (b) the height of the deposit is thereby extended so as to exceed the level of adjoining land (s. 22 (3) (*b*)). Thus one can apparently continue to dump waste materials into existing holes in the ground (caused, for example, by mining or quarrying) until the holes are filled to the surface of the surrounding land.

(3) Control over the display of advertisements is dealt with in detail in the Town and Country Planning (Control of Advertisements) Regulations 1969,[32] made under section 34 of the 1962 Act (now section 63 of the 1971 Act), but without prejudice to the provisions of those regulations, the display of advertisements on the external part of a building which is not normally used for such display is to be treated as a material change of use and therefore development of the building (s. 22 (4)) which provision will have the effect of preventing any recurrence of the decision in *Mills & Rockleys* v. *Leicester Corporation*.[33]

In connection with this provision " advertisement," it may be noted, is very widely defined (in section 290 (1) of the 1971 Act) so as to mean any word, letter, model, sign, placard, board, notice, device or representation, whether

---

[28] *Cole* v. *Harris* [1945] K.B. 474 (C.A.).
[29] *Banks* v. *Cope-Brown* [1948] 2 K.B. 287 (D.C.); *Llewellyn* v. *Hinson* [1948] 2 K.B. 385 (C.A.).
[30] *Langford Property Co.* v. *Goldrich* [1949] 1 K.B. 511 (C.A.).
[31] [1950] A.C. 401.
[32] S.I. 1969 No. 1532; see Chap. 9.
[33] [1946] K.B. 315 (D.C.).

illuminated or not, in the nature of and employed wholly or in part for the purposes of advertisement, announcement or direction, and without prejudice to the foregoing provision the word includes any hoarding or similar structure used or adapted for use for the display of advertisements.

7. Section 23, subss. (2), (3), (4), (5), (6), (7), (8), (9) and (10)

Subsections (2) to (10) inclusive of section 23 of the 1971 Act deal with six types of case which, whilst strictly constituting development, can yet be undertaken without obtaining the planning permission which (were it not for the provisions of these nine subsections) would otherwise be required under the provisions of subsection (1) of section 23.

These six types of case have already been referred to (see pp. 71 and 72) and, in considering them further, comment under the following heads may be offered:

(1) In the first place it will be remembered that, whenever the use of land is mentioned in connection with these six cases, land includes buildings, structures or erections (s. 290 (1)).

(2) Secondly, when, in connection with the first of these six cases, reference is made to land being used " temporarily," it will be remembered that " temporarily " does not necessarily mean for a few years only; it means something that " may, within the reasonable contemplation of the parties, come to an end some day." [34]

(3) Thirdly, it is important to note that, so far as the use of land as a caravan site is concerned, this privilege of freedom from the need to apply for planning permission conferred, by subsections (2), (3) and (4) of section 23 of the 1971 Act, on the first three of these six types of case, does *not* apply to the use of land as a caravan site *unless* the land has been used as a caravan site on at least one occasion during the two-year period ending on March 9, 1960 (s. 23 (7)). What constitutes an " occasion " will be a question of fact; user for one day only would appear to be sufficient.

---

[34] *Burrows* v. *Lang* [1901] 2 Ch. 502.

8. Section 22, subs. (2)

Turning now to subsection (2) of section 22, it is found that
this subsection gives examples of *three operations* and *three uses*
which are *not* to constitute development. These will now be
examined in turn.

As to the three operations, the position is as follows:

(1) The carrying out of works of maintenance, improvement
or other alteration to any building, structure or erection
is not development, *provided* such works affect only
the interior of the building or do not materially affect
its external appearance and are not done by way of
repairing war damage (s. 22 (2) (*a*)).

Thus the carrying out of internal conversions will
not constitute development provided they can be done
without materially affecting the outside of the building
concerned. In this connection it is necessary to bear
in mind that the making of additional windows and
doorways to a building in association with internal
conversion may well be said to affect materially the
external appearance of the building and thereby bring
the internal conversions within the category of development for which consent will be required.

It is to be noted that whilst the carrying out of
internal conversions (as mentioned in the previous
paragraph) may not constitute development, nevertheless any material change in *the use* of the building
consequential upon such conversions *will* itself constitute
development.

It is further to be noted that, since January 1, 1969,
any expansion of a building below ground level (even
if it does not materially affect the external appearance
of the building) *will* constitute development (1971 Act,
s. 22 (2) (*a*)).

(2) The carrying out of maintenance and improvement works
to highways by a local highway authority is not development (s. 22 (2) (*b*)).

(3) The breaking open of streets, etc., for the inspection,
repair or renewal of sewers, mains, pipes, cables, etc.,
by a local authority or a statutory undertaker is not
development (s. 22 (2) (*c*)).

As to the three uses, the position is as follows:

(1) The use of any land or any buildings, structures or erections, within the curtilage of a dwelling-house for purposes incidental to the enjoyment of the dwelling-house as a dwelling-house is not development (s. 22 (2) (*d*)).

Here it is important to note that by virtue of section 290 (1) the word " use " in relation to land does not include the use of land by the carrying out of building operations or any other operations on the land. Thus, it follows that the construction of *new* buildings, structures or erections, even though they are within the curtilage of a dwelling-house, and even though they are to be used in connection with the enjoyment of the dwelling-house as a dwelling-house, does constitute development, although it must be added that much of this sort of " curtilage development " comes within the category of " permitted development " by reason of its being included in Class I of the First Schedule to the Town and Country Planning General Development Order 1963.[35]

As to the meaning of " curtilage," in *Sinclair-Lockhart's Trustees* v. *Central Land Board*[36] the Court of Session held that " the ground which is used for the comfortable enjoyment of a house or other building may be regarded in law as being within the curtilage of that house or building, and thereby as an integral part of the same although it has not been marked off or enclosed in any way. It is enough that it serves the purpose of the house or building in some necessary or reasonably useful way."

(2) The use of land for agriculture or forestry, and the use for any of those purposes of any building, structure or erection occupied with the land so used is not development (s. 22 (2) (*e*)).

Again (and for reasons given above) this provision does not cover *new* agricultural or *new* forestry build-

---

[35] S.I. 1963 No. 709, as amended by later statutory instruments.
[36] (1950) 1 P. & C.R. 195; affirmed (1951) 1 P. & C.R. 320. See also *Stephens* v. *Cuckfield R.D.C.* [1960] 2 Q.B. 373 (C.A.).

ings, structures or erections the construction of which
does constitute development. But the erection of a
great many agricultural and forestry buildings is " permitted development " under Class VI and Class VII
of the First Schedule to the Town and Country Planning
General Development Order 1963.[37]

It will be remembered that " agriculture," by section
290 (1), includes horticulture, fruit growing, seed
growing, dairy farming, the breeding and keeping of
livestock (including any creature kept for the production
of food, wool, skins or fur, or for the purpose of its
use in the farming of land), the use of land as grazing
land, meadow land, osier land, market gardens and
nursery grounds, and the use of land for woodlands
where that use is ancillary to the farming of land for
other agricultural purposes.

(3) The Secretary of State is empowered under section 22
(2) (f) to make an order specifying different classes of
use. Under this authority he has made the Town and
Country Planning (Use Classes) Order 1972 [38] whereby,
in the case of land or buildings used for a purpose of
any class specified in the Order, a change of use to any
other purpose of the same class will *not* constitute
development. This Order is examined more fully in
the following paragraphs.

9. The Town and Country Planning (Use Classes) Order 1972

This Order specifies eighteen different classes of use and when
considering them reference may usefully be made to Ministry Circulars Nos. 42/48, 94/50, 10/60, 5/68 and 97/72. Many of the
expressions used in the Order when dealing with the different Use
Classes are given extended meaning by the definitions in article 2 (2)
of the Order. Certain of these definitions merit special mention
here:

(1) There is, for example, what may be termed a basic
definition of the expression " industrial building " and this
is followed by even more refined definitions of " light industrial

---

[37] S.I. 1963 No. 709, as amended by later statutory instruments.
[38] S.I. 1972 No. 1385.

building," "general industrial building" and "special industrial building."

(2) The word " office " is defined so as to include a bank but not a post office or a betting office.

(3) The word " shop " means a building used for the carrying on of any retail trade or retail business wherein the primary purpose is the selling of goods by retail.

(4) The following, *inter alia*, also constitute shops under the Order: a hairdresser's establishment, an undertaker's establishment, an agency supplying railway, theatre and other tickets, a place for receiving articles for washing, cleaning or repairing.

(5) The following do *not* constitute shops for the purposes of the Order: a fun fair, a garage, a petrol-filling station, an office, a betting office, an hotel, restaurant, snackbar, cafe or any other premises licensed for the sale of intoxicating liquors for consumption on the premises.

With the foregoing definitions in mind, attention may now be paid to article 3 and to the Schedule to the Order, the short effect of which is that (subject to any exceptions specified in the classes themselves and subject also to the important decision in *Corporation of City of London v. Secretary of State for the Environment and Another*) [39] the use of a building for any purpose specified in one of the eighteen classes may be changed to any other purpose falling *within the same class* without the need to obtain planning permission; for any change of use which still leaves the use within its original class does not constitute development under the 1971 Act (s. 22 (2) (*f*)).

The foregoing paragraph (and indeed the whole of the 1972 Order) must now be read in the light of the decision in the *Corporation of London* case just mentioned.[39] This decision fully supports the advice given in Ministry Circular 5/68, para. 23, and demonstrates that conditions attached to a grant of planning permission can validly restrict further changes in the use of land even though such changes would not constitute development by virtue of the provisions of the 1972 Use Classes Order.

Special reference is now made to certain (but not all) of the eighteen Use Classes specified in the Schedule to the 1972 Order.

[39] (1971) 23 P. & C.R. 169.

CLASS I

It follows from the provisions of Class I that, provided a building was used on July 1, 1948, as a shop, it may change its use to a totally different kind of shop without any need of planning permission, provided always that it does not transform itself into a shop for the sale of hot food, a tripe shop, a shop for the sale of pet animals or birds, a cat's-meat shop, or a shop for the sale of motor-vehicles.

Thus a grocer's shop can, without planning permission, become a butcher's shop, or a greengrocer's shop, or a hairdressing establishment, or a ticket agency, or a dry cleaner's receiving office. Whilst it is clear that a grocer's shop cannot, without permission, transform itself into a shop for the sale of hot food, it may be asked whether, conversely, a shop for the sale of hot food can transform itself into a grocer's shop without planning permission. Such a change would, it is submitted, constitute a material change of use but although it is not authorised by the Town and Country Planning (Use Classes) Order 1972,[40] it *is* authorised as " permitted development " under the Town and Country Planning General Development Order 1963,[41] article 3 (1), and the First Schedule, Class III (*b*).

CLASS II

Class II of the Use Classes Order makes it clear that an auctioneer's office (for example) may transform itself into a solicitor's office or into a bank without the need for planning permission. If the predominant use of premises has been as offices, the use of the premises *as a whole* may be as an office and within this use class.[42]

CLASS III

Under Class III of the Order a light industrial building used for a particular purpose may transform itself into a light industrial building used for another type of purpose provided always that it remains throughout a light industrial building as defined in article 2 (2) of the Order. The meaning of " light industrial building " is dealt with in *Crisp from the Fens Ltd.* v. *Rutland C.C.*[43]

[40] S.I. 1972 No. 1385.   [41] S.I. 1963 No. 709.
[42] *Shephard* v. *Buckinghamshire C.C.* (1966) 18 P. & C.R. 419.
[43] (1949) 1 P. & C.R. 48 (C.A.).

CLASS IV

Under this class, a general industrial building may similarly transform itself provided that it remains throughout a general industrial building as defined in article 2 (2) of the Order.   As has already been mentioned, if a use leaps from one class into another class, it puts itself beyond the protection of the Order.   Accordingly, a general industrial building may not, so far as this Order is concerned, so change the purposes for which it is used as to transform itself into a light industrial building, but it is to be noted that such a change *is* authorised, as " permitted development," by the Town and Country Planning General Development Order 1963,[44] art. 3 (1), and the First Schedule, Class III (*a*).

OTHER USE CLASSES

Referring briefly to some of the other eighteen classes, it appears that under Class XIV a hospital can become an institution for old people and under Class XV a health centre can become a day nursery.

So far as this Order is concerned a health centre (being in Class XV) cannot transform itself into a nursing home (which is in Class XIV) for the Order does not authorise a use to leap from one class to another.   But such a change *can* take place independently of the provisions of this Order and without planning permission if it can be proved that the change of use (from a health centre to a nursing home) does not constitute a material change of use.

Similarly, under Class XVI an exhibition hall can become a public library and under Class XVII a theatre can become a cinema. At least one local planning authority who, being wishful to maintain within their area the number of " live " theatres, had given planning permission for the demolition of a theatre and the erection on the site of an office block subject to the condition that the new block would contain within itself " a theatre," was dismayed to find the theatre, which had opened as a " live " theatre, shortly thereafter had changed its use into that of a cinema.   The question here is whether the local planning authority, in granting planning permission for a use which itself fell neatly within Use Class XVII (namely use as a theatre) ought to have added a condition which prevented

[44] S.I. 1963 No. 709.

any change of the theatre into a cinema even though, by virtue of this Order, such a change does not of itself constitute development. (See *Corporation of City of London* v. *Secretary of State for the Environment and Another* [45] and Ministry Circular No. 5/68, para. 23.)

10. Determination of what Constitutes "Development"

From the foregoing paragraphs of this chapter it will be seen that the determination of whether a particular operation or change of use constitutes "development" within the meaning of the 1971 Act may be a nice point.[46] The Act recognises this and makes provision for the determination of doubtful cases by application to the local planning authority (s. 53 (1)), from whose decision there is an appeal to the Secretary of State (ss. 53 (2) and 36). The decision of the Secretary of State may be the subject of further appeal on a point of law to the High Court (s. 247).

The procedure for obtaining a determination under section 53 is contained in article 5A of the Town and Country Planning General Development Order 1963.[47]

In addition to the foregoing manner of ascertaining under section 53 of the 1971 Act what constitutes "development," application may be made to the High Court for a declaration as to whether proposed operations or change of use constitute development and the jurisdiction of the court to make such a declaration is not ousted by section 53 of the 1971 Act: *Pyx Granite Co.* v. *Ministry of Housing and Local Government.*[48]

11. The Meaning of "New Development"

Section 22 of the 1971 Act contains five subsections. The first four of these deal with the definition of "development" and have been dealt with in the foregoing paragraphs of this chapter. It remains to add that subsection (5) of section 22 gives a specialised definition of "new development" which means any kind of development (as defined by section 22 (1) (2) (3) and (4) of the 1971 Act and as discussed in this chapter) other than development specified in the

---

[45] (1971) 23 P. & C.R. 169.
[46] *George Cohen 600 Group* v. *Minister of Housing and Local Government* [1916] 1 W.L.R. 944 (D.C.); *Horwitz* v. *Rowson* [1960] 1 W.L.R. 803.
[47] S.I. 1963 No. 709.
[48] [1958] 1 Q.B. 554 (C.A.); [1960] A.C. 260 (H.L.).

Eighth Schedule to the Act. This latter kind of development (sometimes called " Eighth Schedule Development " or " Existing-Use Development "—it used formerly to be called " Third Schedule Development") is development falling within the ambit of the existing use of land. " New development " is development which goes outside the bounds of existing use. Whilst under the 1971 Act no development (whether new development or not) can be undertaken without planning permission,[49] certain classes of existing-use development (namely, those six classes appearing in Part II of the Eighth Schedule to the Act) have always carried with them a right to compensation in case of a refusal of planning permission (s. 169). Compensation on a refusal of planning permission for *new* development is a much more uncertain affair.[50]

---

[49] See Chap. 8 at p. 88 *et seq.*
[50] See Chap. 16.

Chapter 8

CONTROL OVER THE DEVELOPMENT OF LAND

1. The Need for Planning Permission

ONCE a developer has satisfied himself that that which he proposes to do constitutes development under the Town and Country Planning Act 1971 (a matter which was discussed in the previous chapter), he will bear in mind that he should not undertake such development except with planning permission under Part III of the Act (s. 23 (1)).

Under section 14 of the Town and Country Planning Act 1962 the Minister of Housing and Local Government made the Town and Country Planning General Development Order 1963.[1] This Order is amended by Orders made in 1964, 1965, 1967 and 1968 and is further (quite substantially) amended by the Town and Country Planning General Development (Amendment) Order 1969.[2] These Orders continue in full force and effect under the 1971 Act (s. 293) and may be cited as the Town and Country Planning General Development Orders 1963 to 1969 (1969 Order, art. 1). The 1963 Order itself authorises the carrying out of specified development or classes of development (s. 24 (2) (a)). Permission for any such development (known under the Order as " permitted development ") derives directly from the General Development Order itself and there is no need for a developer undertaking this kind of development to make any application for planning permission in respect thereof.

2. Classes of " Permitted Development "—the General Development Order 1963

Ministry Circulars 67/49, 87/50 and 10/60 contain useful information on General Development Orders which preceded, and are now revoked by, the General Development Order 1963.[1] On the 1963 Order (as later amended) reference may be made to Ministry Circulars 39/67, 55/68 and 12/69.

[1] S.I. 1963 No. 709.
[2] S.I. 1969 No. 276.

Attention is directed to the use in this Order of expressions which are given special and extended meaning by the interpretation provisions of article 2 of the Order.

By virtue of article 3 of the Order planning permission is automatically given for all the twenty-three different classes of development set out in Part I of the First Schedule to the Order, which classes are, accordingly, referred to in the Order under the general heading of " permitted development." If development can be brought within the confines of any one or other of these twenty-three different classes, then no application for planning permission in respect thereof need be made to any local planning authority, the General Development Order itself constituting sufficient planning authorisation therefor.

The automatic planning permission granted for permitted development under the General Development Order is granted subject to one or other, or sometimes both, of the two standard conditions mentioned in Part II of the First Schedule to the Order, and also subject to such particular conditions as are respectively attached to the different classes of development as listed in Part I of the First Schedule to the Order.   The two standard conditions are in the following terms:

1. This permission shall not authorise any development which involves the formation, laying out or material widening of a means of access to a trunk or classified road.

2. No development shall be carried out which creates an obstruction to the view of persons using any highway used by vehicular traffic at or near any bend, corner, junction or intersection so as to be likely to cause danger to such persons.

No useful purpose would be served in setting out here full details of all the twenty-three classes of permitted development. Certain comments, however, may usefully be offered upon a number of these classes.

CLASS I

Development within the curtilage of a dwelling-house.   This class relates to development occurring within the curtilage of a dwelling-house, including the enlargement, improvement or other alteration of the dwelling-house so long as the external cubic content of the original house is not exceeded by more than 1,750 cubic feet or one-tenth, whichever is the greater, subject to a maximum of

4,000 cubic feet.   It is to be noted that a garage, stable, loosebox or coach-house erected within the curtilage is to count as an enlargement of the house, and no part of the enlargement (*e.g.* the garage) is to extend above, or project beyond the front of, the original house.

Under Class I are also authorised a number of other outbuildings frequently to be found within the curtilage of a house, *e.g.* summerhouses, greenhouses, tool sheds, beehives, dog kennels, dovecotes, poultry houses, provided that any such buildings or shelters do not exceed certain limitations in height.

As to the meaning of " curtilage," reference may be made to page 81.

CLASS II

Gates and fences, etc., painting.   Gates, fences, walls and other means of enclosure are authorised by this class provided they do not exceed 4 feet in height when abutting on a road used by vehicles or 7 feet in height in any other case.   External painting of a building is also authorised provided it is not in the nature of an advertisement.

CLASS III

Changes of use.   Under this class is authorised a change of use of a building from use as a " general industrial building " as defined in the Town and Country Planning (Use Classes) Order 1972,[3] to use as a " light industrial building " as therein defined.

There is also authorised the change of use of a restaurant to *any* type of shop (except a shop for the sale of hot food, a tripe shop, a shop for the sale of pet animals or birds, a cat's-meat shop, or a shop for the sale of motor-vehicles) and also a change of use to *any* type of shop from use as a shop for one or other of the five excepted kinds just mentioned.

CLASS IV

Temporary buildings and uses.   Under this class is authorised the erection of buildings, plant and machinery needed temporarily in connection with the carrying out of development (other than mining operations) for which planning permission has been granted or deemed to have been granted under the 1971 Act.

[3] S.I. 1972 No. 1385.

This class also authorises the use of land, *not* within the curtilage of a building or the site of a war-damaged building, for any purpose (except that of a caravan site) on not more than twenty-eight days in total in a calendar year, and the erection or placing of movable structures on the land in connection with such use.[4] The use of a field for an agricultural show and the erection of a marquee, etc., in association therewith, would be authorised as a temporary use under this class.

The effect upon planning permission and enforcement notices[5] of the provision as to twenty-eight days in connection with this class of permitted development was raised in *Postill* v. *East Riding County Council*,[6] in *Francis* v. *Yiewsley and West Drayton Urban District Council*,[7] and in *Cater* v. *Essex County Council*.[8] As a result of the decision in the latter case it appeared impossible to enforce the twenty-eight-day limitation imposed in connection with this class of permitted development, but section 38 (2) of the Town and Country Planning Act 1959 (now section 24 (6) of the 1971 Act) remedied this defect in the law.

CLASS V

Uses by members of recreational organisations.   Under this class land *not* within the curtilage of a dwelling-house may be used for recreation and instruction involving the use of tents (but not caravans) by members of a recreational organisation which holds a certificate of exemption under section 269 of the Public Health Act 1936.

CLASS VI

Agricultural buildings, works and uses.   This class is important from the farmer's point of view for it authorises the carrying out on " agricultural land " of more than one acre *and* comprised in an " agricultural unit " of all the building and engineering operations likely to be undertaken on a normal farm.   The provision and alteration of dwellings, however, are not covered by this class.

---

[4] *Godstone R.D.C.* v. *Brazil* [1953] 1 W.L.R. 1102 (D.C.).
[5] See Chap. 14.
[6] [1956] 2 Q.B. 386 (D.C.).
[7] [1958] 1 Q.B. 478 (C.A.); affirming [1957] 2 Q.B. 136.
[8] [1960] 1 Q.B. 424 (D.C.).

Nor is an aircraft hangar used in connection with the business of breeding and training horses for show-jumping—such business not being requisite for the use of land for agriculture.[9]

" Agricultural land " and " agricultural unit " are defined in article 2 (1) of the General Development Order and should be noted.

Buildings or structures covered by this class are limited in size and height by the particular conditions subject to which planning permission for their erection is permitted by the Order. Moreover, such buildings or structures must be designed for the purposes of agriculture, and thus old bus bodies, tramcars, or railway carriages are not allowed under the permission.

Under this class are also authorised roadside stands for milk churns (but not when they would abut on a trunk road or a classified road) and the winning upon land occupied with agricultural land of minerals reasonably required for the purposes of the agricultural land, e.g. for fertilisation and for the improvement of agricultural buildings.

In those areas of natural beauty specified in the Town and Country Planning (Landscape Areas Special Development) Order 1950,[10] no agricultural development authorised under Class VI may be carried out without notification to the local planning authority, who have fourteen days in which to intervene with requirements as to the design and external appearance of such development. The areas of natural beauty specified in the Order are as follows:

In the county of Caernarvon:
    The urban district of Bettws-y-Coed.
    The rural district of Gwrfai.
    The rural district of Nant Conway.

In the county of Chester:
    The rural district of Tintwistle.

In the county of Cumberland:
    The urban district of Keswick.
    The rural district of Cockermouth.
    The rural district of Ennerdale.
    The rural district of Millom.
    The rural district of Penrith.

[9] *Belmont Farm* v. *Minister of Housing and Local Government* (1962) 13 P. & C.R. 417 (D.C.).
[10] S.I. 1950 No. 729.

In the county of Derby:
    The urban district of Bakewell.
    The rural district of Bakewell.
    The rural district of Chapel-en-le-Frith.

In the county of Lancaster:
    The rural district of Ulverston.

In the county of Merioneth:
    The urban district of Dolgelley.
    The rural district of Dolgelley.
    The rural district of Deundraeth.
    The rural district of Penllyn.

In the county of Westmorland:
    The urban district of Lakes.
    The urban district of Windermere.
    The rural district of North Westmorland.
    The rural district of South Westmorland.

CLASS VII

Forestry buildings and works. Under this class are authorised the carrying out on land used for forestry purposes of building and other operations (but not the building or alteration of dwelling-houses) needed for those purposes, and the making of private roads on such land.

The restrictions of the Town and Country Planning (Landscape Areas Special Development) Order 1950 apply to development authorised by this class if the development is in one of the areas of natural beauty specified in that Order.[11]

CLASS VIII

Development for industrial purposes. This class applies to development carried out by an " industrial undertaker " as defined in the Order (art. 2 (1)), and relates to the provision of certain private roads and railways, sewers, mains, etc.; the installation of certain plant and machinery; the deposit, subject to limitations, of

[11] See above under Class VI.

waste material; and the making of limited additions to industrial buildings. The limited additions may be in the form of extensions or new buildings up to a maximum of one-tenth of the cubic content of the original buildings, but they must not be such as to require a certificate issued by the Secretary of State under section 67 of the 1971 Act and they must not materially alter the external appearance of the premises.

CLASS IX

Repairs to unadopted streets and private ways. Under this class abutting owners (*inter alios*) are authorised to repair the highway (as yet unadopted by the local authority) on which their own premises abut.

CLASS X

Repairs to services. This class authorises the repair of sewers, underground telephone wires, and similar services, by the appropriate authorities.

CLASS XI

War-damaged buildings, works and plant. Under this class is authorised the replacement of war-damaged buildings, works or plant, provided the cubic content thereof is not increased beyond the limits authorised under Class I or Class VIII, and provided further that the replacement does not, except with the permission of the local planning authority, involve any material alteration of the previously existing external appearance.

In connection with development falling within this class, reference should be made to the observations later in this chapter [12] relating to the making of a Direction by the Secretary of State *excluding* certain kinds of development from this particular class of permitted development.

CLASS XII

Development under local or private Acts, or Orders. This class authorises the carrying out (subject to important reservations), as development permitted under the 1971 Act, of any development of

[12] See p. 95.

land which is authorised by a local or private Act, or an Order approved by both Houses of Parliament, provided that the Act or Order designates specifically both the nature of the development and the land upon which it may be carried out.

In *Pyx Granite Co. v. Ministry of Housing and Local Government*,[13] it was held that a company which was authorised by a special Act of Parliament to quarry over a specified area of land did not, as a result of the provisions of Class XII, require express planning permission to carry out further quarrying in the specified area.

CLASSES XIII TO XXIII

These remaining classes of permitted development relate, in the main, to development by local authorities and statutory undertakers (Classes XIII to XX), to the use of aerodrome buildings (Class XXI), to the use of land as a caravan site (Class XXII) [14] and to development required by the conditions of a site licence in force under Part I of the Caravan Sites and Control of Development Act 1960 (Class XXIII).[14]

3. Exclusion from " Permitted Development "

The Secretary of State or a local planning authority may make a direction which will have the effect of removing from the category of permitted development any development specified in the direction (art. 4 (1)). Any such direction made by a local planning authority will require the Secretary of State's approval (art. 4 (2)). Any such direction made under an earlier Development Order and in force on the commencement of the General Development Order 1963 is further continued in force under article 4 (5) of the 1963 Order.

This is important in connection with development falling within Class XI (see above) relating to the replacement of war-damaged buildings, works or plant because some local planning authorities have had this particular class of development *excluded* from the category of permitted development (and thereby made subject to control by the local planning authority) by means of a Direction made and approved under the Town and Country Planning (General Interim Development) Order 1946 (now repealed). In those areas where this has been done, the local planning authority will continue

[13] [1960] A.C. 260 (H.L.).
[14] See Chap. 10.

to have control over the replacement of war-damaged buildings, works and plant, notwithstanding that these matters are included in Class XI of the General Development Order 1963.

4. Method of Applying for Planning Permission

Assuming that development which it is sought to undertake is development within the meaning of the 1971 Act for which planning permission is *not* automatically granted by the General Development Order 1963, then in such case it will be necessary for planning permission to be obtained for it from the appropriate local planning authority (s. 24 (2) (*b*)). Any application to the local planning authority for planning permission must be made in such manner as is prescribed by regulations (s. 25).

Details as to the method of applying for planning permission are dealt with in articles 5, 5A and 5B of the General Development Order 1963 (as amended by the General Development (Amendment) Order 1969). The application is to be made on a form issued by the local planning authority and obtainable from that authority or from the council with whom the application is to be lodged (art. 5 (1)).

In the case of land in the City of London the application is to be lodged with the Common Council of the City, and in the case of other land in the administrative area of Greater London, with the council of the London borough in which the land is situated (art. 5B (1)).

Where the land is not in Greater London the application is to be lodged with the county borough council or with the county district council for the area where the land is situated (art. 5B (1)).

It will be the duty of the council with whom the application is lodged to transmit it (where necessary) to the local planning authority to whom it is made (art. 5B (1)).

The application is to include such particulars as the application form requires to be supplied and is to be accompanied by a plan sufficient to identify the land together with such other plans and drawings as are necessary to describe the development (art. 5 (1)). There must also be lodged such additional copies (not exceeding three) of the application, plans and drawings, as may be required by the directions printed on the application form, and the local planning authority may require such further information as is requisite to enable them to determine the application (*ibid.*).

Either before he buys his land or before he incurs the cost of preparing detailed plans, a developer may wish to know whether his proposed development will be likely to get planning permission if he applies for it. A developer may make an application (art. 5 (2)) for " outline planning permission " which can be granted subject to a condition that there shall be subsequent approval by the local planning authority of any " reserved matters " relating to siting, design and external appearance of buildings (art. 2 (1)). The developer thus gets to know, before he incurs too much expense, whether in principle his proposed development is acceptable to the local planning authority. Once an outline application is granted, the local planning authority are committed to allowing the proposed development in some form or other, the only matters requiring subsequent approval by the authority being such as are specifically reserved in the permission granted on the outline application.

Paragraphs 42–51 inclusive of the Memorandum to Ministry Circular No. 48/59, together with the Appendix, entitled " Notes for Applicants," to that Memorandum, provide guidance not only to local authorities but also to developers seeking to obtain a planning permission for development.

5. Notification of Planning Application to Owners and Agricultural Tenants

An applicant for planning permission does not need to have a legal interest in the land to which the application relates; the application may be made (and frequently is—especially in the case of an application for " outline planning permission " as referred to in an earlier paragraph) by a prospective purchaser or lessee. Formerly the application could be made without the knowledge of the owner of the land,[15] but this is no longer the case.

It was the subject of adverse comment that an application for planning permission could be made behind the back, as it were, of the owner of the land concerned, who thus might never hear anything about the matter at all until there was, for example, an appeal to the Minister against a refusal of planning permission. This state of affairs is now, to some limited extent, remedied by section 27 of the 1971 Act.

---

[15] *Hanily* v. *Minister of Local Government and Planning* [1952] 2 Q.B. 444.

Any application for planning permission *must* be accompanied by a certificate in one or other of four different forms, and if it is not so accompanied, then the local authority receiving it " shall not entertain " it (s. 27 (1)). The choice of which of the four forms of certificate is used depends on the circumstances of the case but section 27 (1) (*a*) (*b*) (*c*) (*d*) of the 1971 Act indicate which form is to be used while article 7 (1) and Part I of Schedule 4 to the Town and Country Planning General Development Order 1963 [16] (as amended by the General Development (Amendment) Order 1969) set out each of the four forms of certificate from which the selection of one is to be made.

These four forms of certificate are referred to in Part I of Schedule 4 to the General Development Order 1963 as (respectively) Certificate A, Certificate B, Certificate C, and Certificate D. If the circumstances of the case require that the certificate shall be in the form of Certificate C or Certificate D, then the certificate *must* contain a statement that a notice (as set out in the certificate itself) has been published on a specified date in a local newspaper circulating in the locality in which the land in question is situated (s. 27 (2)), the form of this notice being set out in Part II of Schedule 4 to the General Development Order 1963.

Whatever form of certificate is used the certificate *must* contain one or other of the alternative statements relating to agricultural holdings set out in section 27 (3) of the 1971 Act.

In any case where the applicant for planning permission is himself either—

(a) the estate " owner " (as defined in section 27 (7) of the 1971 Act) in fee simple of *all* the land comprised in the planning application (s. 27 (1) (*a*)), *or*

(b) entitled to a " tenancy " (which means (s. 290 (1)) a tenancy as defined in the Landlord and Tenant Act 1954) of *all* such land (*ibid.*),

then a certificate in the form of Certificate A will be the appropriate one to use, with the result that the applicant for planning permission will not be under any obligation to give notification of his application to any third party, unless the land comprised in the application constitutes or forms part of an " agricultural holding " (as defined in s. 27 (7) of the 1971 Act), in which case any person who, twenty-

[16] S.I. 1963 No. 709.

one days before the date of the planning application, was a tenant of the agricultural holding must be notified of the application (s. 27 (3) (*b*)).

If, however, the applicant is unable, on the facts, to accompany his planning application with a certificate in the form of Certificate A, then he must accompany it with a certificate in the form of Certificate B, or Certificate C, or Certificate D, as the case may require. If any one of these three kinds of certificate is used, or if the certificate discloses (pursuant to s. 27 (3) (*b*)) that notification of the application has been given to the tenant of an agricultural holding any part of which is comprised in land to which the application relates, then the local planning authority must not determine the application until the end of a period of twenty-one days from the date (as disclosed in the certificate accompanying the application) of the service of the notice of the making of the application or, as the case may be, of the publication of the notice of the making of the application, whichever date is the later (s. 27 (4)). If, during this period of twenty-one days, the authority receive any representation about the application, the authority must take such representation into account before determining the application, provided that the authority are satisfied that the representation is made by a person who is either an " owner " (as defined in s. 27 (7)) of any of the land to which the application relates or is the tenant of an " agricultural holding " (as defined in s. 27 (7)) any part of which is comprised in that land (s. 29 (3) (*a*)).

Having determined the application the local planning authority must give notice of their decision not only to the applicant but to any person who made representations which the authority was obliged to take into account (s. 29 (3) (*b*)).

Any person who issues a certificate which contains a statement which he knows to be false or misleading in a material particular, or who recklessly issues a certificate which is false or misleading in a material particular, is liable on summary conviction to a fine not exceeding £100 (s. 27 (5)).

6. Newspaper Advertisement and Site Notices for
Certain Planning Applications

It is provided in section 26 of the 1971 Act that planning applications in respect of any of those five classes of development prescribed in article 6 of the General Development Order 1963,[17] must be advertised in the local press, and be the subject of a site notice displayed on the land affected by the development, so that representations concerning the development can be sent to the local planning authority within twenty-one days (s. 26 and art. 6 and Sched. 3, Parts I, II and III of the General Development Order 1963 as amended by the General Development Order 1969).

The Secretary of State has stated that this procedure for giving publicity to planning applications will be used only in the case of " very limited types of development which might be considered bad neighbours " and the five classes of development so far prescribed in the General Development Order 1963, are as follows:

  (a) construction of buildings for use as a public convenience;
  (b) construction of buildings or other operations, or use of land, for the disposal of refuse or waste materials;
  (c) construction of buildings or other operations (other than the laying of sewers, the construction of septic tanks serving single dwelling-houses, and works ancillary thereto), or use of land, for the purpose of sewage disposal;
  (d) construction of buildings or use of land for the purpose of a slaughterhouse or knacker's yard;
  (e) construction of buildings and use of buildings for any of the following purposes, namely, as a theatre, a cinema, a music-hall, a dance-hall, a skating-rink, a swimming-bath or gymnasium (not forming part of a school, college or university), a Turkish or other vapour or foam bath, or a building for indoor games.

If any person makes a representation concerning any of the foregoing classes of development and the representation is received by the local planning authority before the end of twenty-one days from the date of the application, then the authority is bound to consider the representation before deciding the application (s. 29 (2)). A person making such a representation is, however, not entitled to appear before the local planning authority but must content himself with expressing his views in writing.

7. Site Notices

If, under the foregoing provisions of the 1971 Act a site notice

[17] S.I. 1963 No. 709.

needs to be displayed, it is the duty of the applicant for planning permission to post the notice on the site (s. 26 (2) (3)) unless he is prevented from doing so by lack of rights of access to the site or of other rights (*ibid.*).

The notice must be posted for not less than seven days during the month immediately preceding the application for planning permission (s. 26 (3) (*b*)), and must be in the form prescribed (s. 26 (3) (*a*) and art. 6 and Sched. 3, Part III of the General Development Order 1963 as amended by the General Development Order 1969). The notice must be firmly fixed and displayed so as to be easily visible by the public without going on the site (s. 26 (4)) and it must state that application for planning permission is to be made (s. 26 (3) (*a*)) and name a place *within the locality* where a copy of the application and of all plans and other documents will be open to public inspection at reasonable hours during a period of not less than twenty-one days after the posting of the notice (s. 26 (6)). It will be noted that it is the applicant's responsibility (and not that of the local planning authority) to make the plans and other documents open for inspection by the public at some place in the locality of the site.

Having done all the foregoing the applicant must sign a certificate (in the prescribed form—s. 26 (9)) to that effect and send it, with his application for planning permission, to the local planning authority who cannot entertain the application in the absence of the certificate (s. 26 (2) (*b*)). If an applicant is unable to carry out all the foregoing requirements he must certify accordingly (*ibid.*).

An applicant issuing a false certificate is liable on summary conviction to a fine of £100 (s. 26 (8)).

An applicant is excused if, without fault or intention of his, a site notice, duly posted, is removed, obscured, or defaced before the requisite seven days have elapsed, *provided* that the applicant has taken reasonable steps for its protection and, if need be, its replacement (s. 26 (5)).

8. Planning Permission in Conservation Areas

Under section 277 of the 1971 Act, local planning authorities are to determine what parts of their areas should be designated as conservation areas, that is, areas of special architectural or historic interest the character or appearance of which ought to be preserved or enhanced.

If any area is so designated the later grant of planning permission for development in the area could be quite a delicate matter. Accordingly, the Secretary of State may give directions to local planning authorities as to the matters which they must consider when dealing with such an application, and as to the consultations with persons or bodies which ought to take place before a decision is made (s. 277).

Where an application for planning permission relates to a conservation area (designated as aforesaid) it must be advertised in the local press and additional publicity must be given to any such application through the medium of " site notices " posted on or near the land to which the application relates (s. 28 (1) and (2)). This will give a further opportunity for representations about the application for planning permission to be made to the local planning authority who must allow time for this to be done (s. 28 (3)). If any representations are made the local planning authority must take them into account when determining the application (s. 29 (4)).

9. Caravans, Offices and Industrial Development

Where development involves the use of land as a caravan site, or the building of offices or the carrying out of industrial development, then in each of these three cases the law has made special provisions relating to the obtaining of planning permission for development.   These special provisions are dealt with later in these pages.[18]

10. By-law Approval for Development

In connection with the need to obtain planning permission under the 1971 Act for all development, a developer must not lose sight of the fact that the code of planning law and the code of public health law still run their separate courses side by side and, accordingly, in addition to whatever planning permission it is necessary to obtain *under planning law* before development is undertaken, it still remains necessary for a developer to obtain, *under public health law* and its associated building by-laws, the approval of the

---

[18] See respectively Chaps. 10, 11 and 12.

appropriate by-law authority to the plans of any buildings involved in his proposed development.

11. Method of Dealing with Applications for Planning Permission

The method of dealing with applications for planning permission once they have been made is again dealt with in the Town and Country Planning General Development Order 1963 [19] (as amended by the General Development (Amendment) Order 1969) and in section 29 of the 1971 Act.

Upon receipt of an application for planning permission the receiving authority must send to the applicant a notification that his application has been received (art. 5B (2)). The actual wording of the notification is set out in Part I of Schedule 2 to the General Development Order 1963.

The period during which a local planning authority must give notice of its decision on the application will be, generally speaking, *two months*, except that in the case of an application affecting a trunk road it will be *three months*, but these periods may be extended by agreement in writing between the parties (art. 5B (3)). In any case the requirement as to these periods is directory and not mandatory and a notice of decision given after the expiration of the statutory period is not ineffective if accepted and acted upon by the applicant.[20]

If the applicant does not hear from the local planning authority within the appropriate period, then he has a right to appeal to the Secretary of State " as if " his application had in fact been refused (s. 37).

In dealing with applications for planning permission a local planning authority must have regard to the provisions of their development plan but are not confined solely to the plan and may have regard to any other material considerations (s. 29 (1)). Moreover, a local planning authority is authorised by the General Development Order 1963 (art. 10), and subject to the directions of the Secretary of State, to ignore, in such cases and subject to such conditions as may be prescribed by the directions aforesaid, the provisions of their development plan and grant permission for development which is contrary thereto (s. 31 (1) (*b*), the 1963 Order,

[19] S.I. 1963 No. 709.
[20] *James* v. *Minister of Housing and Local Government* [1968] A.C. 409 (H.L.).

art. 10, and the Town and Country Planning (Development Plans) Direction 1965 set out in Ministry Circular No. 70/65).

The General Development Order 1963 contains further provisions relating to the giving of directions by the Secretary of State restricting the right of a local planning authority to grant planning permissions (art. 8), and to the holding of consultations with specified bodies before planning permission is given for development affecting trunk roads and special roads (art. 9), or affecting certain other specified matters, *i.e.* land in the area of a neighbouring local planning authority; the amount of traffic using a trunk road or a railway level crossing; a means of access to any road (other than a trunk road) for which the local planning authority is not also the local highway authority; the erection of certain buildings in an area of proposed coal working; development within certain distances of the Royal Palaces or Parks; development of land in an area of special interest notified by the Nature Conservancy under section 23 of the National Parks and Access to the Countryside Act 1949 (art. 11 (1)). The Greater London Council, before granting planning permission, must consult with the Common Council of the City of London or with the council of any London borough affected (art. 11 (1A)). Permission for development of land for agricultural purposes must not be refused or granted subject to conditions without consultation with the Minister of Agriculture (art. 11 (2)). The Secretary of State may direct a local planning authority to consult with named authorities, bodies or persons before dealing with an application for planning permission (art. 11 (3) and (4)).

12. Decision of the Local Planning Authority

The planning decision of the local planning authority may be one of three kinds. The authority may:

(a) grant permission unconditionally, or

(b) grant permission subject to such conditions " as they think fit," or

(c) refuse permission (s. 29 (1)).

The decision of the local planning authority must be in " writing " (the 1963 Order, art. 5 (10)), which expression, by virtue of section 20 of the Interpretation Act 1889, includes printing, lithography, photography, and other modes of representing words in visible form.

If conditions are attached to the grant of permission, or if there is a total refusal of permission, the reasons therefore must be given in writing, together with a notification set out in the terms of Part II of Schedule 2 to the General Development Order 1963 (art. 5B (4)).

A permission for the erection of a building may specify the purposes for which the building shall be used and, if it does not, the building may be used for the purposes for which it was designed (s. 33 (2)).

A grant of planning permission for development may also cover permission for the retention of buildings or works already constructed before the application for permission is made and for the continuance of any use of land instituted before that day (s. 32).

A register of all applications for planning permission and of the local planning authority's decisions is to be kept and to be open for public inspection (s. 34 and art. 14 of the General Development Order 1963 [21] as amended by the General Development Order 1969). The register of planning applications must contain copies of the application and any plans or drawings submitted with them (s. 34 (2)).

Any person interested in buying land may ascertain what planning permission or permissions (if any) have been granted in respect of the land by searching the planning register. Any such search will be additional to the usual conveyancing searches made in registers of local land charges kept under the Land Charges Act 1925.

13. Planning Decisions by Officers of Local Authorities [21a]

Section 4 of the 1971 Act enables a local planning authority to delegate planning functions to any of their officers *if the authority wish to do so.* The authority have a discretion whether to delegate or not. But if they do decide to delegate, then the authority may only delegate (s. 4 (1)) applications of the following kind, namely,

(a) an application for planning permission under Part III of the 1971 Act;

(b) an application for an approval required by a development order or by a condition imposed on the grant of planning permission;

(c) an application for a determination under section 53 of the 1971 Act of the questions whether the carrying out of operations on land or the making of any change in the use

[21] S.I. 1963 No. 709.
[21a] See footnote 19 on page 29.

of land constitutes or involves development of the land and, if so, whether an application for planning permission is required therefor;

(d) an application for consent under an order under section 60 of the 1971 Act to the cutting down, topping, lopping or destruction of trees;

(e) an application for consent under regulations under section 63 of the 1971 Act to the display of advertisements;

(f) an application for an established use certificate under section 94 of the 1971 Act.

The delegation of functions can be made with or without restrictions or conditions (s. 4 (3) (*b*)).

It is to be noted that under section 4 not only may a local *planning* authority delegate planning functions to one of their officers, but a local authority who are not themselves a planning authority but to whom the function of determining planning applications has been delegated under section 3 of the 1971 Act—any such local authority may also delegate to any one of *their* officers the right to determine planning applications (s. 4 (2)), and may also delegate that function to an officer of the local planning authority, provided the latter consents to this (*ibid.*).

Whilst a delegation of power under section 4 can be made to *any* " officer " (the word is not defined in the 1971 Act) of a local authority, the delegation *must* be made to the officer *by name* and not *ex officio* (s. 4 (3)).

If an officer to whom delegated powers have been granted feels that any particular application should not be dealt with by him but should be dealt with by the local authority themselves, then the officer may request this to be done and, if he does so, the local authority will be obliged to determine the application accordingly (s. 4 (4)).

The decision of an officer to whom powers have been delegated by a local authority under section 4 is to be treated *for all purposes* as the decision of the delegating authority, provided the decision is notified in writing to the applicant (s. 4 (5)).

If, in discharging functions which have been delegated to him, the officer does something in respect of which an action is brought against him, then, even though he may not be in a position legally to *require* his employing authority to indemnify him, such authority may nevertheless indemnify the officer against the whole or part of any damages and costs which he may become liable to pay, provided the authority are satisfied that the officer honestly believed that the act complained of was an act which his delegated functions required or entitled him to do (s. 4 (6)).

Hereafter, any reference to a local authority in any enactment is to be construed as referring also to any officer of that authority to whom functions have been delegated by the authority under the 1968 Act (s. 4 (7)).

If a local authority wish to recall any delegation of functions made to one of their officers, they can do so (s. 4 (3) (c)). This can be done at any time and it can be done generally or in respect only of a particular application (*ibid.*). It can, however, only be done without prejudice to anything properly and earlier done by the officer under the terms of the delegation (*ibid.*).

If the delegation of functions is by a local authority acting themselves under delegated powers from a local *planning* authority, and if the delegation of functions is to an officer *of the local planning authority* (as it can be under section 4 (2) (b)), then if the local planning authority withdraw their consent to this arrangement, the delegation of functions to the officer is, *ipso facto*, to be treated as withdrawn (s. 4 (3) (d)).

14. Duration of Planning Permissions

The Town and Country Planning Act 1971 provides, that without prejudice to any revocation or modification, a planning permission to develop land, once granted, will enure for the benefit of the land and of any person for the time being having an interest in the land unless the permission itself otherwise provides (s. 33 (1)). There may thus be more than one permission in existence in respect of the same piece of land.

But a planning permission, whilst it may enure for the benefit of a series of different people in succession, will not itself endure for ever. Indeed, it will not necessarily last until it is revoked. The duration of a planning permission is now controlled by sections 41–44 inclusive of the 1971 Act together with paragraphs 18–22 inclusive of Schedule 24 to the Act.

In considering time limits for planning permissions a distinction has to be made between those permissions granted before April 1, 1969, and those granted on or after that date. April 1, 1969, is the date when the provisions of the Town and Country Planning Act

1968 (which first introduced statutory time limits for planning permissions) came into operation.

(1) Time limits for planning permissions granted before April 1, 1969

Any planning permission granted before April 1, 1969, is deemed to have been granted (if the development to which it relates had not been begun before the beginning of 1968) subject to *a condition* that the development must be begun within five years, namely, before April 1, 1974 (Sched. 24, para. 19).   This condition will not, however, apply to any planning permission which was granted or deemed to be granted before April 1, 1969, subject to an express condition that the development to which it relates should be begun, or be completed, not later than a specified date or within a specified period (Sched. 24, para. 19 (2) (*a*)).

In calculating the period of five years referred to in the above-mentioned condition, no account is to be taken of any period, after April 1, 1969, during which any planning permission to which the condition relates is deemed to be of no effect by reason of paragraph 1 (4) (*a*) of Schedule 12 to the 1971 Act relating to office development in the metropolitan region (Sched. 24, para. 20A).

Thus if a planning permission is a permission granted before April 1, 1969, then, if development pursuant to that planning permission was begun before January 1, 1968, the planning permission does *not* come within the ambit of the 1971 Act at all.   If this is the case, then the planning permission does not come within the ambit of section 44 of the Act either and it follows, therefore, that the development to which the permission relates can *never* be made the subject of a " completion notice " (as to which, see p. 111 below) under section 44 of the Act.

(2) Time limits for planning permissions granted on or after April 1, 1969

For any planning permission granted on or after April 1, 1969, the limitation was formerly dealt with in section 65 of the Town and Country Planning Act 1968, now re-enacted in section 41 of the 1971 Act, under which the limitation is again five years from the grant, or the deemed grant, of planning permission (s. 41 (1) (*a*)).   The development must be begun within this period of five years (s. 41 (2)).   But the five-year period may be varied up or down if circumstances so warrant (s. 41 (1) (*b*)) and it will be for " the authority concerned with the terms of the planning permission " to bring about any variation in the basic five-year period (*ibid.*), this authority being specifically defined in section 43 (4) of the 1971 Act.

It is to be noted that the foregoing provisions relating to the limited duration of planning permissions (whether granted before, or on or after, April 1, 1969) do *not* apply (s. 41 (3)) in the following four cases:

    (a) to any planning permission granted by a development order;

    (b) to any planning permission granted for a limited period (within the meaning of section 30 (2) of the 1971 Act);

    (c) to any planning permission granted under section 32 of the 1971 Act on an application relating to buildings or works completed, or a use of land instituted, before the date of the application; and

    (d) to any outline planning permission (as to which, see section 42 of the 1971 Act).

Any conditions relating to time limits imposed on a grant of planning permission may be the subject of an appeal to the Secretary of State under section 36 of the 1971 Act against the decision of the local planning authority (s. 43 (6)).

If a time limit runs out before that which was required to be done within the limit has actually been carried out, then anything done thereafter is declared to be unauthorised or otherwise out of order (s. 43 (7)).

(*3*) *Time limits for outline planning permissions*

Time limits applicable to outline planning permissions (as defined in section 42 (1) of the 1971 Act) are dealt with separately from those dealt with above.

If an outline planning permission for building or other operations has been granted before April 1, 1969, but the development to which it refers has not been begun before January 1, 1968, then:

    (a) any matter reserved by the permission for later approval must be dealt with within *three years* of April 1, 1969, *and*

    (b) the development itself must be begun within *five years* of April 1, 1969, or within *two years* of " the final approval " of any reserved matter, whichever of these two periods is the longer (Sched. 24, para. 20 (1)).

Such a matter may be said to have been finally approved when either the application for approval is granted by the local planning authority or, in the case of an appeal, when it is granted by the Secretary of State (s. 43 (5) and Sched. 24, para. 21).

It is to be noted that none of the foregoing provisions applying time limits to an outline planning permission granted before April 1, 1969, is to apply if the planning permission is granted subject to an express condition that the development to which it relates is to be begun or completed by a specified date, or that application for approval of any reserved matter is to be made by a specified date (Sched. 24, para. 20 (2)).

In calculating the periods (referred to above) of three years, five years or two years respectively, no account is to be taken of any period, after April 1, 1969, during which any planning permission to which any one of the said periods relates is deemed to be of no effect by reason of paragraph 1 (4) (*a*) of Schedule 12 to the 1971 Act relating to office development in the metropolitan region (Sched. 24, para. 20A).

As to an outline planning permission granted on or after April 1, 1969, the permission is to be granted (and will be deemed to be granted) in a case where the planning authority fails to carry out this requirement (s. 42 (3)) subject to conditions which apply time limits of three years, five years and two years respectively (as mentioned above) (s. 42 (2)) so, however, that " the authority concerned with the terms of the planning permission " (as to which, see section 43 (4)) may vary these time limits (making them shorter or longer) as they consider appropriate (s. 42 (4)). Before varying these time limits the authority must have regard to the provisions of the development plan and to any other material considerations (s. 42 (6)).

Any conditions relating to time limits required by section 42 of the 1971 Act to be imposed in connection with a grant of outline planning permission, or the later approval thereunder of any reserved matter, may be the subject of an appeal to the Secretary of State under section 36 of the 1971 Act against the decision of the local planning authority (s. 43 (6)).

Again, if a time limit included in a grant of outline planning permission runs out before that which was required to be done within the limit has actually been carried out, then anything done thereafter is declared to be unauthorised or otherwise out of order (s. 43 (7)).

(4) *No compensation for time limits*

Compensation is not claimable in respect of a time-limiting condition (s. 147 (3)) and any such condition may also be ignored for certain other purposes relating to compensation and the right to serve a purchase notice (ss. 169 (7), 180 (4) and 237 (5)).

(5) *When is development said to be begun?*

In connection with the foregoing time limits reference is frequently made to the beginning of development. When is a project of development to be regarded as having been begun? This is an important question and the answer is that a project of development must be regarded as having been begun on the earliest date on which a " specified operation " is begun to be carried out (s. 43 (1)). A specified operation (by section 43 (2)) means:

(a) any work of construction in the course of the erection of a building;

(b) the digging of a trench which is to contain the foundations, or part of the foundations, of a building;

(c) the laying of any underground main or pipe to the foundations, or part of the foundations, of a building or to any such trench as is mentioned in the last preceding paragraph;

(d) any operation in the course of laying out or constructing a road or part of a road;

(e) any change in the use of any land, where that change constitutes " material development " (as defined in section 43 (3) of the 1971 Act).

(6) *Termination of planning permissions—completion notices*

But if there are time limits for the *beginning* of development, there are also to be time limits for its *completion*.

The 1971 Act provides for the termination of planning permission by reference to a time limit (s. 44). Local planning authorities are empowered to serve a " completion notice " terminating a planning permission if the development has been begun, but has not been completed, before the expiration of the time limit contained in the permission and it appears unlikely to the local planning authority that it will be completed within a reasonable period thereafter (s. 44 (2)).

The completion notice must be served on the owner and occupier of the land affected and also upon any other person likely, in the opinion of the local planning authority, to be affected by the notice (s. 44 (3) (*a*)).

The completion notice will state that the planning permission will cease to have effect on such date as may be specified in the notice and this date must not be earlier than twelve months from the date of the notice (s. 44 (2)).   If and when the notice ultimately takes effect the planning permission referred to in it will cease to have effect except so far as it authorises development carried out up to and including any such date (s. 44 (5)).

The completion notice will not take effect until confirmed by the Secretary of State, who may substitute a longer period for completion than the period stated in the notice (s. 44 (3) (*b*)).

Any person served with a completion notice may require to be heard by an Inspector (appointed by the Secretary of State) before the Secretary of State confirms the notice (s. 44 (4)).   This require-ment may be made within twenty-eight days of receiving the notice or within such longer period as the notice may state (*ibid.*).

Having served a completion notice a local planning authority may change their mind, in which case they are entitled to withdraw the completion notice.   This can be done at any time before the date on which the notice declares that the planning permission to which it refers is to cease to have effect (s. 44 (6)).

(7) *Renewal of time-limited planning permissions*

In connection with all these time limits it may be remembered that if any particular limit is running out it is always open to a person to apply for a renewal of the planning permission which contains the time limit.   Whether it *will* be renewed is, of course, a matter for the local planning authority and, on appeal, the Secretary of State.   On this matter of renewals the Government position was given by the Minister of State during the Committee Stage of the Bill for the Town and Country Planning Act 1968 (*Hansard*, Standing Committee G, April 4, 1968, col. 956) when he said:

" . . . there is no bar to renewal of the [planning] permission. I accept that cases will arise when, for perfectly good reasons outside his control, the owner will not have been able to start his development within the expected time. It may be due to a falling off of demand in the area and because the builder has stocks of land on his hands. It may be due to difficulties over capital, although if that is so, it does not necessarily follow that he should get an extension, for it may be that he ought to convey the land to somebody who is able to develop it—if it is land which ought, according to proper planning needs, to be brought forward earlier for development. All these are matters which can be considered and adjudicated upon fairly."

15. Conditions Attached to Planning Permissions

Without prejudice to the general right under section 29 (1) of the 1971 Act to grant planning permission subject to such conditions " as they think fit," a local planning authority may specifically grant planning permission subject to conditions:

(a) for regulating the development of *any* land under the control of the applicant, or requiring the carrying out of works on such land if these matters appear to the authority to be expedient in relation to the development for which planning permission is given (s. 30 (1) (*a*));

(b) for requiring the removal of buildings or works, or the discontinuance of any use of land, authorised by the planning permission at the end of a specified period (s. 30 (1) (*b*)) in which case the permission is known as a " planning permission granted for a limited period " (s. 30 (2));

(c) for requiring that the building or other operations permitted by the planning permission shall be *commenced* (not, it will be noted, *finished*) not later than a specified date (s. 30 (3) (*a*)) in which case any operations commenced after that date will be operations commenced and carried out without planning permission (s. 30 (3) (*b*)).

A condition attached to a grant of planning permission must be reasonably certain and intelligently and sensibly related to the planning scheme and proposals for the area.[22]

[22] *Fawcett Properties Ltd.* v. *Bucks C.C.* [1961] A.C. 636 (H.L.).

A condition stipulating for the payment of an annual sum of money to a local planning authority as security for the final fulfilment of a number of conditions subject to which planning permission was granted has been held by the Secretary of State on appeal to be improper, the Secretary of State being advised that the general rule of law in such matters is that no money can be demanded from any person except on distinct authority laid down by statute.[23]

In exercising their discretion to add conditions to a grant of planning permission, a local planning authority cannot do *just as they please* and section 29 (1) of the 1971 Act does not mean this when it says that a planning authority may add to a planning permission such conditions " as they think fit." This means that the conditions must be thought to be " fit " (*i.e.* meet, fit, proper, appropriate, requisite, etc.) *from a planning point of view* and statutory support for this assertion is to be found in subsection (1) itself of section 29 when it enacts that the " authority, in dealing with the application [for planning permission], shall have regard to the provisions of the development plan, so far as material to the application, and to any other material considerations."

It is well settled that a public body holding the privileged position of being able to exercise their discretion when coming to a decision must exercise that discretion reasonably and in good faith.[24]   The exercise of an executive discretion in relation to the attaching of conditions to a grant of planning permission was scrutinised when *Pyx Granite Co. Ltd.* v. *Ministry of Housing and Local Government* was before the Court of Appeal.[25]   In his judgment in the Court of Appeal Lord Denning said [26]:

> " The principles to be applied are not, I think, in doubt. Although the planning authorities are given very wide powers to impose ' such conditions as they think fit,' nevertheless the law says that those conditions, to be valid, must fairly and reasonably relate to the permitted development.   The planning authority are not at liberty to use their powers for an ulterior object, however desirable that object may seem to them to be

---

[23] Case III/16 at p. 12 of the Ministry of Town and Country Planning Bulletin of Selected Appeal Decisions No. III, dated April 1948.
[24] See Lord Greene M.R. in *Associated Provincial Picture Houses Ltd.* v. *Wednesbury Corporation* [1948] 1 K.B. 223 at pp. 228, 233.
[25] [1958] 1 Q.B. 554 (C.A.); reversed upon other grounds [1960] A.C. 260 (H.L.).
[26] *Ibid.* at p. 572.

in the public interest. If they mistake or misuse their powers, however bona fide, the court can interfere by declaration and injunction: see *Sydney Municipal Council* v. *Campbell* [27]; *Roberts* v. *Hopwood* [28]; and *Smith* v. *East Elloe Rural District Council.*" [29]

Further illumination of the kind of condition which may rightly be attached to a planning permission appears in *Fawcett Properties Ltd.* v. *Buckingham County Council.*[30]   In this case in granting planning permission to erect a pair of semi-detached cottages a condition was added that: " The occupation of the houses shall be limited to persons whose employment or latest employment is or was employment in agriculture as defined by section 119 (1) of the Town and Country Planning Act 1947, or in forestry, or in an industry mainly dependent upon agriculture and including also the dependants of such persons aforesaid." The local planning authority stated in writing (as required by the General Development Order 1950, art. 5 (9) (*a*)) their reasons for imposing this condition. When this case was before the Court of Appeal Pearce L.J. (as he then was) said [31]:

> " The council are, by the terms of section 14 of the Town and Country Planning Act 1947 [now section 29 (1) (*a*) of the 1971 Act] entitled to grant permission ' subject to such conditions as they think fit.' The *Wednesbury* case makes it clear that the court will not interfere with that discretion unless it is shown that the authority did not take into account the right considerations, that is, that they disregarded something which they should have taken into account or regarded something which they should not have taken into account. The onus of showing this is on the person seeking to upset the condition imposed by the authority. That onus may be discharged either by showing from the terms of the condition itself that the authority cannot have taken into account the right considerations or by extrinsic evidence to that effect. . . .
>
> " When no reasons are given and decisions of the authority present what Lord Sumner called in another context ' the

[27] [1925] A.C. 338 at p. 343.
[28] [1925] A.C. 578 at p. 613.
[29] [1956] A.C. 736 at pp. 762, 763.
[30] [1959] Ch. 543 (C.A.); affirmed [1961] A.C. 636 (H.L.).
[31] [1959] Ch. 543 at pp. 575, 576.

inscrutable face of a sphinx,' it is hard to discharge such an onus. However, in the case of conditions imposed under section 14 it has been provided (by a statutory instrument [32]) that reasons must be given. No doubt the purpose of that is to help and inform the persons on whom conditions are imposed. Moreover, by the last four lines of section 14 (1) [now section 29 (1) of the 1971 Act, reminding the local planning authority to pay attention to " the provisions of the development plan . . . and to any other material considerations "] indication has been given of the matters which the authority must take into account. But the general principle remains that the condition cannot be upset by this court unless it be shown that the authority have not taken into account the right matters. . . .

" The court will, of course, hold a condition *ultra vires* if it does not ' fairly and reasonably relate to the permitted development,' [33] but in this case it does so relate. Here there is no extrinsic evidence that the authority did not take the right matters into account."

This instructive dissertation by Pearce L.J. may be used as an authoritative yardstick by which to measure the validity of any condition attached to a grant of planning permission for development.

In *Hall & Co.* v. *Shoreham-by-Sea Urban District Council*,[34] a condition which not only required landowners to build a road on their own land but also in effect to grant a public right of way over it without compensation was held by the Court of Appeal to be so unreasonable as to be *ultra vires*.

Assuming that a condition is invalid the question arises: Can the condition subject to which the planning permission has been granted be severed from the permission itself, leaving the latter to stand on its own, free of the inhibiting restrictions caused by the invalid condition? Lord Justice Hodson (speaking *obiter*) in the *Pyx Granite* case said [35]:

" The only remaining question is as to the conditions

[32] Town and Country Planning General Development Order 1950, S.I. 1950 No. 728, art. 5 (9).
[33] See Lord Denning's judgment in *Pyx Granite Co. Ltd.* v. *Ministry of Housing and Local Government* [1958] 1 Q.B. 554 at p. 572.
[34] [1964] 1 W.L.R. 240 (C.A.).
[35] *Ibid.* at p. 578.

imposed by the Minister. I have nothing to add on this subject to the views expressed by my Lord as to the validity of the conditions generally. In any event it would, I think, be impossible to mutilate the Minister's decision by removing one or more of the conditions. The permission given has been given subject to those conditions, and *non constat* but that no permission would have been given at all if the conditions had not been attached. The consequence would be that if any of the conditions imposed were held to be bad as imposed without jurisdiction, the whole planning permission would fall with it, and the respondents would be left without any planning permission at all, for it would not be open to the court to leave the planning permission standing shorn of its conditions, or any of them."

It is worthwhile emphasising that in making the foregoing comment on the inseverability of a planning permission and its attendant conditions and on the wholly annihilating effect of one invalid condition upon an otherwise stainless planning permission, the learned judge was speaking obiter.

On this the comment may be quoted of Roxburgh J. in the Chancery Division in *Fawcett Properties Ltd.* v. *Buckingham County Council* [36] when, after quoting the observations (above) of Hodson L.J., he went on to say:

" So that if there were twenty varied conditions attached to the permission to erect the house, and the house had been erected and yet one of them, however trivial, was *ultra vires*, there would be no planning permission for the erection of that house. Well, that is a very far-reaching obiter dictum and I am glad that I have been absolved from the duty of considering whether it is well-founded."

This particular matter came before the courts in *Hall & Co. Ltd.* v. *Shoreham-by-Sea Urban District Council.* [37]

In this case the Court of Appeal, having held that a certain condition was invalid (as being *ultra vires*), the next question was: could the invalid condition be severed from the planning permission so as to leave the latter otherwise intact? Lord Justice Willmer

[36] [1958] 1 W.L.R. 1161 at p. 1167.
[37] [1964] 1 W.L.R. 240; and see also *Allnatt London Properties* v. *Middlesex C.C.* (1964) 15 P. & C.R. 288.

referred to the remark (quoted above) of Roxburgh J. in the *Fawcett* case about " trivial " conditions but then added " I do not think that any such problem arises in the present case, for here the conditions . . . are fundamental to the whole of the planning permission." Accordingly, it was held that the planning permission itself fell, dragged down by an invalid condition which was fundamental to the permission and not a trivial attachment.

This important matter of the severability of conditions from planning permissions to which they are attached came before the Court of Appeal and thereafter the House of Lords in *Kingsway Investments (Kent) Ltd.* v. *Kent County Council.*[38]

In this case a condition (of a kind which had been attached to almost all outline planning permissions granted by the Kent County Council and other planning authorities since about 1950) provided that the permission " shall cease to have effect " after three years unless the planning authority, having received detailed plans from the developers, *had approved them and had notified their approval* to the developers within the three years, was held by a majority of the Court of Appeal to be unreasonable and invalid, because the approval and the notification would be outside the control of the developer. The court also held (Davies and Winn L.JJ., with Lord Denning M.R. dissenting) that the invalid condition *could* be severed from the outline permission so that the permission remained in existence and could be acted on. The House of Lords, reversing the decision of the Court of Appeal, by a three to two majority held that the condition was valid, and that if the condition were void it could not have been deleted to leave the permission standing since it was of fundamental importance.[39]

It would appear from these decisions that, whether or not a planning permission is to be held wholly bad and of no effect by reason of the invalidity of some condition (or conditions) attached to it is a matter to be decided on a basis of common sense and with particular inquiry as to whether the invalid condition is fundamental or trivial. There is some conflict (as this recent case shows) of judicial opinion on the matter.

The views of the Secretary of State on the attaching of conditions to a grant of planning permission are set out at length in the interest-

---

[38] [1971] A.C. 72; reversing [1969] 2 Q.B. 332.
[39] [1971] A.C. 72.

ing and instructive Circular 5/68 dated February 6, 1968. In paragraph 23 of the Circular the Secretary of State mentions that on a grant of planning permission a condition may be attached which prevents a subsequent change of use to some other use even though, by virtue of the Town and Country Planning (Use Classes) Order 1972, such a change of use would *not* constitute development under the 1971 Act. This view is confirmed in the decision in *Corporation of the City of London* v. *Secretary of State for the Environment and Another*.[40]

16. Appeal to the Secretary of State—Decision by the Secretary of State

There is a right of appeal to the Secretary of State against the decision of a local planning authority (s. 36 (1)) or in respect of the authority's failure to give a decision at all (s. 37). The notice of appeal must be given to the Secretary of State within *six months* of the receipt of the local planning authority's decision or of the expiry of the appropriate period of time within which such decision ought to be given (s. 36 (2) and art. 13 of the General Development Order 1963 [41] as amended by the General Development Order 1969). " Month " is not defined in the General Development Order 1963 but, by virtue of article 2 (2) of the Order, applying section 3 of the Interpretation Act 1889, the expression " month " means a calendar month.

On an appeal to him against the decision of a local planning authority the Secretary of State may allow or dismiss the appeal or may reverse or vary *any* part of the local planning authority's decision and may deal with the application as if it had been made to him in the first instance (s. 36 (3)). Thus appellants will bear in mind that by appealing to the Secretary of State they put before him *the whole* of their application for planning permission and not merely that part of the local planning authority's decision in respect of which they feel aggrieved. In exercising his right to reverse or vary the local planning authority's decision the Secretary of State may himself add more onerous conditions than were imposed by the local planning authority in the first place. Indeed, he may go to the extent of refusing planning permission altogether in a case where,

[40] (1971) 23 P. & C.R. 169.
[41] S.I. 1963 No. 709.

in his view, the local planning authority were wrong in granting the permission.

Before deciding an appeal the Secretary of State must, if either the applicant or the local planning authority so request, afford each of them an opportunity of being heard by a person appointed by the Secretary of State for the purpose—the Secretary of State's Inspector (s. 36 (4)). If the Secretary of State grants such a request, the hearing will be private to the two parties. Neither party can demand a public local inquiry although the Secretary of State frequently decides to hold such an inquiry. (Further discussion on planning inquiries and private hearings held by the Secretary of State in connection with appeals follows in Chapter 15.)

The provisions of the 1971 Act relating to:

(1) the notices to be given to owners and to agricultural tenants (s. 27);

(2) the grant of planning permission (s. 29 (1) and (3)); and

(3) the imposition of conditions affecting other land or requiring the removal of buildings at the end of a specified period (s. 30 (1)),

are made applicable in the case of an appeal to the Secretary of State (s. 36 (5)).

The Secretary of State may decline (s. 36 (7)) to determine an appeal if satisfied that planning permission for the proposed development:

(a) could not have been granted, at all or

(b) could have been granted subject only to the conditions of which complaint is made,

in view of the provisions:

(1) of sections 29, 30, 67 and 74 of the 1971 Act (relating to the determination of planning applications and to industrial development certificates and office development permits); and

(2) of the Town and Country General Development Order 1963 and any directions given under that order.

The decision of the Secretary of State on an appeal " shall be final " (s. 36 (6)) but, notwithstanding this, a " person aggrieved " [42] may within six weeks challenge the decision on a point of law in the

---

[42] As to " persons aggrieved," see *Ealing B.C.* v. *Jones* [1959] 1 Q.B. 384 (D.C.); *R.* v. *Dorset Quarter Sessions Appeals Committee, ex p. Weymouth Corporation* [1960] 2 Q.B. 230 (D.C.); and *Buxton* v. *Minister of Housing and Local Government* [1961] 1 Q.B. 278.

High Court (ss. 242 (1) (*e*), (3) (*b*) and 245 (1) (*b*), (3) (4) (7)).   A local authority may not necessarily be, in this context, a person aggrieved but they may nevertheless be able to challenge the decision on the ground that they are an " authority directly concerned with ... action on the part of the Secretary of State " (s. 245 (2)).

Where any action on the part of the Secretary of State is, on appeal, quashed by the court under section 245 (4) (*b*) of the 1971 Act, it is not open to the court to substitute any other order and the appeal to the Secretary of State revives and is pending.[43]

Notwithstanding the foregoing statutory provisions as to challenge in the High Court, the Secretary of State's decision *may* be quashed on certiorari (as to which, see comment on certiorari appearing, *post*, on p. 127).

Guidance as to the attitude which the Secretary of State might be expected to adopt on appeal being made to him is obtainable from the Bulletins of Selected Appeal Decisions issued from time to time by the Department of the Environment, and also from the " Notes of Planning Decisions " published monthly in the *Journal of Planning and Property Law.*

17. Appeal to Independent Tribunal

The Secretary of State has power (which he has not so far exercised) to provide by a development order that a planning appeal relating to the design or external appearance of buildings or similar matters shall lie to an independent tribunal constituted in accordance with the order instead of to the Secretary of State (s. 50).

18. Appeal to the Secretary of State—Decision by an Inspector

In order to relieve pressure at the Department of the Environment, section 36 (8) of and Schedule 9 to the 1971 Act provide for certain appeals to be heard and *determined* by an Inspector appointed by the Secretary of State.

Schedule 9 to the 1971 Act applies to the following appeals:

    (1) an appeal relating to a planning decision (s. 36 (8));

    (2) an appeal against an enforcement notice (s. 88 (9));

---

[43] *Hartnell* v. *Minister of Housing and Local Government* [1964] 2 Q.B. 510 (C.A.); affirmed [1965] A.C. 1134 (H.L.).

(3) an appeal relating to the certification of an established use (s. 95 (7));

(4) an appeal against a listed building enforcement notice (s. 97 (7));

(5) an appeal against an enforcement notice relating to duties as to replacement of trees (s. 103 (4)); and

(6) an appeal against the refusal of listed building consent, or the grant thereof subject to conditions (Sched. 11, para. 8 (6)).

Out of the whole sum total of all the foregoing types of appeal the Secretary of State may prescribe by regulation certain classes of appeal (Sched. 9, para. 1) and, if he does so prescribe, then *any appeal falling within a prescribed class may be determined by an Inspector appointed for the purpose by the Secretary of State* instead of being determined, as hitherto, by the Secretary of State (*ibid.*).

The Secretary of State has made the Town and Country Planning (Determination of Appeals by Appointed Persons) (Prescribed Classes) Regulations 1970 [44] which set out the following classes of appeals as being suitable for determination by an Inspector (1970 Regulations, art. 3, Sched. 1):

Appeals relating to applications in respect of development by operations

(1) the erection, or the enlargement or other alteration, of a building or buildings for use as not more than 30 dwelling-houses;

(2) the development for residential purposes of land not exceeding 1 hectare (2·47 acres) in extent, where the application for planning permission does not specify the number of dwelling-houses to which it relates;

(3) the erection, or the enlargement or other alteration of buildings to be used for or in connection with any of the following purposes;

(a) a shop,

(b) an office,

(c) a repository or warehouse,

(d) a hotel, boarding house, guest house, residential club, hostel or lodging house,

(e) a petrol filling station,

[44] S.I. 1970 No. 1454.

      (f) the repair of motor vehicles or the garaging of private motor cars,

      (g) religious worship or instruction, or

      (h) the breeding, training or keeping of dogs, cats or horses,

if the aggregate floor space created by the development does not exceed 500 square metres (5,381·55 square feet) and the area of land to which the application relates does not exceed 8,000 square metres (9,567·2 square yards);

  (4) the formation, laying out or widening of a means of access;

  (5) the carrying out of building, engineering or other operations on land for a purpose ancillary or incidental to existing or proposed development of any kind specified in the foregoing or following classes.

Appeals relating to applications in respect of development by change of use

  (6) the change in the use of a building or buildings to use as not more than 30 dwelling-houses;

  (7) the change in the use of a building or buildings to use for or in connection with any purpose specified in Class 3 above, if the aggregate floor space used for such purpose does not exceed 500 square metres (5,381·55 square feet) and the area of land to which the application relates does not exceed 8,000 square metres (9,567·2 square yards);

  (8) the change in the use of land not exceeding 4,000 square metres (4,783·6 square yards) in extent to use for or in connection with any of the following purposes:

      (a) the storage of materials, excluding scrap metal, refuse or waste materials,

      (b) car parking, or

      (c) the display and sale of motor vehicles.

An appeal in any of the foregoing classes will, however, be decided (1970 Regulations, art. 4, Sched. 2) by the Secretary of State if the appeal relates to:

  (1) development to which a direction by the Minister concerned under the provisions of article 8 of the Town and Country Planning General Development Order 1963 (as amended) applies;

  (2) development to which a direction given by the Minister of

Transport or, in Wales, the Secretary of State under article 9 (2) of the General Development Order applies;

(3) development by a local authority;

(4) development by statutory undertakers on operational land or on land in the case of which the circumstances mentioned in section 225 of the 1971 Act apply;

(5) development by the National Coal Board on land of a class specified in regulations made pursuant to section 273 of the 1971 Act;

(6) development for which planning permission has been refused by a local planning authority, or granted by them subject to conditions, where the local planning authority have included in their reasons for such decision the statement that such decision has been made following an expression of views, by a government department or new town development corporation, that the application should not be granted wholly or in part, or should be granted only subject to conditions;

(7) development where the same development or the same land is concurrently the subject or part of the subject of another appeal to the Secretary of State concerned, not being an appeal within any of the classes specified in Schedule 1 to the 1970 regulations, or of an application referred to him, under any provisions of the 1971 Act, or of an order made under section 45 or 51 of the 1971 Act.

The Secretary of State has also made the Town and Country Planning Appeals (Determination by Appointed Persons) (Inquiries Procedure) Rules 1968 [45] dealing with all procedural matters in a case where an Inspector is both hearing and determining a planning appeal.

Even though an appeal falls within a prescribed class and is, therefore, regarded as primarily fit for determination by an Inspector rather than by the Secretary of State, it is open to the Secretary of State, from time to time, by means of directions, to remove from such prescribed class any specified class of appeal in which event the appeal will once again become an appeal suitable only for determination by the Secretary of State and not by an Inspector (1971 Act, Sched. 9, para. 3).

[45] S.I. 1968 No. 1952.

Any Inspector who, under the foregoing arrangements, becomes empowered to determine an appeal is accorded the same powers and duties as the Secretary of State in relation to appeals (1971 Act, Sched. 9, para. 2). Moreover, the parties to such an appeal have similar rights as to being heard by the Inspector as they have by the Secretary of State (*ibid.*).

When an Inspector has been appointed by the Secretary of State to determine an appeal, then the Inspector himself has a discretion (whether or not the parties have asked to be heard), to hold a public local inquiry before he determines the appeal (1971 Act, Sched. 9, para. 5). Such an Inspector is bound to hold such an inquiry if directed to do so by the Secretary of State in any particular case (*ibid.*).

When an appeal has been decided by an Inspector, his decision becomes that of the Secretary of State (1971 Act, Sched. 9, para. 2 (3)).

Where the Secretary of State has appointed an Inspector to determine an appeal the Secretary of State has power, at any time before the appeal is determined, to substitute one Inspector for another if he so wishes (1971 Act, Sched. 9, para. 4).

If, however, one Inspector is substituted for another, then the consideration of the appeal, or any inquiry or hearing in connection with the appeal, if already begun, *must be begun afresh* (1971 Act, Sched. 9, para. 4 (2)) although, in such circumstances, it will not be necessary to give any person the opportunity either of making fresh representations or of modifying or withdrawing representations already made (*ibid.*).

The Secretary of State has power to direct that an appeal which would otherwise be given over for determination by an Inspector shall be withdrawn from such treatment and shall, instead, be referred to the Secretary of State for determination by him in accordance with the procedure at present in force (1971 Act, Sched. 9, para. 3).

Any direction by the Secretary of State restoring to himself the responsibility of determining any particular appeal, must state the Secretary of State's reason for doing so and must be served on the Inspector appointed to hear the appeal (if one has actually been appointed), upon the appellant, upon the local planning authority and also upon any person, being an owner or an agricultural tenant, who has made representations relating to the appeal which the local planning authority are required to take into account (1971 Act, Sched. 9, para. 3 (2)).

If the Secretary of State's reasons for taking the determination of an appeal out of the hands of an Inspector raise matters on which representations have not so far been made, then all parties to the appeal have the right to make further representations and appear and be heard by the Inspector appointed by the Secretary of State for the purpose (1971 Act, Sched. 9, para. 3 (4)).

Similarly, if any party to the appeal had earlier expressed a wish under paragraph 2 (2) of Schedule 9 to the 1971 Act to appear and be heard by the Inspector appointed to determine the appeal, then the Secretary of State, before himself determining the appeal, must afford any such person the right to appear before and be heard by an Inspector appointed by the Secretary of State for the purpose (1971 Act, Sched. 9, para. 3 (4) and (5)).

19. Service of a Purchase Notice

On a refusal, either by a local planning authority or by the Secretary of State, of planning permission, or on the grant thereof subject to conditions, an aggrieved applicant, if an " owner " as defined in section 290 (1) of the 1971 Act (and a freeholder who has let his land for less than a rack-rent is excluded by the definition [46]), may *in certain cases* require his interest in the land to be purchased by the council of the county borough or county district (*i.e.* not necessarily the local planning authority) for the area where the land is situated (s. 180). The requirement must be by a notice in writing called a " purchase notice." Purchase notices are later discussed in detail in Chapter 17.

20. Planning Applications Decided by the Secretary of State in the First Place

Though applications for permission for development will normally be dealt with by local planning authorities, the Secretary of State may require any application to be referred to him for decision by himself (s. 35 and General Development Order 1963, art. 12).[47]   Such applications are sometimes referred to as " called-

---

[46] *London Corporation* v. *Cusack-Smith* [1955] A.C. 337 (H.L.).
[47] S.I. 1963 No. 709.

in applications." This power of determining an application in the first instance is quite distinct from the Secretary of State's power under section 36 of the 1971 Act to determine an appeal against the decision of a local planning authority.

The power of the Secretary of State to call-in an application for planning permission under section 35 of the 1971 Act, covers also an application for approval by a local planning authority of details under the aegis of an outline planning permission earlier granted by the authority (s. 35 (1)).

Before deciding an application for planning permission the Secretary of State must, if either the applicant or the local planning authority so request (General Development Order 1963, art. 12), afford each of them an opportunity of a private hearing before a person appointed by the Secretary of State for the purpose—the Secretary of State's Inspector (s. 35 (5)).

Where an application for planning permission is made direct to the Secretary of State, certain sections of the 1971 Act relating to:
  (1) the publication generally of notices of the planning application (s. 26 (2) and (7));
  (2) the notices to be given to owners and to agricultural tenants (s. 27);
  (3) the grant of planning permission (s. 29 (1) (2) and (3)); and
  (4) the imposition of conditions affecting other land or requiring the removal of buildings at the end of a specified period (s. 30 (1));
are made applicable to the matter (s. 35 (4)).

It is provided that the decision of the Secretary of State " shall be final " (s. 35 (6)) but, as in the case of an appeal to the Secretary of State from the decision of a local planning authority,[48] a " person aggrieved " and a local " authority directly concerned with [the] action on the part of the Secretary of State " may, within six weeks, challenge the Secretary of State's decision in the High Court on a point of law (ss. 242 (1) (*e*), (3) (*a*), and 245 (1) (*b*),(3) (4) (7)).[49]

Notwithstanding the foregoing statutory provisions as to challenge in the High Court, the Secretary of State's decision may be quashed on certiorari on the ground that in making it the Secretary of State has exercised his discretion so unreasonably as not to

[48] See p. 119.
[49] See cases quoted in footnote 42 at p. 120.

amount to an exercise of discretion at all. On this, reference may be made to the judgment of Lord Greene M.R. in *Associated Provincial Picture Houses* v. *Wednesbury Corporation*.[50] A court will not, however, go into the propriety of the policy considerations applied in any particular case.[51]

The inference drawn from *R.* v. *Northumberland Compensation Appeal Tribunal, ex p. Shaw*,[52] that a decision of the Secretary of State could be quashed by certiorari if there is an error of law on the face thereof has now been established as law in *R.* v. *Medical Appeal Tribunal, ex p. Gilmore*.[53] It was said that the remedy of certiorari is not to be taken away by any statute except by the most clear and explicit words. " Final " means only without appeal, and not without recourse to certiorari.

21. Planning Permission for Development by Local Authorities and Statutory Undertakers

The 1971 Act contains special provisions relating to planning permission for development by local authorities and by statutory undertakers (ss. 40, 222–241, 270, 271 and 272).

Much of the development carried out by a local authority or a statutory undertaker in the normal course of their duties as public bodies is covered by Classes XIII to XXI, referred to in the Schedule to the Town and Country Planning General Development Order 1963,[54] and is accordingly " permitted development " under article 3 of that Order.

Under section 42 of the Town and Country Planning Act 1962 (now section 270 of the 1971 Act) the Secretary of State has made the Town and Country Planning General Regulations 1969,[55] Part III of which relates to development by local planning authorities.

22. Revocation or Modification of Planning Permission

It has already been stated that planning permission once given enures (subject to limitations of time contained in the grant of

[50] [1948] 1 K.B. 223 (C.A.).
[51] *R.* v. *East Kesteven R.D.C.* [1947] 1 All E.R. 310 (D.C.).
[52] [1952] 1 K.B. 338 (C.A.).
[53] [1957] 1 Q.B. 574 (C.A.).
[54] S.I. 1963 No. 709.
[55] S.I. 1969 No. 286.

permission itself or imported into the matter by sections 41 to 44 inclusive of the 1971 Act discussed earlier in this chapter) for the benefit of all persons for the time being interested in the land affected (s. 33 (1)) but this, of course, is subject to the right of a local planning authority to revoke or modify a planning permission by means of an order made by the authority and confirmed by the Secretary of State (s. 45).   Before confirming the order the Secretary of State must afford the owner and the occupier of land affected by the order an opportunity of being heard by the Secretary of State's Inspector (s. 45 (3)).

Under section 46 of the 1971 Act certain orders (but not all orders—s. 46 (6)) revoking or modifying planning permissions, which orders are unopposed and unlikely to give rise to claims for compensation, will continue to be made by the local planning authority but will not require confirmation by the Secretary of State (s. 46 and Town and Country Planning General Regulations 1969, reg. 25).[55]

A local planning authority desirous of revoking or modifying a planning permission previously granted by them must do so either:

(a) before building operations authorised by the permission have been completed, in which case the revocation or modification is not to affect so much of the building operations as have been carried out; or

(b) before any change in use of land authorised by the planning permission has taken place (s. 45 (4)).

The validity of an order revoking or modifying a grant of planning permission may, within six weeks, be challenged on a point of law in the High Court by a " person aggrieved " [56] or by an " authority directly concerned " [56] (ss. 242 (1) (*d*), (2) (*a*) and 245 (1) (*a*), (2) (3) (4) (7)).

Compensation may become payable on revocation or modification of a previous planning permission and this is considered in Chapter 16.

On the revocation or modification of a grant of planning permission a purchase notice may, in appropriate circumstances, be served by the owner upon the council of the county borough or county district where the land is situated requiring the purchase of land (s. 188).[57]

---

[56] See p. 120.
[57] As to purchase notices generally, see Chap. 17.

23. Agreements Restricting or Regulating the Development of Land

Irrespective of the powers whereby a local planning authority may control development by the granting or withholding of planning permission therefor, a local planning authority may enter into agreements with landowners restricting or regulating the development of land either permanently or for temporary periods (s. 52). Any such agreement is enforceable against persons deriving title under the person with whom the agreement was originally made (s. 52 (2)) thus avoiding the difficulty which arose in *London County Council* v. *Allen*.[58] The provisions of any such agreement may, however, be overridden by the provisions of a development plan (s. 52 (3)).

24. Stopping Up and Diversion of Highways

So that development may proceed in accordance with planning permission granted under Part III of the 1971 Act, Part X of the Act—sections 209 to 221 inclusive—makes provision for the stopping up or diversion of highways.[59]

What is popularly known as the " planning " method of closing or diverting public streets and roads has been increasingly resorted to in place of the more cumbersome procedure under sections 84 to 91 of the Highways Act 1835. These sections are repealed by the Highways Act 1959, Schedule XXVI, and the stopping up and diversion of highways is now dealt with in Part VI of the Highways Act 1959. It is, however, provided by section 115 of the latter Act that these provisions shall not prejudice a power to stop up or divert a highway contained in any other enactment as, for example, Part X of the 1971 Act.

When the carrying out of development under a planning permission already granted requires that a public highway (whether a carriageway, bridleway or footway) shall be closed up or diverted in some different direction, an order for such treatment can be made by the Secretary of State (ss. 209 and 215). If the highway in question is a footpath or bridleway, the order may also be made (subject—unless the order is unopposed—to confirmation by the Secretary of State (s. 217 and Sched. 20)), by a competent authority

[58] [1914] 3 K.B. 642 (C.A.).
[59] *Harlow* v. *Minister of Transport and Others* [1951] 2 K.B. 98 **(C.A.).**

(s. 210) which means a local planning authority or a local authority functioning under delegated planning power (s. 210 (4)).

The making of a stopping-up or a diversion order for a highway takes time. Accordingly, the Secretary of State can in certain circumstances, make a *draft* order stopping up or diverting a highway notwithstanding that planning permission for the related development has not as yet been actually granted (s. 216). In short, the proceedings for the highway order and for the planning permission can go forward concurrently and this will lead to a saving of time. The highway order cannot, however, be *finally* made unless and until the related planning permission has been granted (s. 216 (5)). The circumstances when this concurrent procedure is available are set out in section 216 (2) (3) and (4).

Another ground for closing or diverting a highway by the Secretary of State is where planning permission is granted for constructing or improving a highway (or the Secretary of State proposes to do this sort of thing) and some *other* highway crosses or enters the route of such highway. In these circumstances an order may be made stopping up or diverting such *other* intruding highway if it appears to the Secretary of State that it is expedient to do so in the interests of safety or in order to facilitate traffic movement (s. 211).

Provision is made whereby, for the purpose of improving amenity, an order can be made by the Secretary of State changing a highway which carried vehicles as well as pedestrians into a highway restricted solely for use by pedestrians with or without horses (s. 212). This could be useful in connection with the provision of what are sometimes called " shopping malls." Action rests in the first place with the local planning authority and the Secretary of State must, before taking action, consult with the highway authority if different from the planning authority (s. 212 (2)). The order, having been made, may be revoked or varied by a subsequent order (1968 Act, s. 92 (8)).

If any such restrictive change in the use of a highway is ordered, compensation for consequential injurious affection may be claimed from the local planning authority (s. 212 (5) and (6)) by any person who has " lawful access " (*i.e.* access authorised by a planning permission or access which needs no such permission (s. 212 (5)) to the highway. The claim for compensation must be made in the manner and within the time (six months) prescribed by regulations

(s. 212 (6) and Town and Country Planning Regulations 1969,[60] (reg. 19).

Where a carriageway is changed into a footpath or a bridleway under the foregoing provisions, a local authority (being " the competent authority "—s. 213 (5)) are given a variety of interesting powers to enable them to improve and beautify the footpath or bridleway (s. 213 (1)–(4)).

Where a local authority have acquired or appropriated land (ss. 214 (2) and 133 (1)) and are holding it for planning purposes (s. 214) the Secretary of State may by order extinguish rights of way over that land, provided alternative rights are given or he is satisfied none is required (s. 214 (1) (a)).   Similarly, if the right of way is a footpath or a bridleway (but not a carriageway) and provided an alternative right of way is given or the local authority are satisfied no such alternative is needed, the local authority may by order extinguish the right of way (s. 214 (1) (b)).   The order of the local authority requires confirmation (unless it is unopposed) by the Secretary of State (s. 217 and Sched. 20).

[60] S.I. 1969 No. 286.

CHAPTER 9

CONTROL OF ADVERTISEMENTS

1. The Advertisements Regulations 1969 and 1972

THE Town and Country Planning (Control of Advertisements) Regulations 1969 [1] as amended by the Town and Country Planning (Control of Advertisements) (Amendment) Regulations 1972 [2] (hereinafter in this chapter referred to as the " Advertisements Regulations ") form a substantial document containing thirty-four regulations and four schedules. They provide a complete *ad hoc* code relating to the display and control of outdoor advertisements.

The sections of the 1971 Act relating to the control of advertisements are sections 63, 64 and 109. In so far as the display of advertisements constitutes development (as to which reference may be made to section 22 (4) of the 1971 Act), no application for planning permission in respect of such development is required, provided the display of the advertisements is in accordance with the Advertisements Regulations (s. 64).

2. Penalties for Breach of Advertisements Regulations

Any person guilty of an offence against the Advertisements Regulations by displaying an advertisement in contravention thereof is liable to a fine of £100 or, in the case of a continuing offence, £5 per day (s. 109 (2) and reg. 8 (1)). With respect to *onus probandi* it is to be noted that a person is deemed to display an advertisement:

(a) if the advertisement is displayed on land of which he is either the owner or the occupier; or

(b) if the advertisement publicises his goods, trade, business or other concern (s. 109 (3)).

But it is open to any such person to prove that the offending advertisement was displayed without his knowledge or consent in which case he will not be guilty of an offence (*ibid.*).

[1] S.I. 1969 No. 1532.
[2] S.I. 1972 No. 489.

3. Definitions

Turning now to the Advertisements Regulations themselves, the word " advertisement " is widely defined by the Regulations and should be specially noted. It means " any word, letter, model, sign, placard, board, notice, device or representation, whether illuminated or not, in the nature of and employed wholly or in part for the purposes of advertisement, announcement or direction (excluding any such thing employed wholly as a memorial or as a railway signal), and without prejudice to the foregoing provision includes any hoarding or similar structure used or adapted for use for the display of advertisements, and references to the display of advertisements shall be construed accordingly " (reg. 2 (1)).

The extent and application of the Regulations is dealt with in regulation 3 whereby they are to apply to the display on land (and " land " includes (reg. 2 (1)) buildings and land covered with water and " building " includes (*ibid.*) any structure or erection or any part of a building structure or erection) of *all* advertisements (reg. 3 (1)) subject to five exceptions as follows:

(a) an advertisement on " enclosed land " (as defined in regulation 3 (2) (*b*)) and not readily visible from outside the enclosure or from within any such part of the enclosure as carries a public right of way or to which the public have access (reg. 3 (1) (*a*));

(b) an advertisement within (reg. 3 (2) (*d*)) a building (which means displayed inside a structure and not outside on a forecourt [3]), subject, however, to the special control provided by regulation 12 with respect to certain advertisements displayed within a building but visible from outside the building (reg. 3 (1) (*b*));

(c) an advertisement displayed upon or inside a vehicle (regs. 3 (1) (*c*) and 3 (2) (*c*)); and

(d) an advertisement incorporated in, and forming part of, the fabric of a building (regs. 3 (1) (*d*) and 3 (2) (*e*)); and

(e) an advertisement displayed on an article for sale, or on the package or other container of the article, or displayed on the pump, dispenser or other container from which the article is sold, provided always that the advertisement relates wholly to the article and is not an illuminated advertisement and does not exceed 0·1 square metre in area (regs. 3 (1) (*e*) and 3 (2) (*a*)).

It is to be noted that for the purpose of (c) of the foregoing

---

[3] *Dominant Sites Ltd.* v. *Berkshire C.C.* (1955) 6 P. & C.R. 10.

exceptions " vehicle " means (reg. 3 (2) (*c*)) a vehicle normally employed as a moving vehicle on a roadway or a railway and also a vessel normally employed as a moving vessel on an inland waterway. Thus omnibuses (provided they keep moving) can carry advertisements both within and without if the managers of these vehicles think fit.

Control under the Advertisements Regulations over the display of advertisements can be considered mainly under two heads, namely, control within Areas of Special Control, and control outside such areas.

4. Areas of Special Control

The definition of an Area of Special Control is dealt with in section 63 (4) (5) of the 1971 Act and in regulations 26 and 27 of, and Schedule 2 to the Advertisements Regulations, and it is for a local planning authority to take the initiative in defining such an area. All local planning authorities are under a duty to consider such definition (reg. 26 (1)). The definition of an Area of Special Control can be achieved by the insertion of appropriate provisions in a development plan or by means of an Order made by the local planning authority and approved by the Secretary of State (s. 63 (4) (5) and reg. 26 (4)). Such an Order may be made by the Secretary of State himself (*ibid.*). Provision is made for advertising the proposal to make such an Order; for the lodging of objections thereto; for the considering of such objections, and for the holding of a public local inquiry or a hearing before the Order is approved or made (s. 63 (5)).

Within an Area of Special Control the general rule will be that no advertisements whatever may be displayed (reg. 27). Such advertisements as are displayed will form exceptions to this general rule (*ibid.*).

The object of regulation 27 (2) of the Advertisements Regulations is to give a wider discretion to local planning authorities in permitting the display of certain advertisements and directional signs within Areas of Special Control in the hope that thereby such authorities might be encouraged to apply special control over most of the countryside and in other places worthy of this protection.[4]

The Secretary of State thinks Areas of Special Control should be reviewed at intervals of not more than, say, five years with a view

[4] Ministry Circular No. 3/60.

to deciding whether adjustments in boundaries should be made, and authorities should in particular consider whether it is reasonable to continue to apply special control in areas which, since special control in the area came into effect, have become substantially built up, especially with industrial or commercial development.

An Order defining an Area of Special Control may be challenged, by a " person aggrieved " or by an " authority directly concerned," [5] within six weeks on a point of law by application in the High Court (ss. 242 (1) (*d*), (2) (*d*) and 245 (1) (*a*), (2) (3) (4) (5) and (7)).

5. Other Areas

With respect to areas which are not Areas of Special Control the general rule is that no advertisements may be displayed without consent, which may be either " express consent " granted by a local planning authority or by the Secretary of State (reg. 6 (1)) or "deemed consent " (reg. 6 (2)), that is to say, consent which is deemed to be granted by the Advertisements Regulations themselves. Deemed consent is applicable to all advertisements falling within Part III of the Regulations.

6. Deemed Consent for Display of Part III Advertisements

Advertisements falling within Part III of the Advertisements Regulations are, first, those coming within the six specified classes given in regulation 14 which cover the following:

Class I.—Functional advertisements of local authorities, statutory undertakers and public transport undertakers (*e.g.*), bus stop signs, signs indicating the way to railway stations, museums, art galleries, etc.

Class II.—Miscellaneous advertisements relating to premises on which they are displayed (*e.g.*), professional, business or trade plates attached to premises where the profession, business or trade is carried on.

Class III.—Certain advertisements of a temporary nature (*e.g.*), " For Sale " or " To Let " boards.

[5] See p. 120.

Class IV.—Advertisements (subject to reservations—reg. 14 (1), Class IV proviso) *on* business premises relating *wholly* to the business carried on or to the goods sold or the services provided, together with the name and qualifications of the person carrying on the business, or selling the goods or supplying the services.[6]

Class V.—Certain advertisements on the forecourts of business premises (*i.e.*), advertisements so displayed but which refer wholly to the matters referred to in Class IV above, provided that the aggregate area of any such advertisements is not more than 4·5 square metres.

Class VI.—Flag advertisements (*e.g.*), a flag bearing only the name or device of the person occupying the building over which it flies.

Any advertisement falling within one or other of the foregoing classes can be excluded from such class by direction of the Secretary of State (reg. 15).

Advertisements falling within Part III of the Advertisements Regulations are, secondly, those coming within regulation 9 relating to:

(a) pending parliamentary or local government elections;
(b) advertisements displayed under statutory obligation (*e.g.*), advertisements relating to the making of compulsory purchase orders under the 1971 Act; and
(c) advertisements in the nature of traffic signs such as traffic lights and " Halt " and " Turn Left " signs.

Thirdly, a local planning authority may display advertisements without express consent upon any land within their area except in an Area of Special Control (reg. 10). The Secretary of State can, however, require the discontinuance of display of any such local planning authority advertisement (*ibid.*).

Fourthly, any advertisement displayed on August 1, 1948, may continue, without express consent, to be displayed (reg. 11).

A local planning authority can require (by serving a " discontinuance notice ") the discontinuance of the display of any advertisement display with deemed consent if they consider it

---

[6] *Cooper* v. *Bailey* (1956) 6 P. & C.R. 261 (D.C.); *Solosigns Ltd.* v. *Essex C.C.* [1956] J.P.L. 904; *Dominant Sites Ltd.* v. *Berkshire C.C.* (1955) 6 P. & C.R. 10; *Arthur Maiden Ltd.* v. *Lanark C.C.* (*No.* 1) [1958] J.P.L. 417.

expedient to do so in the interests of amenity or public safety (reg. 16).

The four Standard Conditions given in Schedule 1, Parts I and II, to the Advertisements Regulations will apply, obligatorily, to all advertisements displayed with deemed consent (reg. 7) with the exception that Standard Condition No. 1 relating to cleanliness and tidiness will not apply (reg. 9 (3)) to an advertisement relating to a pending election and displayed pursuant to regulation 9 (1) (*a*).

7. Express Consent for Display of Advertisements

Where express consent to the display of an advertisement is required (reg. 6 (1)) application therefor can be made to the local planning authority on a form to be supplied by the authority (reg. 17).

Applications for express consent to the display of an advertisement are made (reg. 17 (1)):

(a) where the land is within the City of London, to the Common Council of the City;

(b) where the land is within a London borough, to the council of the London borough; and

(c) where the land is outside Greater London, to the county borough council or county district council for the area in which the land is situated.

In considering an application for express consent a local planning authority is to consider only the interests of amenity and public safety (reg. 5), is under a duty, before granting express consent, to consult certain other authorities (reg. 18) and, subject to these requirements, may

(a) grant consent subject to the three obligatory Standard Conditions set out in Part I of Schedule 1 to the Advertisements Regulations together with such additional and optional conditions (if any) as they think fit to impose, or

(b) refuse consent (reg. 19).

As to the meaning of " amenity," reference may be made to *Re Ellis and Ruislip-Northwood U.D.C.*[7] in which Scrutton L.J. said that " It appears to mean pleasant circumstances, features, advantages."

[7] [1920] 1 K.B. 343 (C.A.).

Every grant of express consent must be for a fixed term which may not be for longer than five years without the approval of the Secretary of State (reg. 20). Nor may the term be shorter than five years, unless so required by the application or considered expedient by the authority, and if no term is specified, then the consent is to have effect as a consent for five years (*ibid.*). If the authority grant consent for less than five years, they must state in writing their reasons for so doing unless the application itself required a consent for less than five years (reg. 20 (2)).

The grant or refusal of express consent must be in writing together with (in the case of a refusal or a grant subject to conditions) the reasons for the decision (reg. 21).

A local planning authority must give their decision on an application for express consent within two months unless such period is extended by agreement in writing made between the authority and the applicant (reg. 21 (2)), and if the decision is not given in the before-mentioned period the application is to be regarded as having been refused (reg. 22 (5)).

Every local planning authority is to keep a register containing particulars of their decisions on applications for express consent (reg. 31).

Provision is made for the revocation or modification of any grant of express consent to the display of an advertisement (regs. 24 and 25).

8. Appeal to the Secretary of State

An applicant for express consent who is aggrieved by the decision of a local planning authority refusing consent or granting the same subject to conditions may appeal to the Secretary of State (reg. 22) within one month (reg. 22 (2)) from the receipt of the notification of the local planning authority's decision. The word " month " is not defined in the Advertisements Regulations but, by virtue of regulation 2 (3), it has the same meaning as in the Interpretation Act 1889, under which it means one calendar month.

The decision of the Secretary of State on an appeal is final (reg. 22 (8)), subject, however, to challenge by a " person aggrieved " [8] or by an " authority directly concerned " [8] within six weeks in the High Court on a point of law (ss. 242 (1) (*e*), (3) (*e*) and 245 (1) (*b*), (2) (3) (4) and (7)).

[8] See pp. 120 and 121.

9. Appeal to Independent Tribunal

The Secretary of State has power (not so far exercised) to provide by regulations that a planning appeal relating to the display of an advertisement shall lie to an independent tribunal constituted in accordance with such regulations instead of to the Secretary of State (s. 50).

10. Fly-Posting

It is to be a condition of every consent to the display of an advertisement under the Advertisements Regulations that such display shall take place only with the permission of the owner of the land or other person entitled to grant permission in relation thereto (reg. 6 (4)). This condition will apply to all consents whether the condition itself is expressly imposed or not (*ibid.*) although it will not apply to statutory advertisements displayed pursuant to regulation 9 (1) (*b*). Breach of this condition, being a contravention of the Advertisements Regulations, is an offence for which a penalty is imposed (reg. 8). Thus fly-posting (which has always been a trespass) becomes an offence prosecutable before a court of summary jurisdiction.

11. " Existing Advertisements "

" Existing advertisements," that is to say, advertisements which were on display on August 1, 1948, may continue to be displayed without express consent (reg. 11) but subject:

(a) to the four Standard Conditions set out in Schedule 1 to the Advertisements Regulations (reg. 7); and

(b) to the requirement as to discontinuance by notice served by a local planning authority (regs. 11 and 16).

12. Compensation

Where, in order to comply with the Advertisement Regulations, works are carried out by any person:

(a) for removing an advertisement which was on display on August 1, 1948; or

(b) for discontinuing the use for the display of advertisements of any site which was being used for that purpose on August 1, 1948, such person may claim compensation with respect to any expenses reasonably incurred by him in carrying out such works (s. 176 and reg. 30). The claim must be submitted in writing to the local planning authority within six months of the completion of any such works (*ibid.*).

13. Miscellaneous Provisions

The Advertisements Regulations contain further provisions dealing with the display of advertisements by local planning authorities (reg. 10), advertisements relating to travelling circuses and fairs (reg. 23), and advertisements displayed within buildings (reg. 12).

The Regulations empower the Secretary of State to call up for decision by himself (instead of by a local planning authority) any matter requiring decision under the Regulations (reg. 28).

14. Saving for Other Statutory Obligations

Neither the Advertisements Regulations nor consents granted under them will have the effect of discharging any obligation or liability relating to the display of advertisements which is imposed or incurred under any other enactment (including a private or local Act or a by-law made under an Act (reg. 2 (1)) in force (reg. 34).

15. Decisions and Advice Relating to Advertisements

When considering the provisions of the 1971 Act relating to advertisements and the Advertisements Regulations, reference may usefully be made to cases decided under earlier legislation relating to the display of advertisements. Such cases are accordingly listed as follows:

(1) *United Billposting Co.* v. *Somerset C.C.* (1926) 24 L.G.R. 383 (D.C.);

(2) *Gloucester Billposting Co. Ltd.* v. *Hopkins* (1932) 30 L.G.R. 488;

(3) *Royle* v. *Orme* (1932) 30 L.G.R. 494;

(4) *Horlicks Ltd.* v. *Garvie* [1939] 1 All E.R. 335 (D.C.);

(5) *Mills & Rockleys Ltd.* v. *Leicester Corporation* [1946] K.B. 315 (D.C.);

(6) *More O'Ferrall Ltd.* v. *Harrow U.D.C.* [1947] K.B. 66 (D.C.);

(7) *Borough Billposting Co.* v. *Manchester Corporation* [1948] 1 All E.R. 807 (D.C.);

(8) *Dominant Sites Ltd.* v. *Hendon Borough Council* [1952] 2 All E.R. 899 (D.C.).

Useful advice as to control over the display of advertisements is to be found in Ministry Circulars 3/60, 11/60, 27/60 and 11/62.

CHAPTER 10

Note: In this chapter all section references are references to the Caravan Sites and Control of Development Act 1960 unless otherwise stated.

CONTROL OVER CARAVANS

1. Summary

ONE particular form of development, namely, the use of land as a site for caravans caused more litigation under the Town and Country Planning Act 1947 between the years 1948 and 1960 than any other kind of development and in 1960 Parliament decided that there should be a new *ad hoc* statutory form of control relating solely to caravans. The outcome of this was the enacting of Part I of the Caravan Sites and Control of Development Act 1960. Part I of the Act (relating to caravan sites) contains thirty-two sections, none of which (except sections 21 and 22) is affected in any way by the Town and Country Planning Act 1971. On the other hand, Part II of the 1960 Act (relating to the enforcement of planning control over development generally) is repealed and superseded by Part V of the 1971 Act.

Thus the *ad hoc* statutory form of control over caravans and caravan sites introduced in 1960 continues to be found in Part I of the Caravan Sites and Control of Development Act 1960 and not in the Town and Country Planning Act 1971. This *ad hoc* form of control over caravans (which comprises a system of licensing of caravan sites by the councils of county boroughs and county districts) is a form of control which functions over and above (*i.e.* in addition to) the general control of development through the medium of planning permission granted under Part III of the Town and Country Planning Act 1971 and the enforcement provisions of Part V of that Act.

In short, planning permission for caravan sites is just as essential as ever it was, but a caravan site must now satisfy not only the Town and Country Planning Act 1971 but also the licensing provisions of Part I of the Caravan Sites and Control of Development Act 1960.

Part I of the Caravan Sites and Control of Development Act

143

1960 did not originally apply to the County of London (s. 31 now repealed) but it was extended to Greater London as from April 1, 1965, by the London Government Act, 1963, Sched. 17, para. 21.

The control of local authorities over movable dwellings by means of licences granted under the Public Health Act 1936 is now abolished in so far as it relates to caravans (s. 30). The Minister of Housing and Local Government could, by order made before August 29, 1962, repeal or amend any local enactment which appeared to him to be either superseded by or inconsistent with the 1960 Act (s. 27).

It should be mentioned that the Caravan Sites Act 1968 was enacted primarily to restrict the eviction of occupiers of caravans from caravan sites and to secure the establishment of such sites by local authorities " for the use of gypsies and other persons of nomadic habit." This Act, accordingly, does not fall within the general stream of town planning legislation and is not therefore referred to in this chapter except in so far as it enacts a slight variation in the definition of " caravan "—a matter briefly referred to below.

2. Site Licences for Caravans

Under the 1960 Act the general rule is that no land may be used as a caravan site unless and until a site licence has been issued by the local authority (*i.e.* the council of a borough or urban or rural district or the Common Council of the City of London (s. 29)) to the occupier of the land comprising the site (s. 1 (1)). If an occupier of land contravenes this requirement he is liable, on a first offence, to a fine of £100 and on a second or subsequent offence to a fine of £250 (s. 1 (2)). In this context an occupier of land is (s. 1 (3)) the person who, by virtue of an estate or interest held by him in the land, is entitled to possession of the land or would be so entitled but for the rights of any other person under any licence granted in respect of the land; provided, however, that where land amounting to not more than four hundred square yards in area is let under a tenancy entered into with a view to the use of the land as a caravan site, the expression " occupier " means, in relation to that land, the person who would be entitled to possession of the land but for the rights of any person under that tenancy.

A " caravan site " is any land in which a caravan is stationed *for human habitation*, together with land used in conjunction therewith (s. 1 (4)).

" Caravan " means any structure (not being a tent or a railway carriage standing on a railway) designed or adapted for human habitation which is capable of being moved from one place to another (by being towed or transported) including a motor-vehicle so designed or adapted (s. 29 (1)), but this definition is *not* to include (Caravan Sites Act 1968, s. 13) a " twin-unit caravan " if its dimensions exceed any of the following limits, namely:

(a) length: 60 feet;
(b) width: 20 feet;
(c) overall height of living accommodation: 10 feet.

3. Application for, and Issue of, a Site Licence

An application for a site licence must be made in writing by the occupier of the land to the borough or district council in whose area the land is situated (s. 3 (1)). The application must give (s. 3 (2)) the particulars required by the Secretary of State in the Caravan Sites (Licence Applications) Order 1960.[1]

Faced with an application for a site licence, the local authority (provided there has been a grant of planning permission *otherwise* than under and by virtue of a development order) (s. 3 (3)) *must* issue the same within two months of receiving the particulars referred to in the previous paragraph or within such extended period as may be agreed (s. 3 (4)) unless the applicant has had a site licence revoked (s. 9) within the previous three years (s. 3 (6)).

It is to be emphasised that a site licence is to be issued if, and only if, the requisite planning permission for the use of land as a caravan site has already been formally granted by the local planning authority who, before doing so, must first consult with the site licensing authority (Town and Country Planning Act 1971, s. 29 (5) (6)). Thus the general rule under the 1960 Act is that if there is in being the requisite planning permission for use of land as a caravan site, then the issue of a site licence under the 1960 Act for such land *must* follow—the real sting of the 1960 Act lying not in the granting or the withholding of a site licence, but in the number and style of conditions which may be attached to a site licence. If

[1] S.I. 1960 No. 1474.

there is no such requisite planning permission in being, then the application for a site licence *must* be refused (s. 3 (3)).

If a site licence is not issued within the appropriate two months period (s. 3 (4)) to an applicant who is entitled to receive one, no offence is committed by the applicant under section 1 of the 1960 Act pending the issue of the site licence (s. 6).

A register of site licences is to be kept by every site licensing authority and is to be open to public inspection (s. 25 (1)).

4. Transfer of Site Licence

The holder of a site licence who ceases to occupy the caravan site may, with the consent of the local authority, transfer it to the new occupier of the site (s. 10 (1)). The transferee must be the occupier of the site (*ibid.*). The name of the transferee must be endorsed on the site licence (s. 10 (2)) and an appropriate entry made in the register of site licences (s. 25 (2)).

The object of the need to get the local authority's consent to any transfer of a site licence is simply to secure that the local authority get to know of any transfer which might take place. Usually there will be no question of the local authority refusing consent to a transfer because if they did the new occupier of the site could at once apply for a new site licence in his own name and, if planning permission to station caravans on the site was still in existence, the site licence to the new occupier could not be refused. If, however, the local authority took the view that the arrival of a new occupier provided a convenient occasion for reviewing the conditions attached to the site licence, they could refuse the transfer and leave it to the new occupier to apply for a new site licence in his own name, and to this new site licence the local authority could attach new conditions.

5. Duration of Site Licence

In general a site licence cannot be issued for a limited period (s. 4 (1)). The governing factor is again the planning permission subject to which the site licence is issued. Only if the governing planning permission is for a limited period may the site licence be granted for a limited period only—a period which *must* expire when the planning permission itself expires (*ibid.*).

Any variation in the governing planning permission made by

the Secretary of State on appeal to him under section 36 of the Town and Country Planning Act 1971 will require the making of appropriate alterations in the site licence to ensure that its terms comply with the period (if any) for which the planning permission (as varied on appeal) is to subsist (s. 4 (2)).

6. Conditions Attached to Site Licence

A local authority has a wide discretion as to the attaching of conditions to a site licence but conditions must be such as the authority think it (a) necessary or (b) desirable to impose on the occupier of the land in the interests of:

(1) caravan dwellers on the site itself; or

(2) any other class of persons; or

(3) the public at large (s. 5 (1)).

In deciding what conditions (if any) to attach to a site licence a local authority must have regard (s. 5 (6)) to the " Model Standards for Caravan Sites " (with respect to the layout of caravan sites and the provision of facilities, services and equipment in connection therewith) which have been issued by the Secretary of State under powers contained in the 1960 Act (ibid.).

Without prejudice to a local authority's power to impose conditions generally, a local authority is specifically authorised (s. 5 (1)) to impose conditions:

(a) for restricting the occasions on which caravans are stationed on land for human habitation, or the total number of caravans which are so stationed at any one time;

(b) for controlling, whether by reference to size, to state of repair or to any other feature (other than the materials of which the caravans are constructed), the types of caravan which are stationed on land;

(c) for regulating the positions in which caravans are stationed on land for human habitation and for prohibiting, restricting, or otherwise regulating, the placing or erection on such land, at any time when caravans are so stationed, of structures and vehicles of any description whatsoever and of tents;

(d) for securing the taking of any steps for preserving or enhancing the amenity of land on which caravans are stationed for human habitation, including the planting and replanting of the land with trees and bushes;

(e) for securing that, at all times when caravans are stationed on land, proper measures are taken for preventing and detecting the outbreak of fire, and adequate means of fighting fire are provided and maintained;

(f) for securing that adequate sanitary facilities, and such other facilities, services or equipment as may be specified by the local authority, are provided for the use of persons dwelling in caravans and that, at all times when caravans are stationed on land for human habitation, any such facilities and equipment are properly maintained.

No condition, however, may be imposed controlling the types of caravan by reference to the materials of which the caravans are constructed (s. 5 (2)).

A condition which *must* be attached to a site licence is that requiring a copy of the site licence to be conspicuously displayed on the site unless the site is restricted to three caravans or less (s. 5 (3)). Against this particular condition there is no appeal (s. 7 (1)).

A condition attached to a site licence is perfectly valid notwithstanding that it requires the carrying out of works which the holder of the site licence is not entitled to carry out as of right (s. 5 (5)). The holder must either acquire such a right or forgo the use of the land as a caravan site.

A condition attached to a site licence may require the doing of works on the site by the occupier within a specified period and may prohibit the bringing of caravans on the site until such works are completed to the satisfaction of the local authority (s. 5 (4)). If the works are not so completed within the specified period, the local authority may do the works and recover the cost thereof from the occupier who is in default (s. 9 (3)).

If an occupier of land fails to comply with any condition attached to a site licence, he is liable on a first offence to a fine of £100 and on a second or subsequent offence to a fine of £250 (s. 9 (1)). On a third or subsequent conviction for breach of a condition the court (*i.e. not* the local authority) may make an order revoking the site licence (s. 9 (2)). If the site licence is so revoked the local authority may not issue a further licence to the offending occupier until a period of three years has elapsed (s. 3 (6)).

7. Appeal Against Conditions Attached to Site Licence

Within twenty-eight days of the issue of a site licence, there is a right of appeal to a magistrates' court by a person aggrieved [2] by a condition attached to a site licence (s. 7 (1)) and the court, if satisfied that the condition is " unduly burdensome," [3] may vary or cancel the condition (*ibid.*).

" Unduly burdensome " is an expression not defined in the 1960 Act. The question whether a condition is " unduly burdensome " is the only matter which the court is entitled to consider and in doing so the court must have regard to the Secretary of State's " Model Standards for Caravan Sites " (s. 7 (1)).

8. Alteration of Conditions Attached to Site Licence

A local authority may at any time and of their own volition (but only after allowing the licence holder an opportunity of making representations) alter, by variation or cancellation of existing conditions or by the imposition of new conditions, the conditions attached to a site licence (s. 8 (1)).   The licence holder may himself apply for an alteration of such conditions (s. 8 (2)).   In either case the local authority must not alter the conditions without first having regard to the Secretary of State's " Model Standards for Caravan Sites " (s. 8 (4)).

The holder of a site licence who is aggrieved [4] by any alteration of site licence conditions or by the local authority's refusal to agree to his application for an alteration of conditions may appeal to a magistrates' court (s. 8 (2)) and the court in considering the matter must have regard to the Secretary of State's " Model Standards for Caravan Sites " (s. 8 (4)).

When site licence conditions are altered, the licence holder must, if required, deliver up his site licence to the local authority for amendment [5] (s. 11 (1)) and if he fails, without reasonable excuse, to do so, he is liable to a fine of £10 (s. 11 (2)).

---

[2] As to " a person aggrieved," see *Ealing Corporation* v. *Jones* [1959] 1 Q.B. 348 at p. 390 (D.C.); *R.* v. *Dorset Q.S. Appeals Committee, ex p. Weymouth Corporation* [1960] 2 Q.B. 230 (D.C.); and see p. 120.

[3] See *Owen Cooper Estates* v. *Lexden and Winstree R.D.C.* (1964) 16 P. & C.R. 233 (D.C.); *Esdell Caravan Parks* v. *Hemel Hempstead R.D.C.* [1966] 1 Q.B. 895 (C.A.).

[4] As to persons aggrieved, see p. 120.

[5] *Turner* v. *Garstang R.D.C.* (1965) 17 P. & C.R. 218.

9. Temporary Exemptions for Existing Caravan Sites

The 1960 Act contains special provision (ss. 13 to 20) relating to caravan sites in existence when the 1960 Act came into operation on August 29, 1960 (s. 50 (4)).   Such " existing sites " (as defined in section 13) were temporarily relieved of the need to obtain a site licence but application for such a licence had to be made not later than October 29, 1960 (s. 14).   Further exemption until November 29, 1960, was accorded (s. 15) to certain sites which were in being on August 29, 1960, but which were nevertheless technically not " existing sites."

10. Permanent Exemptions from Requirements as to Site Licences

All the foregoing provisions of this chapter relating to the need of a caravan site to be granted a site licence under the 1960 Act have no application (s. 2) to a number of caravan sites more particularly described in the First Schedule to the Act.

Briefly, the 1960 Act has no application to the following eleven uses of land, namely:

(1) the use of land within the curtilage of a dwelling-house as a caravan site, such use being incidental to the enjoyment of the house;

(2) the use of any land as a site for a caravan for a period including not more than two nights, by a person travelling with the caravan, provided:

  (a) that at the time there is no other caravan for human habitation on the land (including any adjoining land in the same occupation); and

  (b) that during the previous twelve months there has not been any such caravan on such land on more than twenty-eight days;

(3) the use as a caravan site of land comprising at least five acres (including any adjoining unbuilt land in the same occupation), provided that during the previous twelve months:

  (a) there has not been any caravan for human habitation on any part of the land on more than twenty-eight days; and

    (b) there have not been more than three such caravans on the land at any one time;

(4) the use as a caravan site of land occupied and supervised for the purposes of recreation by an " exempted organisation," *i.e.* an organisation for promoting recreational activities which has been granted a certificate of exemption by the Secretary of State under paragraph 12 of the First Schedule to the 1960 Act;

(5) the use by not more than five caravans at a time of land where a certificate has been issued by an exempted organisation approving it for use by its members;

(6) the use as a caravan site under the supervision of an exempted organisation in connection with a meeting of its members, lasting not more than five days;

(7) the use of agricultural land as a caravan site for seasonal accommodation of agricultural workers employed on land in the same occupation;

(8) the use of any land as a caravan site for seasonal accommodation of forestry workers employed on land in the same occupation;

(9) the use as a caravan site for the accommodation of persons employed in connection with building or engineering operations on the same or adjoining land;

(10) the use as a caravan site by a travelling showman (being a member of an organisation of travelling showmen recognised by a certificate of the Secretary of State) either travelling for the purposes of his business or in winter quarters (October–March);

(11) the use as a caravan site of land occupied by the borough or district council.

The Secretary of State may, by order, exclude particular land from any of the foregoing exemptions numbered (2) to (10) inclusive (Sched. 1, para. 13).

11. Provision of Caravan Sites by Local Authorities

Local authorities (including in this context county councils (s. 24 (8)) have power to provide caravan *sites*, to manage them and make charges for the use of them, to provide services and facilities in connection therewith (s. 24 (1) (2) (3) (4)) and to acquire land compulsorily (s. 24 (5) (6)).   A local authority have no power to provide caravans (s. 24 (7)).

12. Caravans on Commons

A rural district council may by order prohibit (s. 23 and Sched. 2), either absolutely or except in specified circumstances, the stationing of caravans on a common including a town or village green (s. 23 (8)).   Any person stationing a caravan in contravention of such an Order is liable on summary conviction to a fine of £10 (s. 23 (3)).

The need for the foregoing provision against stationing caravans on a common arises from the fact that in the case of commons there may be no occupier who could be said to " cause or permit . . . the use of land as a caravan site " as mentioned in section 1 of the 1960 Act and, accordingly, no offence under that section could be committed.   The provisions of section 23 of the Act are thus complementary to the site licensing system set up by the rest of Part I of the Act—a system which presupposes the existence of an identifiable occupier.

These powers of a rural district council do not apply (s. 23 (1)) to commons or waste land falling under section 193 of the Law of Property Act 1925.   As that section mainly applies to urban commons the exercise of powers of control under section 23 of the 1960 Act is limited to *rural* district councils.

13. Protection for Occupiers and Entry on Land

An authorised officer of a local authority may (on giving twenty-four hours' notice to the occupier) enter upon a caravan site, or upon land with regard to which an application for a site licence has been made, in connection with the discharge of the local authority's powers under the 1960 Act (s. 26).   Any person wilfully obstructing such an officer in the execution of his duty is liable to a fine of £5 (s. 26 (5)).

Where an occupier of land grants to another a licence (not to be confused with a " site licence " granted by a local authority) to use land as a caravan site, or where land of not more than 400 square yards is the subject of a tenancy for use as a caravan site (in which two cases the licensor or the lessor remains (s. 1 (3)) the

" occupier " of the land) then if, in either of these cases, the licensee or the tenant does anything which would amount to an offence under the 1960 Act if done by the occupier, the occupier may terminate the licence or the tenancy and retake possession of the land notwithstanding the terms of the licence or tenancy (s. 12). Such an occupier may enter on the land and do any works necessary in order to comply with a site licence granted in respect of such land by a local authority (*ibid.*).

CHAPTER 11

CONTROL OVER OFFICES

THE building of offices is a form of development which is subject (at least for the time being) to additional *ad hoc* control over and above that furnished by general town planning control. This special control for offices springs from the Control of Office and Industrial Development Act 1965. This Act had two separate and distinct functions, one of which was commercial and the other industrial. It was Part I of the Act which imposed restrictions on office development. Part I of the Act is now replaced by sections 73 to 86 of the Town and Country Planning Act 1971 and is discussed in this chapter while Part II of the Act (relating to industrial matters) is replaced by sections 66 to 72 of the 1971 Act and is dealt with in Chapter 12.

Sections 73 to 86 of the 1971 Act, relating to office development, are referred to in the 1971 Act as " these provisions " (ss. 85 (1) and 73 (7)). They are provisions which translate into legislative effect the clamp-down on office building which was promised in the Government Paper of November 4, 1964, entitled " Offices—A Statement by Her Majesty's Government."

1. Office Development Permits to Ensure Further Restriction on Offices

There had been (long before 1964) an outcry from certain quarters that there were too many new offices being built in London. In view of the fact that no new office block could be built in London (or anywhere else in the country for that matter) without planning permission first being obtained, this criticism really meant that too many planning permissions for offices were being granted by the local planning authorities who, presumably, were functioning within the ambit of their approved development plans. In these circumstances the Government applied further restrictions on office building by enacting new law now to be found in sections 73 to 86 of the 1971 Act.

Just as under earlier town planning legislation it had been (and still is, by virtue of ss. 66–72 of the 1971 Act) necessary, in the case of industrial development of a certain size,[1] for a developer to have not only planning permission from the local planning authority but also an industrial development certificate (an I.D.C.) from the Secretary of State, so, under the 1971 Act, a builder of office premises which exceed in office floor space " the prescribed exemption limit "[2] (s. 75 (1) (7) (8)) will need to have, in addition to the customary planning permission, an office development permit (an O.D.P.) from the Secretary of State.   Indeed, any planning application for office premises of a size beyond the exemption limit *will be of no effect* (and the local planning authority will therefore be precluded from doing anything at all with it) unless it is accompanied by an office development permit (s. 74 (1)).

2. The Secretary of State's Discretionary Powers

The Secretary of State has a complete discretion whether to issue or to withhold an office development permit, but in exercising this discretion he must have particular regard to the need for promoting a better distribution of office employment in Great Britain (s. 74 (3)).   There is no appeal against a refusal to grant an office development permit and no compensation is payable on such refusal.

3. Restrictions Attached to an Office Development Permit

The Secretary of State may attach restrictions (s. 77 (1)) on the grant of an office development permit.

The restrictions must be such as the Secretary of State " considers necessary or expedient " and may, for example, include restrictions as to the period within which an application for planning permission for the office development may be made or as to the persons by whom the application may be made (s. 77 (1)).   If the planning application is made otherwise than in accordance with restrictions attached to the office development permit, then the application is to be treated as if it were not accompanied by the requisite office development permit (*ibid.*) which means, of course, that the application will be a nullity.

[1] See Chap. 12.
[2] See p. 159.

The 1971 Act makes no provision for appeal against any restrictions attached to an office development permit and no provision is made for payment of compensation in respect of any such restriction.

4. Conditions Attached to an Office Development Permit

The Secretary of State may in addition to restrictions (as mentioned above), attach conditions to an office development permit if he so desires, but the conditions must be such as he considers appropriate in the exercise of his discretion under section 74 (3) of the Act (s. 77 (2)) by which, as mentioned earlier, he is to have particular regard to the need for promoting the better distribution of office employment (s. 74 (3)).

There is no provision in the 1971 Act for any appeal against conditions attached to an office development permit nor for the payment of compensation in respect of any condition so attached.

It is worthy of special note that, whilst conditions which the Secretary of State may impose may be such (s. 77 (3)) as could *not* be imposed as planning conditions under the 1971 Act, these conditions *must* nevertheless be imposed by the local planning authority if and when they come to grant planning permission for the office development in respect of which the office development permit has earlier been issued by the Secretary of State (s. 77 (4)). The local planning authority may, of course, attach planning conditions of their own if they so desire (*ibid.*), provided such conditions are not inconsistent with the Secretary of State's conditions (s. 82 (4)), which are obligatory. If, however, the local planning authority fail to carry the Secretary of State's conditions into any relevant planning permission granted by the authority, the planning permission will not thereby be invalidated but will be *deemed* to have been granted subject to the Secretary of State's conditions (s. 77 (5)).

When any condition attached by the Secretary of State to an office development permit is carried forward into any grant of planning permission (thereby becoming a planning condition as well as a Secretary of State condition):

(1) the 1971 Act removes (s. 82 (1) (2) and (3)) the right of appeal against such a condition which would otherwise have been available under section 36 of the Act;

(2) the 1971 Act excludes any compensation which might other-

wise have been payable under the Act in respect of such a planning condition (s. 147 (3));

(3) the 1971 Act prevents the condition being made the basis of the service of a purchase notice (s. 185) calling for the compulsory purchase of land under the provisions of s. 180 of the 1971 Act;

(4) on an appeal to the Secretary of State against an enforcement notice relating to the condition, the Secretary of State can ignore the appeal in so far as it claims that planning permission free of the condition ought to have been granted (s. 88 (8)) and the enforcement procedure can go ahead without being held up by the appeal;

(5) an enforcement notice relating to contravention of the condition must be taken as having been served on the owner and the occupier of land to which it relates if in fact it is served on the owner and occupier of that particular part of the building where the contravention occurred (s. 87 (5));

(6) if the condition is one which could and would have been attached in the ordinary course to a planning permission, the grant of permission may include a certificate to this effect (s. 82 (3)) and if it does then the Secretary of State, on a planning appeal made to him under section 36 of the 1971 Act, is not required to entertain the appeal (*ibid.*) and the condition will continue to function even after the operation of sections 73 to 86 of the 1971 Act come to an end (s. 86 (3)).

5. Temporary Duration of Office Restriction—How Long is " Temporary "?

" These provisions " (*i.e.* ss. 73–86) of the 1971 Act relating to office development have a limited duration and are due to expire on August 4, 1977 (s. 86 (1) as amended by the Town and Country Planning (Amendment) Act 1972, s. 5) but Parliament can in the meantime, if it so desires, determine otherwise (*ibid.*). Thus, at this moment of writing, there is no knowing precisely how long these additional restrictions on office development will continue except that, under the 1971 Act as it now reads, they will not extend beyond August 4, 1977.

6. What is an Office?—What does the Act Catch?

Having outlined the sort of additional control which can be imposed under " these provisions " of the 1971 Act over and above general town planning control consideration must now be given to the question of what is the sort of office development which is caught by sections 73 to 86 of the 1971 Act.

Development which, under the Act, will need an office development permit from the Secretary of State before any planning application in respect of it can be made to the local planning authority, is development which *consists of or includes* (s. 74 (1)):

(a) *the erection of a new building* containing office premises; or

(b) *the extension or alteration of an existing building* by the addition of, or the conversion of premises into, office premises; or

(c) *a change of use* whereby premises which are not office premises become office premises.

It will be noted that the expression " office premises " appears frequently in the foregoing paragraph. This important expression is given a whole section to itself (s. 73) in order that its meaning may be made clear.

" Office premises " *means* (s. 73 (1)):

(a) premises whose " sole or principal use " (as to which, see s. 73 (2) (3) and (4)) is to be use as an office or for office purposes; or

(b) premises which are to be occupied together with premises referred to in (a) *and* which are to be occupied wholly or mainly for the purposes of the activities carried on in the premises referred to in (a).

The foregoing definition leads to the further questions of what constitutes " office purposes " and what is " clerical work." The 1971 Act, without specifically defining the meaning of either of these expressions, does go so far as to declare what these expressions *include* (s. 73 (5)), and the position is that " office purposes " *includes*:

(1) the purpose of administration,

(2) the purpose of clerical work,

(3) the purpose of handling money,

(4) the purpose of telephone and telegraph operating, and

(5) the purpose of operating computers.

The Act continues with the explanation that " clerical work " *includes*:

(1) writing,
(2) book-keeping,
(3) sorting papers,
(4) filing,
(5) typing,
(6) duplicating,
(7) punching cards or tapes,
(8) machine calculating,
(9) drawing of matter for publication, and
(10) the editorial preparation of matter for publication.

Thus the net is wide and the Act, by virtue of the definitions elaborated above, will cover office development of any conceivable kind. However, the Secretary of State may (s. 73 (6)) by order ensure that premises which, under the foregoing definitions, would constitute " office premises " for the purposes of the Act, shall be removed from that category. The Secretary of State can thus narrow the definition; he has no power to widen it.

7. Offices Exempted from the Act—The Prescribed Exemption Limit

Having discussed what is " an office " to which the 1971 Act applies, the next question is: is there any exemption from the general rule? The answer is yes. No office development permit is needed if the office floor space to be created by the proposed development, together with office floor space in any " related development," does not exceed " the prescribed exemption limit " (s. 75 (1)). This limit was originally 3,000 square feet in *all* areas (s. 75 (7)) but the limit may be increased or decreased by order made by the Secretary of State (s. 75 (8)) provided it is never decreased to less than 1,000 square feet (*ibid.*).

In areas *outside* " the metropolitan region " the prescribed exemption limit was raised to 10,000 square feet as from July 27, 1967, by the Control of Office Development (Exemption Limit) Order 1967.[3] The limit was raised to 10,000 square feet as from February 25, 1969, for areas *within* the metropolitan region but

[3] S.I. 1967 No. 1087.

outside Greater London (Control of Office Development (Exemption Limit) Order 1969 [4]).   Since December 16, 1970, the limit has been raised in respect of *all* areas to 10,000 square feet and the Orders of 1967 and 1969 (above quoted) have been repealed (Control of Office Development (Exemption Limit) Order 1970).[5]

" Office floor space " means (s. 85 (3)) gross floor space as ascertained by external measurement.

The meaning of the expression " related development " is complex indeed.   Briefly, it means (s. 75 (2)) development either:
- (a) in the same building as that for which planning permission is being sought; *or*
- (b) in a contiguous or adjacent building which is part of the same project, or for the purposes of the same undertaking, as the proposed development for which planning permission is being sought,

provided the development (in either case) fulfils certain conditions (s. 75 (2) (3) or (4) (5) and (6)).

The object of all this is the very logical one of precluding office development on a piecemeal basis each bit of which is below " the prescribed exemption limit."   It is the aggregate which counts.

8. In which Areas does Control of Offices Operate?

Sections 73 to 86 of the 1971 Act relating to control of office development do not apply everywhere at the same time and the first question is to find out whether, for the time being, " these provisions " (s. 73 (7)) have any application at all in an area where it is proposed to carry out office development.

" These provisions " apply automatically to all land within " the metropolitan region " (s. 74 (4) (*a*)).   They can be applied to other areas of Great Britain outside the metropolitan region by means of orders made (or varied) from time to time by the Secretary of State (ss. 74 (4) (*b*), 287 (3)).   The Secretary of State has made four such Orders, namely, the Control of Office Development (Designation of Areas) Order 1965,[6] a similarly named Order of 1966,[7] the Control of Office Development (Designation of Areas) (Variation) Order

[4] S.I. 1969 No. 174.
[5] S.I. 1970 No. 1824.
[6] S.I. 1965 No. 1564.
[7] S.I. 1966 No. 888.

1969,[8] and a similarly named Order of 1970.[9] These Orders, taken together, apply to large areas of England and Wales which are comparatively thickly populated. The Secretary of State may also, by order, extract the metropolitan region (or any part of it) from the operation of " these provisions " of the 1971 Act (s. 74 (4)).

Any conditions attached to a planning permission as a result of office development control will lapse if and when the area, in which the planning permission operates, ceases to be controlled by those provisions of the 1971 Act relating to office development (s. 82 (6) as amended by the Town and Country Planning (Amendment) Act 1972, s. 6).

9. The Metropolitan Region—Where is it?

What then is this important area known as " the metropolitan region? " It is important to ascertain whether land on which it is proposed to build offices is, or is not, within the metropolitan region not only because the office control provisions of the 1971 Act apply to land within that region automatically but, additionally and more importantly, because certain of the retrospective provisions of the Act (Sched. 12) also apply to office building in the metropolitan region but not elsewhere.

The metropolitan region comprises (s. 85 (1)) all the area of Greater London *plus* all the areas set out in Schedule 13 to the Act and it may well come as a surprise to learn that places as far apart (westwards–eastwards) as Aldershot and Southend-on-Sea and (northwards–southwards) as Luton and Horsham, are within this region for the purposes of the 1971 Act.

The Greater London area means the area of all the thirty-two London Boroughs which came into operation on April 1, 1965, together with the City of London and the Inner and Middle Temples. This is by virtue of the definition of " Greater London " as enacted in section 2 (1) of the London Government Act 1963.

10. Greater London—Retrospective Restrictions

In its effect on the metropolitan region the 1971 Act breaks new ground in the controversial field of retrospective legislation. This is the effect of section 83 of the Act (as read with the whole of Sched.

---

[8] S.I. 1969 No. 173.
[9] S.I. 1970 No. 1823.

12 to the Act) dealing with office development in the metropolitan region in any case where planning permission for such development was granted before August 5, 1965, the date of the passing of the Control of Office and Industrial Development Act 1965.

In Greater London where application was made before August 5, 1965, for planning permission for development involving

(a) the erection of a new building containing office premises, or

(b) the extension of an existing building by the addition of office premises,

then, any planning permission granted on that application will be of no effect without the additional grant of an office development permit (Sched. 12, para. 1 (4)) unless the planning permission was granted before November 5, 1964,[10] and either

(a) the new building, or the extension of the existing building, was erected *before* November 5, 1964, or

(b) a building contract for such new building or extension was made *before* November 5, 1964 (Sched. 12, para. 1 (1) (3) (4)).

A " building contract " means a contract (other than a lease) which is made between an owner of land and a person who, in the course of business, undertakes to erect or extend a building on the land, such business consisting wholly or mainly in the execution of building operations or of building operations plus engineering operations (s. 85 (1)).

The onus of proving that a building contract was in fact made *before* November 5, 1964, rests upon the party who alleges it was so made (Sched. 12, para. 1 (5)).

The Secretary of State is given very full powers to call for information and documents within not less than twenty-eight days to enable him to ascertain whether a building contract for the erection or the extension of a building had in fact been made before November 5, 1964 (Sched. 12, para. 5).   The notice by the Secretary of State calling for this information may be served upon:

(a) the applicant for planning permission, or

(b) the owner of the land affected, or

(c) the person carrying out, or about to carry out, building operations under the building contract (Sched. 12, para. 5 (1)).

---

[10] November 5, 1964, is the date mentioned in the Government Paper of November 4, 1964, entitled, " Offices—A Statement by Her Majesty's Government."

Any person failing to comply with the Secretary of State's notice is liable on summary conviction to a fine of £100 (Sched. 12, para. 5 (3)). Any person who knowingly supplies false information, or who recklessly makes a false statement in supplying information, is liable on summary conviction to a fine of £100 or imprisonment for three months or both, and on conviction on indictment such a person is liable to a fine or imprisonment for two years or both (*ibid.*). In the case of an offence committed by a company any director, manager, secretary or other similar officer of the company may be proceeded against and punished along with the company if the offence by the company is proved to have been committed with the consent or connivance of such person or as a result of his neglect (s. 285).

Again, in Greater London any grant of planning permission before August 5, 1965, for a change of use which has the effect of creating office floor space (Sched. 12, para. 1 (2) (*a*)) will be of no effect without the additional grant of an office development permit (Sched. 12, para. 1 (4)) unless the grant of planning permission was before November 5, 1964 (Sched. 12, para. 1 (2) (*a*), (3) and (4)).

11. The Metropolitan Region Outside Greater London—Retrospective Restrictions

In the metropolitan region outside Greater London, where planning application for office development was made before August 5, 1965, any planning permission granted on that application will be of no effect without the additional grant of an office development permit (Sched. 12, para. 1 (4)) unless the planning permission was granted before November 5, 1964 (Sched. 12, para. 1 (2) (*b*), (3) and (4)).

12. Revitalisation of Suspended Planning Permissions in the Metropolitan Region

It will be seen from the foregoing paragraphs dealing with the whole of the metropolitan region (including Greater London) that in a number of cases a planning permission for office development, even though granted before August 5, 1965, the date of the passing of the Control of Office and Industrial Development Act 1965, is of no effect until an office development permit is granted by the Secretary of State in respect of the office development included in the planning permission. When this is done the planning permission again becomes fully effective (Sched. 12, para. 2).

In connection generally with the retrospective provisions of the 1971 Act relating to planning permissions for office development which were granted before August 5, 1965, it must be remembered that any such planning permission must be acted upon before the expiration of five years from April 1, 1969 (s. 292 (1) and Sched. 24, paras. 19 and 20), but in calculating that period of five years no account is to be taken of any period during which such a planning permission was ineffective for lack of an office development permit (s. 292 (1) and Sched. 24, para. 20A).

13. Saving in the Metropolitan Region for Development less than 3,000 Square Feet

In any case in the metropolitan region (including Greater London) where, in accordance with the retrospective provisions of the 1971 Act above discussed, a planning permission for office development has been granted before August 5, 1965, that planning permission will continue to be good notwithstanding the retrospective provisions of the Act, provided that any office floor space to be created by the development does not exceed 3,000 square feet (Sched. 12, para. 1 (3)).

14. Mixed Development—Factories with Offices

A scheme of development may comprise at one and the same time industrial development as well as office development. If it does, then the requirements of sections 67 and 68 of the 1971 Act, relating to the grant by the Secretary of State of industrial development certificates, must be complied with as well as the requirements of the 1971 Act relating to the grant by the Secretary of State of office development permits (s. 76 (1)).

In Greater London if, in a case of mixed industrial and office development, an industrial development certificate was duly issued and planning permission was granted *before* November 5, 1964, then such mixed development is excluded from control under the provisions of the 1971 Act relating to office development notwithstanding that no building was erected, or (as the case may be) no building contract for the development was made, before November 5, 1964 (Sched. 12, para. 3).

Sections 70 and 71 of the 1971 Act allow conditions to be attached to an industrial development certificate granted by the Secretary of State in respect of " industrial development." Any conditions so attached may, in the case of mixed development—partly industrial and partly office—include conditions relating not only to industrial matters but also to the amount of office space to be contained in the industrial building (s. 70 (3) (*b*)).

Accordingly when, in a case of mixed development, an industrial development permit is required under section 67 of the 1971 Act and an office development permit under section 74 of the Act, provision is made that, notwithstanding the requirements of section 74 of the Act, no office development permit will be needed provided the industrial development certificate contains all requisite conditions relating to office development (s. 76 (2)). Dual control of office development is thus avoided.

15. Buildings not Needing an Office Development Permit— Restrictions on Use

There remains the matter of the building which is erected in circumstances which do not call, at the time of erection, for any office development permit. What about, for example, some later change of use of the building if such change of use happens to be a change to office purposes? Can this be freely done? The answer is no; there are restrictions.

In the case here envisaged, if the building is in the metropolitan region, there are retrospective restrictions. In such a case if planning permission for the erection of the building was granted before August 5, 1965, but after November 4, 1964, then such grant of planning permission will be deemed to be subject to a condition that the building shall not at any time contain office floor space which exceeds 3,000 square feet (s. 83 and Sched. 12, para. 7).

In the case of planning permission granted on or after August 5, 1965, for the erection of a building on land in an area to which the office development restrictions of the 1971 Act for the time being apply (in other words, whether the building is within or without the metropolitan region), then, subject to the two exemptions in section 78 (4) of the Act, if the building will have a floor space of twice (or more than twice) the " prescribed exemption limit," the planning permission must contain a condition (s. 78 (2)) providing that the use of the building shall be restricted so that it never at any time contains office floor space in excess of the " prescribed exemption limit " (s. 78 (3)) as that limit stood at the date of the grant of planning permission (s. 81 (2)). If the local planning authority forget the aforesaid condition the grant of planning permission is still valid and the condition is deemed by the Act to be attached to it (s. 81 (1)).

The foregoing restrictions relating to office floor space introduced into a building which did not need to have an office development permit for its *erection*, are applied, in general, to a planning permission granted for the *alteration* or *extension* of a building where no office development permit is required for such alteration or extension (ss. 79 and 81).

Corresponding provisions are applied in the case of a planning permission for the erection of not one building but of two or more buildings where no office development permit is required (ss. 80 and 81).

16. Planning Permission to Retain Building for Office Purposes—Restrictions

Under section 32 of the 1971 Act application can be made for planning permission to retain a building (or continue a use) for which planning permission has not yet been obtained, thereby regularising *ex post facto* a situation not in order town-planning-wise.

If, in a case where such an application is made, an office development permit would have been required for the original development, the application will be of no effect unless accompanied by an office development permit (s. 74 (1) (2) and (3)).

In the metropolitan region, in the case of a planning permission granted under section 32 (2) of the 1971 Act before August 5, 1965, there are retrospective restrictions. In such a case the planning permission is suspended until an office development permit is obtained (s. 83 and Sched. 12, para. 6) *unless*:

(a) in the case of a building in Greater London, the building was erected before November 5, 1964, or a building contract was made before that date (*ibid.* incorporating Sched. 12, para. 1 (1) (3) and (4)); or

(b) in the case of a building in the metropolitan region but outside Greater London, the planning permission was granted before November 5, 1964 (*ibid.* incorporating Sched. 12, para. 1 (2) (3) and (4)).

17. Enforcing Restrictions on Office Development

The additional control over office development imposed by the 1971 Act will be enforced under, and in accordance with, the enforcement procedure enacted in Part V of the Act.

The 1971 Act, however, has had to create special enforcement procedure regarding certain developments in Greater London which are subject to retrospective control under the retrospective provisions of the Act.

It will be remembered that under Schedule 12 to the Act in Greater London planning permission for office development, even though granted before August 5, 1965 (the date of the passing of the Control of Office and Industrial Development Act 1965), may nevertheless be of no effect unless and until an office development permit in respect of the development is granted by the Secretary of State under section 74 of the Act.

In such circumstances the Act provides that, if the office development is commenced notwithstanding the lack of planning permission, an enforcement notice (under the provisions of Part V of the Act) may be served only by, or on the direction of, the Secretary of State (s. 83 and Sched. 12, para. 4 (2)) and may require building operations to be discontinued forthwith (Sched. 12, para. 4 (3)). The notice may be served upon any person who, in pursuance of a building contract to which he is a party, is carrying out office construction (*ibid.*). The notice will take effect *immediately it is served* (Sched. 12, para. 4 (4)) and this is so even though an appeal against it is lodged under the appeal procedure of Part V of the Act (*ibid.*). An appeal against this sort of enforcement notice can still be made but it must be made within a period, to be specified in the notice, which is not less than twenty-eight days after the service of the notice (Sched. 12, para. 4 (5)). The appeal can be only upon those grounds specified in Schedule 12, para. 4 (7) to the 1971 Act (Sched. 12, para. 4 (6) and (7)).

A person who fails to comply with such an enforcement notice (*i.e.* a person who does not stop office building immediately) is liable to a fine of £100 (Sched. 12, para. 4 (8)). If, after a first conviction, such a person further offends against the enforcement notice by recommencing building operations, whether immediately or after an interval, he is liable to a penalty of £20 per day for each day on which he continues to offend (Sched. 12, para. 4 (9)).

If, after an enforcement notice has been served, any requisite office development permit is issued, or planning permission is granted authorising operations to which the enforcement notice relates, then in either of these circumstances the enforcement notice becomes automatically spent (Sched. 12, para. 4 (10)).

An enforcement notice which is still outstanding when the office control provisions of the 1971 Act come to an end (on August 4, 1977, unless Parliament orders otherwise—s. 86 (1)) will forthwith cease to have any effect (s. 86 (4)).

18. Location of Offices Bureau

Under the Location of Offices Bureau Order 1963,[11] which was made under the powers of the Minister of Town and Country Planning Act 1943, assistance and advice is given to the Secretary of State about the location of offices from a town planning point of view.

Under the 1963 Order it is the general duty of the Bureau to encourage the decentralisation and diversion of office employment from congested areas in Central London to suitable centres elsewhere and to take such steps as may be necessary for this purpose.   In discharging its functions the Bureau must comply with such directions of a general character as the Secretary of State may give.

[11] S.I. 1963 No. 792.

CHAPTER 12

CONTROL OVER INDUSTRIAL DEVELOPMENT

1. Erection of Industrial Buildings—Secretary of State's Industrial Development Certificate

The building of factories (industrial development) is a form of development which (like offices) is subject to special control over and above that afforded by general town planning control as established by the Town and Country Planning Act 1971. The statutory authority for this special control is to be found in sections 66 to 72 of the 1971 Act.

Sections 67 and 68 of the 1971 Act provide that, if development involves the erection of an industrial building, or the change of use of premises into use as an industrial building, then, if the industrial building together with any " related development " (s. 68 (4)) comprises more than 5,000 square feet (s. 68 (1)) of " industrial floor space " (s. 68 (3)) and is of any class prescribed (s. 67 (1)) by regulations made by the Secretary of State, the certificate of the Secretary of State that the erection of the industrial building can be carried out consistently with the proper distribution of industry (s. 61 (1) (3)) must be first obtained.

In considering whether any development for which an industrial development certificate has been applied for is development which can be carried out consistently with the proper distribution of industry, the Secretary of State must have particular regard to the need for providing employment in " development areas " (s. 67 (3) (7)), that is to say, in areas for the time being specified under section 15 of the Industrial Development Act 1966 under which section the Secretary of State has made the Development Areas Order 1966.[1]

The Secretary of State, acting under the Town and Country Planning (Erection of Industrial Buildings) Regulations 1966,[2] has prescribed *all* classes of industrial buildings as falling within the ambit of section 67 of the 1971 Act. For this purpose the expression

[1] S.I. 1966 No. 1032.
[2] S.I. 1966 No. 1034.

169

" industrial building " is defined (s. 66) as meaning a building used or designed for use

(a) for the carrying on of any process for or incidental to any of the following purposes, namely:

    (i) the making of any article or of part of any article, or

    (ii) the altering, repairing, ornamenting, finishing, cleaning, washing, freezing, packing or canning, or adapting for sale, or breaking up or demolition, of any article, or

    (iii) without prejudice to the foregoing paragraphs, the getting, dressing or preparation for sale of minerals or the extraction or preparation for sale of oil or brine; and

(b) for the carrying on of scientific research, being a process or research carried on in the course of a trade or business. For the purposes of this definition the expression " building " includes a part of a building and " article " means an article of any description, including a ship or vessel (*ibid.*).

The figure of 5,000 square feet of industrial floor space referred to in section 68 (1) of the 1971 Act is capable of alteration under the provisions of section 69 of the Act. The Secretary of State has made the Town and Country Planning (Industrial Development Certificates: Exemption) (No. 2) Order 1972 [3] which increases the exemption limit for industrial development certificates from 5,000 square feet to 10,000 square feet in areas of England specified in the Schedule to the Order and from 10,000 square feet to 15,000 square feet in the rest of England and in Wales.

The areas specified in the Schedule to the 1972 Order are:

    (1) Greater London;

    (2) The administrative counties of Bedford, Berkshire, Buckingham, Essex, Hampshire, Hertfordshire, Kent, Oxford, Surrey, East Sussex, West Sussex;

    (3) The municipal borough of Poole;

    (4) The county boroughs of Bournemouth, Brighton, Canterbury, Eastbourne, Hastings, Luton, Oxford, Portsmouth, Reading, Southampton and Southend-on-Sea.

The Town and Country Planning (Industrial Development Certificates: Exemption) (No. 2) Order 1972 came into operation on July 19, 1972.

[3] S.I. 1972 No. 903.

The Secretary of State has also made the Town and Country Planning (Industrial Development Certificates) Regulations 1972 [4] which came into operation on July 20, 1972. These regulations now provide that an industrial development certificate shall no longer be required in respect of an industrial building in any area set out in the Schedule to the regulations (to which reference should be made). The areas described in the Schedule are the areas specified as development areas by the Development Areas Order 1966.[5]

The application for the Secretary of State's certificate should be made before any application for planning permission for the industrial building is made to the local planning authority, because any such application for planning permission is *of no effect* unless a copy of the certificate issued by the Secretary of State is furnished to the local planning authority along with the application for planning permission (s. 67 (1)). There is no appeal against a refusal of the Secretary of State to issue such a certificate.

2. Retention of Buildings for Industrial Purposes

If an industrial development certificate would be required for the erection of a building, then an application under section 32 of the 1971 Act for planning permission to retain the building as an industrial building will be *of no effect* unless accompanied by an industrial development certificate (s. 67 (2) and (5)).

3. Restrictions or Conditions Attached to Industrial Development Certificates

The Secretary of State may attach restrictions to an industrial development certificate and any application for planning permission must accord with such restrictions (s. 70 (1)).

The Secretary of State may likewise attach conditions to an industrial development certificate (s. 70 (2) (3)). Such conditions may go beyond those which could be imposed under the 1971 Act on a grant of planning permission (s. 70 (4)) and must be carried forward by the local planning authority into any planning permission later granted for industrial development (s. 70 (5)). If not so carried forward the conditions will be *deemed* to have been

---

[4] S.I. 1972 No. 904.
[5] S.I. 1966 No. 1032.

carried forward (s. 70 (6)). If there is any inconsistency between conditions obligatorily attached to a planning permission (as being derived from a Certificate granted by the Secretary of State) and other conditions attached to the planning permission by the local planning authority, the obligatory conditions will prevail (s. 71 (3)).

There is no appeal under section 36 of the 1971 Act against a condition obligatorily attached to a grant of planning permission because it was included in an industrial development certificate issued by the Secretary of State (s. 71 (2)). Again, the attaching of any such condition to a planning permission cannot give rise to any claim for compensation (s. 147 (3)) nor can it ever be the basis for serving a purchase notice (s. 180 (4)).

4. Refusal of Industrial Development Certificate—Consequences

Where the Secretary of State refuses to issue an industrial development certificate (against which refusal there is, as already stated, no appeal) with the result that any application for planning permission for industrial development is of no effect (s. 67 (1)), the local planning authority must nevertheless consider whether they would have refused to grant the planning permission sought by the application had the latter been in order (s. 72). If satisfied that they would have so refused to grant planning permission, they must serve a notice on the applicant informing him accordingly (*ibid.*).

Such a notice will operate as a refusal of planning permission for the purposes of (s. 72 (1)):

(1) allowing the applicant to serve upon the appropriate local authority a purchase notice [6] in accordance with section 180 of the 1971 Act requiring the purchase of his land (s. 191 (2));

(2) making a claim for compensation under Part VII of the Act [7] (s. 151); and

(3) allowing a review of the local planning authority's decision by the Secretary of State acting under sections 38 and 39 of the Act, with a view of avoiding the payment of compensation (s. 72 (2)).

[6] See Chap. 17.
[7] See Chap. 16.

5. The Need to Take Account of " Related Development "

In considering, in connection with any proposed industrial development, whether the proposed development will overreach the permitted limit of 5,000 or, as the case may be, 3,000 square feet of industrial floor space, the permitted limit is to be applied not only to the *proposed* industrial development itself but also to any " related development " (s. 68 (1)).

The definition of " related development " is involved; it is to be found in section 68 (4) (5) (6) and (7) of the 1971 Act.

The object of these complex provisions is to render it impossible to escape the need for an industrial development certificate by carrying out a project of industrial development on a piecemeal basis at different times, such development being, nevertheless, all part and parcel of a related whole.

CHAPTER 13

CONTROL OVER TREES AND WOODLANDS, SPECIAL BUILDINGS AND WASTE LAND

A. TREES AND WOODLANDS

1. Tree Preservation Orders

THE 1971 Act makes provision for the preservation of trees, groups of trees or woodlands by means of Tree Preservation Orders. Such an Order (which operates independently of any development plan whether in course of preparation or in operation) is made by a local planning authority (s. 60). The Order needs confirmation by the Secretary of State (s. 60 (4)) except when no objection to it is lodged (s. 60 (5) (c)).

Before making a Tree Preservation Order a local planning authority must be satisfied that it is expedient so to do *in the interests of amenity* (s. 60 (1)). In other words, matters of amenity are the only relevant factors for consideration in connection with the making of a Tree Preservation Order.[1]

2. Effect of a Tree Preservation Order

When in force a Tree Preservation Order will prohibit the cutting down, topping, lopping or wilful destruction of trees except with the consent (which may be given subject to conditions) of the local planning authority (s. 60 (1) (a)). It may also provide for the replanting of any woodland area which is felled in the course of forestry operations permitted by, or under, the Tree Preservation order (s. 60 (1) (b)) and for the payment by a local planning authority of compensation in respect of damage or expenditure caused or incurred in consequence of any refusal of consent by the local planning authority to the cutting down, topping or lopping of trees protected by the Order or arising out of the granting of any such consent subject to conditions (s. 174 and see *Cardigan Timber Co.* v. *Cardiganshire* C.C.[2]).

[1] As to the meaning of " amenity," see *Re Ellis and Ruislip-Northwood U.D.C.* [1920] 1 K.B. 343 (C.A.).   [2] (1957) 9 P. & C.R. 158 (L.T.).

As to applications for a local authority's consent under a Tree Preservation Order, the Order may apply the provisions generally of Part III of the 1971 Act relating to applications for planning permission for development and appeals to the Secretary of State in connection therewith (s. 60 (1) (*c*), 2 (*a*)). There is, however, in this instance, no need to give publicity to the application under section 26 of the 1971 Act nor to notify owners and agricultural tenants under section 17 of the Act (s. 60 (2) (*a*)).

A purchase notice requiring the purchase of the applicant's land may, in appropriate circumstances, be served in the event of any consent under a Tree Preservation Order being refused (ss. 60 (2) (*b*) and 191 (1)).[3]

3. Procedure for a Tree Preservation Order

The procedure for the making of a Tree Preservation Order is dealt with (s. 60) in the Town and Country Planning (Tree Preservation Order) Regulations 1969 [4] whereby the Order must be made in the form (or substantially in the form) set out in the Schedule to the 1969 Regulations (reg. 4) and must define the trees, groups of trees or woodlands to which it relates and for that purpose must include a map (*ibid.*).

On making the Order the authority must deposit for inspection, in the locality of the trees, a certified copy of the Order and the map (reg. 5 (*a*)) and send copies of these to the Conservator of Forests and the District Valuer together with a list of persons affected (reg. 5 (*b*)).

The local planning authority must serve a copy of the Order upon owners and occupiers of land affected by the Order, and on any other person known to them as being entitled to work by surface working any minerals in the land affected by the Order, or to fell any trees or woodlands affected by the Order (reg. 5 (*c*)).

With the copy of the Order there must also be served a notice stating (reg. 5 (*c*) (i) to (v)) the grounds for making the Order, the place where it can be inspected by the public, that objections and representations about the Order may be made to the Secretary of State within twenty-eight days of the service of the notice, that if no objections or representations are " duly made " (or, if made, are

---

[3] As to purchase notices generally, see Chap. 17.
[4] S.I. 1969 No. 17.

withdrawn) the Order, after forty-two days, may be confirmed (without modification) by the authority which made it, and the effect of any direction (included in the Order) that the Order shall take effect immediately and before confirmation (s. 61). The local planning authority must give the Secretary of State a certificate that the foregoing requirements have been complied with (reg. 8 (1) (iv)).

Every objection or representation must state both the particular trees or woodlands to which it refers and also the grounds of the objection, and unless it does these things and is received by the Secretary of State within the twenty-eight days above-mentioned, it will not be " duly made " (reg. 7).

Before confirming a Tree Preservation Order the Secretary of State must take into consideration any objections or representations which have been " duly made," and if he holds a public local inquiry into the matter (and he is not obliged to do so) he must also take into consideration his Inspector's report of the inquiry (reg. 8).

In a case of urgency (*e.g.* where there is danger of the imminent felling of trees) a Tree Preservation Order, as made by the local planning authority, may contain a direction that section 61 of the 1971 Act shall apply to it in which event the Order will forthwith operate provisionally for a period of six months or until, in the meantime, the Secretary of State either confirms the Order or notifies the authority that he will not do so (s. 61 (2)).

If no objections or representations about a Tree Preservation Order are made (or, if made, are withdrawn) then, not less than forty-two days from the service of notices of the making of the Order, the Order may be confirmed (but without any modification) by the authority which made it (s. 60 (5) (*c*) and reg. 6 (1)).

Notice of the confirmation of a Tree Preservation Order must be served on all owners and occupiers of land affected by it and on all those entitled to fell trees, or work by opencast workings minerals, which are affected by the Order (regs. 6 (2) and 9).

Tree Preservation Orders are registrable as local land charges under rule 3 of the Local Land Charges (Amendment) Rules 1948.[5]

A " person aggrieved " [6] by, or an " authority directly concerned " [6] with, the making of a Tree Preservation Order, or a

___

[5] S.I. 1948 No. 1283.
[6] As to meaning of these expressions, see pp. 120 and 121.

decision of the Secretary of State (whether it is a decision on appeal or a decision by him in first instance) relating to an application for consent under such Order, may, within six weeks, challenge, on a point of law, the validity of the Order or the decision of the Secretary of State by application to the High Court (ss. 242 (1) (*d*) (*e*), (2) (*c*), (3) (*e*) and 245).

On such an application the High Court may quash the Order or decision if satisfied that the Order or decision is not within the powers of the 1971 Act or that the interests of the applicant have been substantially prejudiced by failure to comply with the requirements of the Act (s. 245 (4)).   In addition the court may quash or (where applicable) suspend the operation of the Order or the decision in whole or in part (s. 245 (5)).

4. Penalties for Contravention of a Tree Preservation Order

If any person contravenes the provisions of a Tree Preservation Order he is liable on a summary conviction to a fine not exceeding £50 and in the case of a continuing offence to an additional fine not exceeding 40s. per day (s. 102 (2) (3)).   But if the offence is that of cutting down or wilfully destroying a tree, or topping or lopping a tree in a manner which is likely to destroy it, the fine is £250 or twice the value of the tree whichever is the greater (s. 102 (1)).

Nothing in a Tree Preservation Order is to apply (s. 60 (6)) to the cutting down, topping or lopping of a tree:

(1) which is dying or dead or has become dangerous; or

(2) in accordance with statutory obligations; or

(3) so far as necessary to prevent or abate a nuisance.

5. Further Duties in Relation to Trees

When granting planning permission for development, a local planning authority must impose conditions, and make Tree Preservation Orders whenever appropriate, to secure the preservation or planting of trees (ss. 59 and 60 (3)).

The owner of land on which a tree (the subject of a Tree Preservation Order) dies, or is removed or is destroyed in contravention of the Order, is required to replace the tree unless the local planning authority absolve him from this responsibility (s. 62).

The local planning authority are empowered to enforce these provisions subject to appeal to the Secretary of State and to a further appeal (on law only) to the courts (ss. 103 and 246).

B. BUILDINGS OF SPECIAL ARCHITECTURAL OR HISTORIC INTEREST

1. Lists of Special Buildings

With a view to guiding local planning authorities in the preservation of buildings of special architectural or historic interest the Secretary of State is to compile lists of such buildings (s. 54 (1) (2) (3)) and supply copies of such lists to councils of the county boroughs and county districts affected (s. 54 (4) (5)). Any copy so supplied is to be registered in Part X of the register of local land charges (s. 54 (6)) kept under the Land Charges Act 1925, in the manner prescribed in rule 15 of the Local Land Charges Rules 1966.[7]

The owner and occupier of a listed building must be informed that the building has been listed (s. 54 (7)) but the Secretary of State is not obliged to consult either the owner or the occupier before listing any building though he must consult with such persons as appear to him appropriate as having special knowledge of, or interest in, such buildings (s. 54 (3) and Town and Country Planning (Listed Buildings) Regulations 1968 [8]).

The Secretary of State must keep open for free inspection copies of all lists prepared by him and a local authority must likewise keep open for such inspection any portion of a list relating to their area (s. 54 (8)).

The doing of any act causing, or likely to result in, damage to a listed building is an offence punishable with a fine of £100 (s. 57 (1) (2)). If a person, convicted of this offence, fails to prevent further damage resulting from the offence he is liable to a daily penalty of £20 (s. 57 (3)).

A local authority may carry out works urgently necessary for the preservation of an unoccupied listed building after giving seven days' notice to the owner (s. 101).

[7] S.I. 1966 No. 579.
[8] S.I. 1968 No. 1910.

The Secretary of State may make *loans* as well as grants under section 4 of the Historic Buildings and Ancient Monuments Act 1953 for the preservation of historic buildings (Civic Amenities Act 1967, s. 4).

2. Building Preservation Notices for Unlisted Buildings

Where a building is not listed under the 1971 Act but nevertheless appears to a local planning authority to be of special architectural or historic interest and it is threatened with demolition or alteration, the local planning authority may serve on the owner and occupier of the building a " building preservation notice " which subjects the building, for a maximum of six months, to the same protection and provisions as if it were listed (s. 58).

During this period of six months the local planning authority may ask the Secretary of State to consider including the building in a list (s. 58 (1)) compiled or approved under the 1971 Act. If the Secretary of State does so include it, or if he notifies the local planning authority in writing that he does not intend so to include it, then the building preservation notice at once ceases to have effect (s. 58 (3)). If the Secretary of State does in fact decline to list the building, the local authority may not within the next twelve months serve any further building preservation notice in respect of the building (s. 58 (5)).

In a case where a building preservation notice ceases to have effect but the building to which the notice relates does not become a listed building—in other words, where the efforts of the local planning authority have failed—provision is made for the payment of compensation for loss or damage caused by the service of the building preservation notice (s. 173).

3. Unlisted Buildings in Conservation Areas

A local planning authority may designate as a conservation area any part of their area which is of special architectural or historic interest the character or appearance of which it is desirable to preserve or enhance (s. 277). Once this is done then protection for *unlisted* buildings in the conservation area is now available under section 7 of and Schedule 2 to the Town and Country Planning (Amendment) Act 1972, which section and Schedule are to be construed as one with the 1971 Act (1972 Act, s. 7 (8)). A local planning authority can, with the consent of the Secretary of State, control the demolition of any unlisted building in a conservation area in the interests of preserving the character or appearance of the area (1972 Act, s. 7 and Sched. 2).

4. Listing of Buildings replaces Building Preservation Orders

The listing of a building under the 1971 Act is the key to its further protection under the extensive provisions of Part V of the 1971 Act and the Town and Country Planning (Listed Buildings) Regulations 1968.

Under sections 30 and 31 of the Town and Country Planning Act 1962 a building of special architectural or historic interest could be given protection if it were made the subject of a building preservation order made by a local planning authority and approved by the Secretary of State. If it were merely included in a list of buildings of special architectural or historic interest under section 32 of the 1962 Act it did not receive the same amount of protection.

Under the 1971 Act there are no more building preservation orders but every building which was subject to such an order on January 1, 1969, but was not listed under the 1962 Act, will be deemed (s. 54 (10)) to be a building listed under the 1971 Act. The Secretary of State may at any time direct that this arrangement shall cease to have effect (s. 54 (10)) but before he does so he must consult with the local planning authority and with the owner and with the occupier of the building (s. 54 (11)).

5. A Set of New Expressions

Part IV of the 1971 Act creates a number of entirely new expressions relating to special buildings. These expressions are seven in number as follows: " listed building " (s. 54 (9)); " listed building consent " (s. 55 (2)); " listed building purchase notice " (s. 190 (5)); " listed building enforcement notice " (s. 96 (2)); " building preservation notice " (s. 58 (1)); " repairs notice " (s. 115 (1)); and " direction for minimum compensation " (s. 117 (4)).

6. How to List a Building

Under the 1971 Act, when consideration is given to the question of whether or not a building should be listed, the Secretary of State may take into account not only the building itself but also its relationship to other buildings and the desirability of preserving features associated with it but not actually forming part of the building itself (s. 54 (2)). Thus, it is not solely the building which is to be considered but the entire *mise en scéne*.

When the 1971 Act is talking about a listed building, it is also talking about any object or structure fixed to a building or forming part of the land and comprised within the curtilage of the building (*ibid.*).

7. Listed Building Consent for a Listed Building

Under the 1971 Act it is an offence, punishable by imprisonment or fine or both (s. 55 (1) (5)), to demolish, alter or extend a listed building without a written grant of consent known as " listed building consent " (s. 55 (2)) granted by the local planning authority or by the Secretary of State. A listed building consent may be granted either with or without conditions (s. 56 (4) (5)) and must be distinguished from any grant of planning permission which may, or may not, also be required in the circumstances of any particular case (ss. 55 (2) and 56 (2)). Sometimes an appropriately worded planning permission will itself constitute a listed building consent (s. 56 (2)).

In deciding whether or not to grant planning permission or listed building consent with respect to the building of special architectural or historic interest, special regard must be paid to the desirability of preserving the building or of preserving any features of special architectural or historic interest which the building possesses (s. 56 (3)).

Any person carrying out works to a listed building in breach of conditions subject to which the requisite listed building consent was granted commits an offence (s. 55 (4)) punishable by imprisonment or fine or both (s. 56 (5)).

It is a defence to proceedings for an offence relating to a listed building to prove that any works carried out on the building were urgently necessary in the interests of safety or of health, or for the preservation of the building, and that notice in writing of the need for the works was given to the local planning authority as soon as reasonably practicable (s. 55 (6)).

8. Buildings Exempt from Protection

Certain ecclesiastical buildings and ancient monuments are exempted from these provisions relating to the protection of buildings (s. 56 (1)), but it is now clear that a building used as the residence of a minister of religion and from which he performs the duties of his office is to be treated as not being an ecclesiastical building (*ibid.*). Thus clergy houses are brought within the protection of the 1971 Act even though churches used for church purposes are not (*ibid.*).

9. Applications, Appeals and Revocations relating to Listed Building Consents

An application for listed building consent will be made in the first place to the local planning authority although the Secretary of State may direct that the matter shall be dealt with by him instead of by the local planning authority (s. 56 (6)).

The detailed procedure for the making of such an application, and as to appeals to the Secretary of State in the case of a decision which is unsatisfactory to the applicant, are contained in Part I of Schedule 11 to the 1971 Act (s. 56 (6)) and in the Town and Country Planning (Listed Buildings) Regulations 1968.[9]

Provision is made as to the revocation or modification of listed building consent by the local planning authority or by the Secretary of State, and as to compensation to be paid in any such cases, and details of these provisions are to be found in Part II of Schedule 11 to the 1971 Act (s. 56 (6)) and in the aforementioned Listed Buildings Regulations 1968.

10. Purchase Notices for Listed Buildings

If, having made an application for listed building consent in respect of a building and having got a decision which either refuses consent or attaches conditions to the grant of consent, or where listed building consent is revoked or modified—if in any of these circumstances the owner of the building—and indeed of certain land attached to the building (s. 190 (3))—claims that in its present state the listed building has become incapable of a reasonably beneficial use, then he may serve a purchase notice (s. 190 (1)) called in the

---

[9] S.I. 1968 No. 1910.

1971 Act a " listed building purchase notice " (s. 190 (5))—requiring the appropriate local authority to purchase the listed building.

Details as to proceedings following the service of a listed building purchase notice are contained in Schedule 19 to the 1971 Act (s. 190 (1) and Listed Buildings Regulations 1968).

If the application for listed building consent is an application not to demolish a building but merely to carry out alterations or extensions, and the application is refused, then in certain instances compensation is to be paid to the owner by the local planning authority (s. 171 and Listed Buildings Regulations 1968).

11. Enforcement Notices for Listed Buildings

It has already been mentioned that it is an offence to demolish, alter or extend a listed building without first obtaining listed building consent (s. 55 (1) (4)). If unauthorised works to a listed building are carried out, then the local planning authority, in addition to taking proceedings for the offence, may serve upon the owner an enforcement notice (s. 96)—called in the 1971 Act a " listed building enforcement notice " (s. 96 (2)). Details as to the method of service, and the taking effect, of a listed building enforcement notice are given in section 96 of the 1971 Act and, as to appeals against such a notice, in section 97 of and Schedule 9 to the Act.

In the event of non-compliance with the terms of a listed building enforcement notice, the local planning authority may recover penalties from the person in default (s. 98) and this might include a subsequent owner (s. 98 (2) (3)).

In addition the Secretary of State and the local planning authority may themselves take steps to implement an enforcement notice which has not been complied with by the person on whom it was served (s. 99) whilst the Secretary of State has the power to direct a local planning authority to take enforcement action or to take it himself (s. 100).

12. Compulsory Acquisition of Listed Buildings

Provision is made in the 1971 Act whereby local authorities (whether or not they are local planning authorities), or the Secretary of State, may acquire compulsorily any listed building which is not being properly preserved (s. 114). This power of acquisition may not be exercised until at least one month after the service upon the owner of the building of a " *repairs notice* " specifying the work which is considered to be necessary for the proper preservation of the building (s. 115).

Any person having an interest in a listed building which it is proposed to acquire compulsorily can apply to a magistrates' court for the area in which the building is situated to stay the proceedings under the compulsory purchase order (s. 114 (6)), and if the court is satisfied that reasonable steps have in fact been taken for properly preserving the building, the court may make an order accordingly (*ibid.*). Against any such order a person aggrieved has a right of further appeal to the Crown Court (s. 114 (7)). Thus the question of whether or not proper and reasonable steps have been taken for preserving the building is a matter which will be argued out before the magistrates in the first place and the Crown Court in the second.

Section 59 of the Town and Country Planning Act 1968 (a section not repealed by the 1971 Act) makes an amendment to the Acquisition of Land (Authorisation Procedure) Act 1946, Schedule 1, paragraph 12, under which an order for the compulsory acquisition of land containing an ancient monument is subject to Special Parliamentary Procedure unless the Minister of Public Building and Works gives a certain certificate. Formerly, these arrangements applied to a listed building under the Town and Country Planning Act 1962 but this is no longer to be the case unless the listed building is, at the same time, an ancient monument under the ancient monuments legislation (1968 Act, s. 59).

13. Compensation on Acquisition of Listed Buildings

If a listed building is compulsorily acquired the compensation to be paid to the owner of the building will, in general, disregard the depressive effect of the fact that the building has been listed (s. 116).

If, however, it is established that the building has been allowed *deliberately* to fall into disrepair for the purpose of justifying redevelopment of the site, then provision is made whereby there will be included in the compulsory purchase order authorising the acquisition of the building by the local authority, a direction for what is referred to as " minimum compensation " (s. 117 (1) (2) (3)).

The effect of the inclusion in the compulsory order of a direction for minimum compensation is that the local authority will be able to buy the listed building compulsorily but at a price which disregards any profit which might have accrued from the redevelopment of the site (s. 117 (4)). Thus the effect of a direction for minimum compensation is to put a ceiling on the amount which the owner can get. In short, in the circumstances here discussed, " minimum compensation " represents the maximum amount receivable.

Against a direction for minimum compensation there is a right of appeal to the magistrates' court acting for the area where the building is situated (s. 117 (5)) with a further appeal to the Crown Court (s. 117 (6)).

14. Miscellany

The procedures relating to the preservation of special buildings are applied to the buildings of local planning authorities (s. 271) and also to Crown land (s. 266).

If a local authority desires to make a grant under the Local Authorities (Historic Buildings) Act 1962 towards the expenses of repairing or maintaining a special building, then under the Town and Country Planning Act 1968 this grant may be made at the local authority's discretion and without the consent of the Secretary of State (1968 Act, s. 58, which is not repealed by the 1971 Act).

C. CONTROL OF WASTE LAND

Section 65 (together with ss. 104–107) of the 1971 Act empowers a local planning authority to take action with regard to neglected land which has become unsightly or offensive. Under section 65, if serious injury to amenity [10] is caused by the condition of any garden, vacant site or other open land, the local planning authority may serve on the owner and occupier of that land a notice requiring abatement of the injury by the taking of such steps as may be specified in the notice within such period as may be so specified. Whether land is a " garden, vacant site or other open land " is a question of fact depending on the circumstances of the particular case.[11]

A notice under section 65 does not require confirmation by the Secretary of State but he may give directions to local planning

---

[10] See *Re Ellis and Ruislip-Northwood U.D.C.* [1920] 1 K.B. 343 (C.A.).
[11] *Stephens* v. *Cuckfield R.D.C.* [1960] 2 Q.B. 373 (C.A.).

authorities who must conform to them when taking action under the section (s. 65 (1)).

The notice will take effect (subject to challenge in a magistrates' court under s. 105 of the 1971 Act) at the end of the period (not less than twenty-eight days after service of the notice) specified in the notice (s. 65 (2)). If, at the end of that period, the requisite steps have not been taken, any person who does anything which has the effect of continuing or aggravating the injury caused by the condition of the land will be liable to a penalty not exceeding £50 (s. 104 (2)).

Expenses incurred in complying with the notice under section 65 are deemed to be incurred for the person who caused or permitted the land to be made the subject of the notice (s. 107 (2)).

If, within the requisite period, a notice under section 65 has not been complied with, the local planning authority may itself enter in the land and take the appropriate action to comply with the notice, the cost of so doing being recoverable by the authority from the person who is then the owner of the land (s. 107 (1)).

Regulation 21 of the Town and Country Planning General Regulations 1969 [12] applies sections 276, 289, 292 and 294 of the Public Health Act 1936 to the steps required to be taken to comply with a notice under section 65 (ss. 107 (3) and 91 (3) (4)).

A notice under section 65 may be the subject of an appeal to a magistrates' court (s. 105) with a further appeal to the Crown Court (s. 106). The notice is of no effect pending the final determination or withdrawal of the appeal (s. 105 (3)). The magistrates' court may correct any informality, defect or error in the notice if satisfied that it is not a material matter (s. 105 (4)). In determination of the appeal the magistrates' court must give directions for giving effect to the court's decision (s. 105 (5)).

The grounds of appeal to the magistrates' court may be any of the following (s. 105 (1)), namely:

(1) that the condition of the land does not cause serious injury to amenity;

(2) that the condition of the land is the ordinary result of development which is not a contravention of Part III of the 1971 Act;

(3) that the land in question is not a garden, vacant site or other open land;

12 S.I. 1969 No. 286.

(4) that the requirements of the notice exceed what is necessary for preventing serious injury to amenity; and

(5) that the period allowed for the taking of the steps required by the notice falls short of what should reasonably be allowed.

CHAPTER 14

THE ENFORCEMENT OF PLANNING CONTROL

1. Enforcement Control where Planning Permission Required

(1) *Service of enforcement notice*

The enforcement of planning control over the development of land is dealt with in Part V of the Town and Country Planning Act 1971.

Section 87 of the 1971 Act provides for the serving of enforcement notices. A local planning authority may serve an enforcement notice in any instance where it appears to the authority that there has been *a breach of planning control after the end of 1963* (s. 87 (1)). The authority are not *obliged* to serve an enforcement notice whenever it appears that there has been a breach of planning control. The authority must always consider whether it is *expedient* to serve such a notice having regard to:

(a) the provisions of the development plan, and

(b) any other material considerations (*ibid.*).

" Breach of planning control " is specially defined (s. 87 (2)) and relates to any development carried out, whether before or after the 1971 Act without planning permission, or to development which fails to comply with conditions or limitations subject to which planning permission for the development was granted.

(2) *The four-year rule*

The reference to " after the end of 1963," is worthy of note. December 31, 1963, was just about four years prior to the publication of the Town and Country Planning Bill on December 19, 1967 —the Bill which became the Town and Country Planning Act 1968.

Under the law as it formerly stood under the Town and Country Planning Act 1962, it was well known that if irregular development could continue in being for a period of four years without getting itself subjected to an enforcement notice, then such development became automatically legitimated from a town planning point of view by the effluxion of time, namely, the period of four years.

Thereafter, under the 1962 Act, no enforcement notice could be served in respect of such development.

This is still the position under the 1971 Act (s. 87 (3)) *if* the development complained of consists of:

(a) the carrying out without planning permission of building, engineering, mining or other operations in, on, over or under land; *or*

(b) the failure to comply with any condition or limitation which relates to the carrying out of such operations and subject to which planning permission was granted for the development of that land; *or*

(c) the making without planning permission of a change of use of any building to use as a single dwelling-house.

In other words, the effect of section 87 (3) of the 1971 Act is that in the case of development which involves *not operations* but only *change of use*, there is no time limit whatsoever on the service of an enforcement notice except in the single instance (s. 87 (3) (*c*)) where the change of use constitutes a change of use of a building into use as a single dwelling-house in which instance the four-year rule continues to apply.

It follows from the foregoing that if *any* originally irregular development has contrived, not later than December 31, 1967, to " make the grade " by persisting for four years and thereby getting itself in order in the eyes of town planning law then no enforcement notice can touch it.

After the commencement on April 1, 1969, of Part II of the 1968 Act it is to be noted that if change-of-use development is irregular at its inception no passage of time will make it regular. At all times it will be open to the local planning authority to serve an enforcement notice notwithstanding that four, six, ten or, indeed, any other number of years have passed since the change-of-use development was originally carried out. The one exception to this rule is change of use of a building into use as a single dwelling-house (s. 87 (3) (*c*)); this sort of development " makes the grade " after four years' existence without challenge by enforcement notice.

(3) *Service, contents and taking effect of enforcement notice*

Under the 1971 Act an enforcement notice *must* be served on the owner and the occupier of the land to which it relates and also upon any other person who has an interest in the land, which interest, in the opinion of the authority, is materially affected by the notice (s. 87 (4) (5)).

The enforcement notice must specify (s. 87 (6)):

     (a) *the matters* which are alleged to constitute a breach of planning control, *i.e.* the facts on which the local planning authority relies as justifying the service of the notice;

     (b) *the steps* required by the local planning authority to be taken to remedy the breach; and

     (c) *the period for the compliance* with the notice which period is to be calculated as from the date when the notice takes effect.

The 1971 Act provides specifically that the steps which an enforcement notice can require to be taken may include:

    (a) the demolition or alteration of buildings or works;

    (b) the discontinuance of any use of land; or

    (c) the carrying out on land of any building operations or other operations (s. 87 (7)).

An enforcement notice *will take effect* (subject to appeal to the Secretary of State under section 88 of the 1971 Act) at the end of such period as is specified in the notice and this period must not be less than twenty-eight days after the service of the notice (s. 87 (8)).

There is no prescribed form of enforcement notice and there has been much litigation about the form and content of such a notice.

An enforcement notice must specify clearly and accurately the development which it is alleged has been carried out without planning permission or, in the case of a breach of conditions or limitations, the matters on which it is alleged that conditions or limitations subject to which planning permission was originally granted have not been complied with.[1] A notice which ignored the fact that planning permission had been granted for a limited period (which had expired at the time of the service of the notice) was held to have proceeded on a false basis and, accordingly, to be invalid.[2] But the failure to state the reason why the acts com-

---

[1] *Keats* v. *L.C.C.* [1954] 1 W.L.R. 1357 (D.C.); *Lincolnshire (Parts of Lindsey) C.C.* v. *Wallace Holiday Camp* [1953] 2 Q.B. 178 (D.C.); *East Riding C.C.* v. *Park Estate (Bridlington)* [1957] A.C. 223 (H.L.); *Miller-Mead* v. *Minister of Housing and Local Government* [1963] 2 Q.B. 196 (C.A.) where Upjohn L.J. said that the test is " does the notice tell him (the person on whom it is served) fairly what he has done wrong and what he must do to remedy it."

[2] *Francis* v. *Yiewsley & West Drayton U.D.C.* [1958] 1 Q.B. 478 (C.A.).

plained of amounted to development was held not to invalidate the notice (*ibid.*).

A local planning authority are not estopped from serving an enforcement notice in respect of development simply because one of their chief officers has stated that planning permission was not required for that development—*Southend-on-Sea Corporation* v. *Hodgson (Wickford) Ltd.* [1962] 1 Q.B. 416. This case illustrates, generally, the danger of relying on statements made (doubtlessly in good faith) by the planning officer of a local planning authority. It is the decision of *the authority* which counts and the authority are not bound to accept the advice of their planning officer.

The contents and wording of enforcement notices in cases where caravan sites have been used seasonally (*i.e.* year after year but, in each instance, for part of the year only) or for more than the permitted number of caravans, have been the subject of much argument and litigation.[3]

It will be seen that an enforcement notice must specify *two periods*—one being the period at the end of which the notice takes effect (s. 87 (8)) and the other being the period within which specified steps are to be taken for securing compliance with the notice (s. 87 (6) (*c*)). An enforcement notice which does not thus specify two periods is a nullity.[4] The two periods may be sufficiently clearly indicated though not expressly stated.[5] If an enforcement notice is invalid by reason of not specifying the two periods aforesaid, the recipient is not estopped from challenging the validity of the notice by reason of having applied to the local planning authority for planning permission on the basis that the notice is valid, and having appealed to the Secretary of State against the refusal by the local planning authority of his application.[6]

An enforcement notice is registrable as a local land charge.[7]

---

[3] *Webber* v. *Minister of Housing and Local Government* [1968] 1 W.L.R. 29 (C.A.); *Brookes* v. *Flintshire C.C.* (1956) 6 P. & C.R. 140 (D.C.); *Taylor* v. *Eton R.D.C.* (1957) 9 P. & C.R. 430 (D.C.); *Guildford R.D.C.* v. *Fortescue & Others* and *Guildford R.D.C.* v. *Penny* [1959] 2 Q.B. 112 (C.A.).

[4] *Burgess* v. *Jarvis & Sevenoaks R.D.C.* [1952] 2 Q.B. 41 (C.A.); *Mead* v. *Chelmsford R.D.C.* [1953] 1 Q.B. 32 (D.C.); *Godstone R.D.C.* v. *Brazil* [1953] 1 W.L.R. 1102 (D.C.). For further decisions on the matter of an enforcement notice being a nullity, see *Findlow* v. *Lewis* [1963] 1 Q.B. 151; *Noble* v. *Armitage* (1962) 182 E.G. 209; *Miller-Mead* v. *Minister of Housing and Local Government* [1963] 2 Q.B. 196 (C.A.); *Bambury* v. *Hounslow L.B.C.* [1966] 2 All E.R. 532 (D.C.).

[5] *Wilkinsons' Executors* v. *Leeds Corporation* (1952) 3 P. & C.R. 222.

[6] *Swallow & Pearson* v. *Middlesex C.C.* (1953) 3 P. & C.R. 314.

[7] Local Land Charges (Amendment) Rules 1966, No. 579, r. 8.

There will not usually be any question of removing an enforcement notice from the register after there has been compliance with the notice, since the notice is not discharged by such compliance (s. 93 (1)).

A local planning authority may extend the time for compliance with an enforcement notice *before* the specified time has expired (s. 89 (6)), but an extension *after* that time is an act of grace without legal consequences.[8]

(4) *Withdrawal of enforcement notice*

A local planning authority may withdraw an enforcement notice at any time *before it takes effect* and, if they do, they must forthwith give notice of the withdrawal to every person on whom the notice was served (s. 87 (9)).   This is a useful provision.   There had been doubt as to whether an enforcement notice once served could in law be withdrawn by the local planning authority even if the local planning authority wished to do so.

The withdrawal of an enforcement notice does not in any way preclude the service of a second one in respect of the same matter (s. 87 (9)).

(5) *Appeal against enforcement notice*

Appeals against enforcement notices are dealt with in section 88 of the 1971 Act.   The appeal is to the Secretary of State and it can be made at any time, provided the notice has not come into effect (s. 88 (1)).   The appeal may be made (*ibid.*) by—

(a) a person on whom the notice has been served; or

(b) any other person having an interest in the land.

An appeal may be made on any one or other of the following seven grounds (s. 88 (1)):

(a) that planning permission ought to be granted for the development to which the notice relates or, as the case may be, that a condition or limitation alleged in the enforcement notice not to have been complied with ought to be discharged;

(b) that the matters alleged in the notice do not constitute a breach of planning control;

(c) in the case of a notice relating to development involving

---

[8] *Joyner* v. *Guildford Corporation* (1954) 5 P. & C.R. 30 (county court decision).

operations (in which case the four-year rule applies), that the four-year period has in fact elapsed;

(d) in the case of a notice relating to development (change-of-use development) to which the four-year rule does not apply, that the breach of planning control complained of occurred before the beginning of 1964;

(e) that the enforcement notice was not served as required by section 87 (4) of the 1971 Act;

(f) that the steps required by the notice to be taken exceed what is necessary to remedy any breach of planning control;

(g) that the specified period for compliance with the notice falls short of what should reasonably be allowed.

The appeal is made by notice in writing to the Secretary of State and the notice must indicate not only *the grounds* of the appeal but must also state *the facts* on which the appeal is based (s. 88 (2)). On any such appeal the Secretary of State must, if either the appellant or the local planning authority so wish, afford to each of them an opportunity of appearing before an Inspector appointed by the Secretary of State for the purpose (*ibid.*).

If an appeal is lodged the enforcement notice, naturally, becomes of no effect pending either the final determination or the withdrawal of the appeal (s. 88 (3)).

On the appeal the Secretary of State may correct any informality, defect or error in the enforcement notice if he is satisfied it is not material (s. 88 (4) (*a*)) and, in a case where failure to serve the notice upon a person entitled to receive the notice under section 87 (4) of the 1971 Act would generally have been a ground for allowing the appeal, the Secretary of State may, nevertheless, disregard this slip if he is satisfied that the person who has not been served has not been substantially prejudiced thereby (s. 88 (4) (*b*)).

On hearing the appeal the Secretary of State has wide powers to give all such directions as are requisite for giving effect to his decision, whatever the decision may be (s. 88 (5)).   Amongst other things the Secretary of State may give directions for quashing an enforcement notice or for varying its terms in favour of the appellant (*ibid.*) and he may himself grant planning permission for the development to which notice relates or, as the case may be, he may discharge conditions or limitations subject to which planning permission for that development was granted (s. 88 (5) (*a*)).   In addition he may determine any purpose for which land which is the subject of the appeal may, in the circumstances obtaining at the time of the determination, be lawfully used having regard to any past use thereof and to any planning permission relating to the land (s. 88 (5) (*b*)).

In considering whether to grant planning permission the Secretary of State *must* pay attention to the provisions of the development plan so far as they are material to the subject-matter of the enforcement notice and also to any other material considerations (s. 88 (6)).

Any planning permission granted by the Secretary of State, as a result of an appeal against an enforcement notice, may be granted by him subject to such conditions as he thinks fit (s. 88 (6) (*b*)), and may include permission to retain or to complete any buildings or works with or without complying with a condition attached to a previous planning permission (s. 88 (6) (*a*)).

If, on hearing an appeal against an enforcement notice, the Secretary of State discharges a condition or limitation he may substitute another condition or limitation for it, whether more or less onerous (s. 88 (6)).

Any planning permission granted by the Secretary of State on appeal against an enforcement notice will be final (s. 88 (7) (*b*)), and, for the purposes of the local planning authority's register of planning permissions, the Secretary of State's decision is to be treated as the decision of the local planning authority (s. 88 (7) (*c*)).

Where a notice purporting to be an enforcement notice is one relating to non-compliance with conditions or with limitations attached to a grant of planning permission, the validity of the notice is not to depend on whether the non-compliance to which the notice relates was in fact a non-compliance with conditions or with limitations or with both (s. 243 (5)).   If the notice has referred to " conditions " or to " limitations " or even to both of these things, then the notice is to be construed as applying to conditions or to limitations (or to both) as the facts of the case require (*ibid.*).

Once a person has appealed to the Secretary of State against an enforcement notice, neither he nor anyone else will be entitled, in any other proceedings instituted after the appeal, to claim that the enforcement notice was not duly served on the person who appealed against it (s. 110 (2)).   This is a matter which must be taken on the appeal to the Secretary of State or not at all.

If, after service of an enforcement notice, planning permission is granted for the retention of buildings or works, or for continuance of a use of land, to which the notice relates, the notice ceases to have effect (s. 92 (1) (2)) but this is without prejudice to the liability of any person for an offence in respect of a failure to comply with the enforcement notice before it ceased to have effect (s. 92 (3)).

On an appeal against an enforcement notice the Secretary of State has power to award costs to either of the parties to the appeal (s. 110 (1)).

When the Secretary of State has given his " decision " (s. 246 (5)) on the appeal made to him against the enforcement notice, then:

(1) the appellant himself, or

(2) the local planning authority, or

(3) any person on whom the enforcement notice has been served,

may either appeal against the decision on a point of law to the High Court or require the Secretary of State to state and sign a case for the opinion of the High Court (s. 246 (1)).

At any stage of the proceedings on an appeal to the Secretary of State, the Secretary of State may himself take the initiative and state any question of law which arises during the proceedings in the form of a special case for the decision of the High Court (s. 246 (2)) from whose decision there will be a further appeal to the Court of Appeal (*ibid.*).

An appeal to the High Court from the decision of the Secretary of State can only be on a question of law. The court will not interfere with a finding on a question of fact or degree unless it can be said that the decision made thereon could not properly have been reached.[9]   The onus of proof is on the appellant.[10]

(6) *Stop notices for development involving operations*

Once an enforcement notice is served, the local planning authority may, at the same time (or at any time thereafter but before the enforcement notice takes effect), serve the further notice known as a " stop notice " (s. 90 (1)). The stop notice must refer to the enforcement notice to which it is dependent and must have a copy of such enforcement notice annexed to it (*ibid.*).   This provision is aimed at those appellants who, in time past, have been prepared to adopt delaying tactics in order to drag out as long as possible the ultimate determination of an appeal against an enforcement notice.

This stop notice procedure does *not* apply to development which

---

[9] *East Barnet U.D.C.* v. *British Transport Commission* [1962] 2 Q.B. 484 (D.C.).
[10] *Nelsovil* v. *Minister of Housing and Local Government* [1962] 1 W.L.R. 404 (D.C.).

comprises only change of use (s. 90 (1)) except where the alleged breach of planning control is the deposit of refuse or waste materials, in which case the stop notice procedure does apply (s. 90 (2)).

The effect of a stop notice is to prohibit any person on whom it is served from carrying out or continuing any specified operations (*i.e.* operations specified in the stop notice) on the land to which the enforcement notice relates, provided such operations are operations which are *either*

(a) alleged by the enforcement notice to be in breach of planning control, *or*

(b) are so closely associated with such operations as to constitute substantially the same operations (s. 90 (1)).

A stop notice may be served on any person who appears to the local planning authority to have an interest in the land, or to be concerned with the carrying out and continuance of operations upon the land, affected by the enforcement notice (s. 90 (3)).

A stop notice (s. 90 (4)):

(a) must specify the date on which it is to take effect and this may not be earlier than three, nor later than fourteen, days from the day on which it is served;

(b) in relation to any person served will take effect on the date specified within it (as the date for taking effect) or will take effect on the third day after the date on which it is served, whichever is the later; and

(c) will cease to have effect when the enforcement notice either takes effect or is withdrawn or quashed.

Any person who fails to comply with the provisions of a stop notice is guilty of an offence and liable on summary conviction to a fine not exceeding £400 or, on conviction on indictment, to a fine of unrestricted amount (s. 90 (5)). If the offence is continued after conviction. then for every day on which it is continued such a person is liable to a further fine of not more than £50 on summary conviction and to a further fine of unlimited amount on conviction on indictment (*ibid.*).

A stop notice is not invalidated by reason of the fact that the enforcement notice to which it relates was not served precisely as required by section 87 (4) of the 1971 Act, if it is shown that the local planning authority took all reasonable steps to effect proper service of the enforcement notice (s. 90 (6)).

A local planning authority may at any time withdraw a stop notice by serving notice to that effect on persons served with the stop notice (s. 90 (7)).

(7) *Compensation for loss or damage due to stop notice*

Provision is made (but only in certain, and not in all, circumstances) for compensation for *loss or damage directly* due to a stop notice (s. 177 (1)). Compensation will be payable (s. 177 (2)) when (and only when):

(a) the enforcement notice to which the stop notice is related is itself quashed on any of the grounds mentioned in paragraphs (*b*), (*c*), (*d*) or (*e*) of section 88 (1) of the 1971 Act (as to which, see above at pages 192 and 193); *or*

(b) the allegation in the enforcement notice on which the prohibition in the stop notice is dependent (see s. 177 (3)) is not upheld by reason of the enforcement notice being varied on one or other of the four aforementioned grounds; *or*

(c) the enforcement notice is withdrawn by the local planning authority (but not if this is done because planning permission is granted for development to which the enforcement notice relates or for the retention or continuance of such development freed of any condition or limitation subject to which a previous planning permission was granted); *or*

(d) the stop notice itself is withdrawn.

When is a prohibition in a stop notice to be treated as dependent on an allegation in an enforcement notice? The answer is that it is to be so treated if, and to the extent that, the operations to which the prohibition in the stop notice relates are either the same as those alleged in the enforcement notice to constitute a breach of planning control, or are so closely associated with them as to constitute substantially the same operations (s. 177 (3)).

Claims for compensation for loss or damage due to a stop notice must be made (s. 177 (4)) to the local planning authority in the manner prescribed and within the time (six months from the decision which gives rise to the claim) prescribed by regulation 19 of the Town and Country Planning General Regulations 1969.[11] Any such loss or damage may include a sum payable for breach of

[11] S.I. 1969 No. 286.

contract caused by the taking of action necessary to comply with the stop notice (s. 177 (5)).

In respect of any contract entered into *on or before* December 31, 1969, *a contractor*, prohibited by a stop notice from carrying out his obligations to a developer, has a statutory right (as distinct from any contractual right that may be negotiated between the parties) to compensation from *the developer* (s. 90 (8)).

(8) *Certification of established use of land*

As already explained, the 1971 Act (re-enacting the Town and Country Planning Act 1968) provides for the abolition of the four-year time limit on the service of an enforcement notice in respect of any development which constitutes an unauthorised change of use unless such change of use is the change of use of a building to use as a single dwelling-house, in which case the four-year time limit continues to function (s. 87 (3) (*c*)).

It has been recognised that this abolition of the four-year rule in the case of any unauthorised change-of-use development could lead to difficulties in the future because it will be open to a local planning authority *at any time* in the future—that is to say, days, months or even years ahead—to challenge a use of land as being unauthorised. If such challenge does not take place until many years after the commencement of the use of which complaint is made, it may well be that, at that time in the far future, it will be difficult for the person enjoying the use complained of to prove that such use was earlier established at a time which makes it immune from challenge.

Accordingly, sections 94 and 95 of and Schedule 14 to the 1971 Act make provision whereby a use of land may, on application, be certified by a local planning authority as *an established use* (s. 94 (2)) in which event the applicant is entitled to receive from the local planning authority an " established use certificate " (s. 94 (4)).

A use of land is to be regarded as established (s. 94 (1)) if:

> (a) it was begun before the beginning of 1964 without planning permission and has continued ever since the end of 1963; *or*
>
> (b) it was begun before the beginning of 1964 under a planning permission granted subject to conditions or limitations which have either never been complied with at all or have not been complied with since the end of 1963; *or*

(c) it was begun after the end of 1963 as the result of a change of use which did not require planning permission and since the end of 1963 there has been no change of use which did require planning permission.

The benefit of this procedure is, of course, that an established use, certified as aforesaid, is not liable to challenge under the enforcement procedure of section 87 of the 1971 Act because under that section an enforcement notice may be served only in respect of a breach of planning control occurring " after the end of 1963 " (s. 87 (1)).

It should be emphasised that these provisions relating to the certification of established uses are relevant only in the case of change-of-use development in respect of which the four-year limitation rule has been abolished by the 1971 Act.

Where the four-year rule continues to apply, as it does (s. 87 (3)) in the case of development which involves either the carrying out of operations affecting land or a change of use of a building to use as a single dwelling-house, then the four-year rule may continue to be relied upon by a developer in the future just as it always has been relied on under the Town and Country Planning Act 1947 and all its successors; this position is not affected by the certification procedure here discussed.

Any person who claims that a particular use of land in which he has an interest has become established can apply to the local planning authority for an established use certificate (s. 94 (2)) provided, however, that no such application can be made in respect of the use of land as a single dwelling-house, or in respect of any use of land which is not actually subsisting at the time of the application (*ibid.*).

An established use certificate may be granted either by a local planning authority under section 94 of the 1971 Act or by the Secretary of State under section 95 of the Act and in either event the grant may relate to the whole or part only of the land specified in the application, or to one or more uses in a case where the applicant claims to have more than one established use for the same piece of land (s. 94 (3)).

If, on application for a certificate, the local planning authority are satisfied that the applicant's claim is made out, then they *must* grant him an established use certificate (s. 94 (4)). If they are not so satisfied, then they *must* refuse the application (*ibid.*).

The application must be dealt with by the local planning authority within a period to be prescribed by a development order or within such extended period as may be agreed between the applicant and the local planning authority, and if not granted within such period the application is deemed to be refused (s. 94 (5)).

Detailed provisions as to:

(1) the method of applying for an established use certificate;

(2) the method of appealing against a refusal of a certificate; and

(3) the form of such a certificate,

are given in section 94 (6) of and Schedule 14 to the 1971 Act.

If the local planning authority refuse a certificate the applicant may appeal to the Secretary of State (s. 95 (2)), who may grant or refuse the certificate (*ibid.*) and whose decision is final (s. 95 (5)). Before determining such an appeal the Secretary of State must give the applicant and the local planning authority (if either so desire) an opportunity of being heard by a person appointed by the Secretary of State (s. 95 (4)).

Once granted, an established use certificate is, as regards any matters stated within it, to be conclusive for the purposes of any appeal to the Secretary of State against any enforcement notice served in respect of the land to which the established use certificate relates, provided that the enforcement notice was served after the date on which the established use certificate was granted (s. 94 (7)).

An established use certificate is an important document. Thus any person who, with a view to obtaining such a certificate, knowingly or recklessly makes a false statement or, with intent to deceive, produces a false document or withholds material information, is liable on summary conviction to a fine not exceeding £400 or, on conviction on indictment, to imprisonment not exceeding two years or to a fine of unlimited amount or to both (s. 94 (8)).

For the purpose of being recorded in the Register of Decisions on Planning Applications kept by a local planning authority under section 34 of the 1971 Act an application for an established use certificate is to be regarded as an application for planning permission (s. 94 (4) and Sched. 14, para. 6).

(9) " *Established use certificates* "—*grant by Secretary of State*

Any application for an established use certificate made, as it always will be in the first place, to a local planning authority, may be called in by the Secretary of State in order that he may deal with it instead of the authority (s. 95 (1)).

Where the Secretary of State declines to grant an established use certificate he may, instead, grant planning permission for the use in respect of which the application for an established use certificate was made (s. 95 (3) (6)).

Any decision by the Secretary of State on a called-in application for an established use certificate is final (s. 95 (5)).

(10) *Enforcement action by local planning authority*

If an enforcement notice which has come into operation requires specified steps to be taken (other than the discontinuance of a use of land) and those steps are not taken within the period specified in the notice (or within such extended period as the local planning authority may allow), the authority may enter on this land affected by the notice and carry out, by means of the demolition or alteration of buildings or works, the requirements of the enforcement notice and, having done so, may recover as a simple contract debt their reasonable expenses of so doing (ss. 91 and 111). Any such expenses may become a charge on the land (s. 91 (5)).

The action for recovery of expenses incurred by a local planning authority in carrying out the requirements of an enforcement notice is taken against the person who is the owner (as defined in section 290 (1) of the 1971 Act) of the land at the date when it is sought to recover the expenses (s. 91 (1)).

It will be noticed that a person against whom an action for the recovery of expenses is taken may not necessarily be the person who improperly carried out, without planning permission, the development of which complaint is made or who broke the conditions or limitations subject to which planning permission was originally granted, because action for the recovery of expenses is to be taken against " the person who is then the owner of the land " (s. 91 (1)). Any expenses, however, which are incurred either by an owner or occupier of land in complying with an enforcement notice, or any sums paid by an owner of land under section 91 of the 1971 Act in respect of the expenses of a local planning authority in taking steps to enforce the provisions of an enforcement notice, are deemed to have been incurred by, or to have been paid for the use and at the request of, the person by whom the development was originally carried out (s. 91 (2)) to whom recourse for reimbursement must be

H.O.—7*

made by any subsequent owner or occupier of the land who incurs expenses as a result of the service upon him of an enforcement notice.

The provisions of sections 276, 289, 292 and 294 of the Public Health Act 1936 apply, with the necessary modifications, in relation to steps required to be taken by an enforcement notice (s. 91 (4) and the Town and Country Planning General Regulations 1969,[12] reg. 21).

A person who, without a grant of planning permission, reinstates or restores any building or work which has already been demolished or altered in compliance with an enforcement notice, is liable to a penalty of £400 (s. 93 (5)).

(11) *Penalties for non-compliance with enforcement notice*

In addition to the powers of the local planning authority to " step in " and carry out the requirements of an enforcement notice (s. 91), it is provided that where the notice requires specified steps (other than the discontinuance of a use of land) to be taken, the person who was the owner of the land at the time the notice was served shall, if the aforementioned steps are not duly taken, be liable to a fine of £400 on summary conviction or a fine of unlimited amount on conviction on indictment (s. 89 (1)).

Such a person, if he has ceased to be the owner of the land before the end of the time allowed for complying with the enforcement notice, may, on giving at least three *clear* days' notice to the prosecution, have the person who had then become the owner of the land brought before the court (s. 89 (2)).   If the original defendant proves that the failure to comply with the enforcement notice was due, in whole or in part, to the default of the subsequent owner, then the latter may be convicted and the original owner, if he proves that he himself took all reasonable steps to secure compliance with the order, *must* be acquitted (s. 89 (3)).

If a person, having been convicted under any of the above provisions for non-compliance with an enforcement notice, then fails to do everything in his power to comply with the notice as soon as practicable, he is liable to a further daily penalty of £50 on summary conviction or a fine of unlimited amount on conviction on indictment (s. 89 (4)).

[12] S.I. 1969 No. 286.

Where an enforcement notice requires the discontinuance of a use of land, or compliance with conditions or limitations attached to a grant of planning permission, then if any person uses the land, or carries out operations in contravention of the notice, he will be liable to a fine of £400 on summary conviction or a fine of unlimited amount on conviction on indictment together with (if the prohibited use is continued) a daily penalty of £50 on summary conviction or a fine of unlimited amount on conviction on indictment (s. 89 (5)).

(12) *Continuing efficacy of enforcement notice against subsequent development*

Compliance with the terms of an enforcement notice does not discharge the notice (s. 93 (1)). Thus the resumption of a use of land, after that use has been discontinued in compliance with an enforcement notice, will constitute a further contravention of the notice (s. 93 (2)). Similarly, if development of land, by way of reinstating or restoring buildings or works which have been demolished or altered in compliance with an enforcement notice, is carried out, the enforcement notice is deemed to apply to such reinstated buildings or works " notwithstanding that its terms are not apt for the purpose " (s. 93 (3)).

Where the local planning authority propose to take enforcement action under section 91 of the 1971 Act in respect of such irregularly reinstated buildings or works, they must give not less than twenty-eight days' notice of their intention to the owner and occupier of the land affected (s. 93 (4)).

2. Enforcement Control over Authorised Development

The provisions of this chapter have so far dealt with the enforcement of planning control over *unauthorised* development, *i.e.* development which wholly lacks planning permission, or development which is in breach of conditions or limitations subject to which planning permission was granted. In the case of such unauthorised development the remedy (as already discussed) is by way of an enforcement notice.

But the proper planning of land may, from time to time, require the removal or prohibition of development originally undertaken *with* planning permission and in entire compliance with planning

control. Accordingly, a local planning authority may by Order, confirmed by the Secretary of State, require the alteration or removal of any authorised building or the discontinuance of any authorised use of land (s. 51) but if this is done compensation, assessed (s. 178) in accordance with the Land Compensation Act 1961, will be payable to any person in respect of damage caused by:
    (a) the depreciation in the value of his interest in the land;
    (b) the disturbance of his enjoyment of the land (s. 170 (2) (4)). Such a person may also claim compensation for expenses reasonably incurred by him in complying with the requirements of a local planning authority respecting authorised development (s. 170 (3)).

Claims for compensation must be made in writing within six months of the order of the local planning authority (Town and Country Planning General Regulations 1969,[13] reg. 19).

The validity of an Order made under section 51 of the 1971 Act may be challenged on a point of law within six weeks by application in the High Court by any person aggrieved [14] by the Order or by any authority directly concerned [14] with the Order (ss. 242 (1) (d), (2) (b) and 245 (1) (2) (3) (4) (7)).

If any person, without planning permission, uses land in contravention of an Order made under section 51 of the 1971 Act he will be liable to a fine of £400 on summary conviction or a fine of unlimited amount on conviction on indictment (s. 108 (1)) together with a daily penalty of £50 on summary conviction or a fine of unlimited amount on conviction on indictment (*ibid.*).

In addition the local planning authority may, in default, take any steps required to be taken under the Order for the alteration or removal of buildings or works (s. 108 (2)) and may sell materials removed (accounting for the proceeds of sale) under the authority of section 276 of the Public Health Act 1936 as applied by section 108 (2) of the 1971 Act.

3. Enforcement of Control over Listed Buildings

Under section 54 of the 1971 Act the Secretary of State may prepare lists of buildings of special architectural or historic interest with a view to guiding local planning authorities as to their functions under the 1971 Act in relation to such buildings.

[13] S.I. 1969 No. 286.
[14] As to a "person aggrieved" or an "authority directly concerned," see pp. 120 and 121.

The enforcement of control over a listed building is discussed in Chapter 13.[15]

4. Enforcement of Control over Waste Land

Under section 65 of the 1971 Act a local planning authority may serve on the owner and on the occupier of land a notice requiring the taking of specified steps to abate the serious injury to amenity caused by the condition of any garden, vacant site or other open land.[16]   Subject to appeal to a magistrates' court, a " notice under section 65 " will take effect at the end of such period (which may not be less than twenty-eight days after the service of the notice) as may be stated in the notice (s. 65 (2)).

The enforcement of control following the service of a notice under section 65 is discussed in Chapter 13.[17]

5. Enforcement of Tree Preservation Orders

The making of a Tree Preservation Order for the preservation of trees and woodlands is dealt with earlier in Chapter 13.[18]   So far as enforcement is concerned it needs only to be stated here that if any person contravenes the provisions of a Tree Preservation Order he is liable to a fine of £250 or twice the value of the tree (whichever is the greater) if the offence is cutting down or wilfully destroying a tree, or topping or lopping it in such a way as to be likely to destroy it (s. 102 (1)), or a fine of £50 if the offence is otherwise (s. 102 (2)).   For a continuing offence there is a further fine on summary conviction of £2 per day (s. 102 (3)).

6. Enforcement of Control over Advertisements

Advertisement control has been discussed earlier in Chapter 9.[19]

A local planning authority may require the removal of any advertisement displayed in contravention of the Town and Country Planning (Control of Advertisements) Regulations 1969 [20] (as

[15] See Chap. 13, p. 183.
[16] See Chap. 13, p. 185.
[17] See Chap. 13, p. 186.
[18] See Chap. 13, p. 174.
[19] See Chap. 9, p. 133.
[20] S.I. 1969 No. 1532.

amended by the Town and Country Planning (Control of Advertisements) (Amendment) Regulations 1972 [21]) or the discontinuance of the use of any advertising site used in contravention of those Regulations (s. 109 (1)). The authority have power under the 1969 Regulations to require the discontinuance of the display of advertisements displayed with deemed consent in order to remedy injury to amenity or danger to the public (reg. 16).

To secure such removal or discontinuance the 1969 Regulations apply, with adaptations, the provisions of Part V of the 1971 Act relating to enforcement notices (s. 109 (1)).

It is to be remembered that a person is deemed to display an advertisement if:

(a) the advertisement is displayed on land of which he is the owner or occupier, or

(b) the advertisement gives publicity to his goods, trade, business or other concerns

unless in either case such person proves that the advertisement was displayed without his consent or knowledge (s. 109 (3)).

A person who displays an advertisement in contravention of the 1969 Regulations is liable to a fine of such amount (not exceeding £100) as may be prescribed by regulations and, in the case of a continuing offence, to a daily penalty of such amount (not exceeding £5) as may be prescribed by regulations (s. 109 (2) and the 1969 Regulations, reg. 8).

The former power to serve an enforcement notice in respect of a contravening advertisement has not been continued under the 1969 Regulations. In some cases, however, the display of an advertisement may amount to development under section 22 (1) and (4) of the 1971 Act and, if not in accordance with the 1969 Regulations, planning permission will not be deemed granted under section 64 of the Act, in which case the normal enforcement procedure under the 1971 Act will apply.

[21] S.I. 1972 No. 489.

CHAPTER 15

PLANNING INQUIRIES—PROCEDURE RULES

1. Rules of Procedure

THE holding of public local inquiries is now a well-known and accepted part of the administrative process relating to town planning control over the development of land. Such an inquiry may, for example, be held in connection with the approval by the Secretary of State of a development plan (or of an amendment to a development plan) under the Town and Country Planning Act 1971, or of a compulsory purchase order for land under the Acquisition of Land (Authorisation Procedure) Act 1946, or of a designation order for the site of a new town under the New Towns Act 1965, or in connection with an appeal to the Secretary of State (under section 36 of the 1971 Act) against a planning decision or (under section 37 of the Act) in default of the giving of a planning decision, or (under sections 63 (2) (c) and 60 (2) (a) of the Act) against a decision relating to the display of an advertisement.

The Report[1] of the Committee on Administrative Tribunals and Enquiries (the Franks Committee) recommended in July 1957 that in connection with these inquiries a " code or codes of procedure for Inquiries should be formulated by the Council on Tribunals (later established under the Tribunals and Inquiries Act 1958 which is now repealed and replaced by the Tribunals and Inquiries Act 1971) and made statutory; the procedure should be simple and inexpensive but orderly." The result of their recommendations was the enacting of a statutory provision (now contained in section 11 of the Tribunals and Inquiries Act 1971 which enables the Lord Chancellor, after consultation with the Council on Tribunals, to make rules of procedure for " statutory inquiries," as defined in section 19 (1) and (2) of the Tribunals and Inquiries Act 1971, held by or on behalf of the Secretary of State. The Lord Chancellor has made the Town and Country Planning (Inquiries Procedure) Rules 1969[2] and the Compulsory Purchase by Local Authorities (Inquiries Procedure) Rules 1962.[3]

[1] Cmnd. 218 of 1957.
[2] S.I. 1969 No. 1092.   [3] S.I. 1962 No. 1424.

2. Scope of the Rules

The scope of these two sets of Rules needs to be noted. The Planning Inquiries Rules 1969 apply (rule 2) to public inquiries (and also to private hearings):

(1) in connection with *applications* for planning permission referred to the Secretary of State under section 35 of the 1971 Act and *appeals* to the Secretary of State under sections 36 and 37 of the 1971 Act against a planning decision relating to development;

(2) in connection with applications for consent or appeals under tree preservation orders;

(3) in connection with applications for consent or appeals relating to listed building consents under Schedule 11 to the 1971 Act;

(4) in connection with applications for consent under the Town and Country Planning (Control of Advertisements) Regulations 1969,[4] relating to the display of advertisements and appeals to the Secretary of State under those Regulations.

The Compulsory Purchase Order Rules apply to public inquiries and private hearings into compulsory purchase orders made under the Acquisition of Land (Authorisation Procedure) Act 1946. Thus they do *not* apply to orders made under Part III of the Housing Act 1957, or under the New Towns Act 1965.

3. The Town and Country Planning (Inquiries Procedure) Rules 1969

The 1969 Rules exclude (rule 2 (3)) from the operation of the Rules all appeals given over (under the 1971 Act) for determination by Inspectors [5] instead of by the Secretary of State except that in a case where the Secretary of State recovers (under Sched. 9, para. 3, to the 1971 Act) the right to determine an appeal himself, then the 1969 Rules will again apply to the proceedings.

If an appeal is dealt with by an Inspector instead of by the Secretary of State, then the procedure will be regulated *not* by the 1969 Rules but by the Town and Country Planning Appeals (Determination by Appointed Persons) (Inquiries Procedure) Rules 1968.[6] These Rules follow closely the provisions of the 1969 Rules

[4] S.I. 1969 No. 1532.
[5] See Chap. 8, p. 122.
[6] S.I. 1968 No. 1952.

and make provision as to procedure for all those classes of planning appeals which can be transferred for determination by Inspectors under Schedule 9 to the 1971 Act. These 1968 Rules are referred to again at the end of this chapter.

The rest of this chapter is devoted mainly to an examination of the Planning Inquiries Rules 1969.

(1) *Importance of Planning Inquiries Rules 1969*

The Franks Committee advocated the provision of a right of appeal to a court of law whenever certain irregularities occurred in connection with a town planning appeal. In consequence of this, section 245 of the 1971 Act provides for challenging the validity of the Secretary of State's decision in a planning appeal on the ground that his action is *ultra vires* or that any of " the relevant requirements " have not been complied with (ss. 245 (1) (*b*), (3) and 242 (3) (*b*)). The expression " the relevant requirements " means (s. 245 (7)), *inter alia*, any requirements of the Tribunals and Inquiries Act 1971 *or of any rules made under that Act*. Thus *all* the requirements of the Town and Country Planning (Inquiries Procedure) Rules 1969 [7] become " relevant requirements " and if any one of these is not now properly observed, any decision of the Secretary of State which derives from them may be challenged in a court of law under section 245 of the 1971 Act. Thus the need for a close observance of the requirements of the Planning Inquiries Rules 1969 is a matter of the greatest importance.

(2) *Town planning appeals—their importance*

Town planning appeals increase both in importance and in number. Today the value of land depends pre-eminently on the kind of planning permission for development which can be got for it. Planning permission for development, once granted, runs with the land (s. 33 (1)) and every owner of land (except the owner who neither wishes to sell nor to develop his land) has every incentive for seeking to obtain the most generous grant of planning permission which it is possible to obtain. This has led to an increasing number of appeals to the Secretary of State against refusals of planning permission or against the grant of planning permission subject to conditions.

[7] S.I. 1969 No. 1092.

Not every appeal which is made to the Secretary of State is sustained to the end. Often a compromise is reached between the aspirations of the developer and the requirements of the local planning authority. The national figures for the last few years show how appeals have grown in number; they also show that the odds against winning an appeal are hardening with the years.[8]

The rewards which attend success are often sufficiently attractive to make an appeal seem a worth-while effort to an applicant seeking planning permission to develop his land. Rural land with the benefit of planning permission for development may be worth £1,000 per acre; without such permission it may fetch only £100 per acre. Any payment of compensation for a refusal of planning permission is usually a mere consolation prize compared with the rich rewards which follow in the wake of a grant of planning permission for development.

(3) *Procedure before inquiry*

Turning now to the Town and Country Planning (Inquiries Procedure) Rules 1969,[9] it will be found that the Rules begin to function with a letter from the Secretary of State addressed to the local planning authority, which expression includes (rule 3 (1)) not only the local planning authority for the area in which the land is situated but also any local authority to whom planning functions have been delegated by the local planning authority.

On being notified by the letter from the Secretary of State of the application or appeal to the Secretary of State, the local planning authority must forthwith inform the Secretary of State and the appellant (rule 4 (1)) of the names and addresses of any third parties who have made representations to the local planning authority under sections 26, 27 or 28 of the 1971 Act, these being the sections which require an applicant for planning permission to give notice of his application in the case of certain types of " bad neighbour " development (s. 26) or, if the applicant is *not* the owner of the land affected by the application, require him to serve notice of his application upon the owner of the land and upon any agricultural tenant of the land (s. 27) or which require the local planning authority to

---

[8] See Department of the Environment, *Statistics for Town and Country Planning* (Series I Planning Decisions—No. 4 Statistics of decisions on planning applications 1971 England and Wales).

[9] S.I. 1969 No. 1092.

advertise in the local press and publish a site notice in the case of development in a conservation area (s. 28). Such third parties are referred to in the 1969 Rules as " section 17 parties " (rule 3 (1)) because their rights in this context originally arose from section 17 of the Town and Country Planning Act 1962.

Where there is in force a direction by either the Minister of Housing and Local Government or the Minister of Transport restricting the grant of planning permission for the development which it is sought to carry out, the Minister shall, on hearing from the local planning authority that the direction is a relevant matter in the appeal, send a statement in writing giving the reasons for the making of the direction (rule 4 (2)).

If the Secretary of State decides to hold a public local inquiry in connection with the application or appeal he must fix a date, time and place for the holding of the inquiry and he must give not less than 42 days' notice in writing of this to the applicant or, as the case may be, the appellant, to the local planning authority and to all section 17 parties (rule 5 (1)).

With the written consent of the applicant (or the appellant) and the local planning authority the Secretary of State may give such shorter notice for the holding of the inquiry as may be agreed and he may vary the time or place fixed for the inquiry where he thinks it necessary or advisable (*ibid.*).

The Secretary of State may require the local planning authority to publicise the holding of the inquiry (rule 5 (2)), and where the land involved in the inquiry is under the control of the applicant (or appellant) the latter must, if requested by the Secretary of State, affix firmly on the land a public notice of the inquiry (rule 5 (3)).

(4) *Written statement of submissions*

Next comes the written statement of submissions. This statement is most important.

In the case of a referred application to the Secretary of State, the Secretary of State must, not later than 28 days before the inquiry, serve on the applicant, on all section 17 parties and on the local planning authority, a written statement of his reasons for directing that the application be referred for decision to him and of any points likely to be relevant to a consideration of the application (rule 6 (1)). If a government department has expressed in writing to the Secretary of State views on the application these views must be communicated to the persons and parties aforesaid (*ibid.*).

In the case of an appeal to the Secretary of State, the local planning authority must, not later than 28 days before the inquiry, serve on the appellant and all section 17 parties a written statement of any submission the authority propose to put forward at the inquiry (rule 6 (2) (3)).   The written statement must be accompanied by:

(i) a list of all the documents (including maps and plans) to which the authority intend to refer, or which they intend to put in evidence, at the inquiry, and

(ii) a notice stating the times and place at which such documents may be inspected (rule 6 (4)).

A reasonable opportunity for such inspection must be afforded to the appellant and all section 17 parties all of whom must be allowed, where practicable, to take copies of the documents (*ibid.*).   *Any other person interested* must also be given a reasonable opportunity to inspect the aforementioned documents and, where practicable, to take copies of such documents and of the local planning authority's written statement (rule 6 (5)).

The written statement given by the local planning authority must mention any direction made by the Secretary of State or by the Minister of Transport Industries restricting the grant of planning permission for the development sought to be carried out and must include a copy of any such direction and the reasons for its making (rule 6 (3)).

Where a government department has expressed in writing to the local planning authority the view that the application for planning permission should not be granted or should be granted only subject to conditions, then, if the local planning authority propose to rely on any such expression of view at the inquiry, they must include the view of the government department in their written statement and must supply a copy of the statement to the government department concerned (rule 6 (3)).

But if the Secretary of State and the local planning authority have to give a written statement about their case *before* the inquiry opens (in other words, if they have to give away their case to " the other side " before the shouting starts!) so also will this have to be done by the applicant (or appellant) if, *but only if*, the Secretary of State so requires (rule 6 (6)).   It is a matter of Ministerial policy

whether an applicant (or appellant) shall be called upon to do for
" the other side " what the other side are bound in all cases themselves to do for the applicant (or appellant).

(5) *Representatives of the Secretary of State at the inquiry*

Where the Secretary of State has given a direction restricting the
grant of planning permission for the development which it is sought
to carry out, the applicant (or appellant) may, not later than 14 days
before the opening of the inquiry, apply in writing to the Secretary
of State for a representative of his department to be available at the
inquiry (rule 8).   In such a case the Secretary of State must make a
representative available at the inquiry who is there to answer
questions elucidating the reasons given by the Secretary of State for
making the direction, provided always that such questions are not,
in the opinion of the Inspector holding the inquiry, questions
directed to the merits of government policy (*ibid.*).   Such a representative of the Secretary of State is not *called* as a witness by any
party appearing at the inquiry.   He attends at the inquiry by
direction of the Secretary of State and he is there to answer questions
put by anybody attending the inquiry.

(6) *Representatives of other government departments at the inquiry*

Where either:

    (1) the Minister of Transport Industries has given a direction
        restricting the grant of planning permission for the
        development which it is sought to carry out; or

    (2) Where any government department has expressed in
        writing to the local planning authority the view that the
        application for planning permission should not be
        granted or should be granted only subject to conditions
        and the local planning authority (as required by rule
        6 (3)) have set out such view in their written statement—

then, in either of the foregoing cases, the applicant (or appellant)
may, not later than 14 days before the opening of the inquiry, apply
in writing for a representative of the Minister of Transport Industries
or of the other government department concerned to be available at
the inquiry (rule 9 (1)), and appropriate arrangements must be
made accordingly (rule 9 (2)).

The representative of a government department attending the
inquiry in the foregoing circumstances must state the reasons for

the direction or the view referred to in the previous paragraph; he must give evidence and be subject to cross-examination to the same extent as any other witness (rule 9 (3) (4)), provided, however, that the Inspector taking the inquiry must disallow any question which, in his opinion, is directed to the merits of government policy (rule 9 (5)).

(7) *Who may appear at the inquiry*

The persons *entitled as of right* under the Planning Inquiries Rules 1969 to appear at the inquiry are (rule 7 (1)):

(a) the applicant (or appellant);
(b) the local planning authority (within the meaning of section 1 of the 1971 Act) for the area in which the land is;
(c) where the land is in a united district for which a joint planning board has been constituted under section 1 (4) of the 1971 Act, the council of the administrative county in which the land is;
(d) where the land is *not* in Greater London or in a county borough, the council of the county district in which the land is, or the Council of the Isles of Scilly, as the case may be;
(e) section 17 parties;
(f) where the land is in an area designated as the site of a new town, the development corporation of the new town;
(g) any persons on whom the Secretary of State has required notice to be served under rule 5 (2) (*b*) of the 1969 Rules.

It will be noted that rule 7 (1) (*d*) does *not* cater for any authority within the area of Greater London.   The reason for this is that the 1969 Rules are modified in their application to Greater London by Rule 16.   Rule 16 (*d*) sets out the provisions which apply to authorities in Greater London in substitution for the provisions of rule 7 (1) (*d*).

In addition to the foregoing parties and persons who appear at the inquiry *as of right* the Inspector may, at his discretion, allow *any* other person to appear (rule 7 (2)).

Where there are two or more persons having a similar interest in the matter under inquiry, the Inspector may allow one or more persons to appear for the benefit of some or all of the persons so interested (rule 7 (4)).

(8) *Procedure at the inquiry*

Except as otherwise provided in the Planning Inquiries Rules 1969 the Inspector taking the inquiry can, at his discretion, choose the procedure to be followed at the inquiry (rule 10 (1)).

Unless the Inspector with the consent of the appellant otherwise determines, the appellant will have the responsibility of beginning (that is to say speaking first) at the inquiry and he will also have the right of finally replying, whilst all other persons, whether *entitled or merely permitted* to appear at the inquiry, will be heard in such order as the Inspector may determine (rule 10 (2)).

The appellant, the section 17 parties and also the local planning authority are *entitled* freely to call evidence at the inquiry and to cross-examine any person giving evidence, but any other person appearing at the inquiry may call evidence and cross-examine only to such extent as the Inspector permits (rule 10 (3)). The distinction here made may well, in practice, turn out to be more apparent than real because it is inconceivable that an Inspector would in any way obstruct any person who has anything to say or bring out which is germane to the inquiry.

The Inspector may neither require nor permit the giving or production of evidence which is contrary to the public interest (rule 10 (4)) but, subject to the protection accorded to a witness representing a government department—who may not be asked questions touching the merits of government policy (rules 8 and 9 (5))—any evidence may, at the discretion of the Inspector, be admitted at the inquiry (rule 10 (4)). The Inspector may also direct that documents put in evidence may be inspected by any person *entitled or permitted* to appear at the inquiry and that facilities may be afforded to such a person to take or obtain copies of such documents (*ibid.*).

An important provision in the Rules is that which empowers the Inspector to allow both the local planning authority or the applicant (or appellant) to add to the submissions set out in their written statement served (under rule 6) earlier in the appeal and also to alter, or to add to, any list of documents which accompanied the written statement, so far as any such alterations or additions may be said to be necessary to determine the issues between the parties (rule 10 (5)). But if any such alteration or addition is made then the Inspector must give the local planning authority, the applicant (or appellant) and the section 17 parties an adequate opportunity of considering any fresh submission or document, and to enable this to be done he must, if need be, adjourn the inquiry, in which case he may make a recommendation in his report as to the payment of additional costs incurred by any such adjournment (*ibid.*). Thus, those who fail to put into their written statement matters which, later, they wish to raise at the inquiry, may find that whilst they are able to do this they can only do it on making themselves responsible for any additional costs thereby caused.

If a person who is *entitled* to appear at the inquiry fails to appear the Inspector may, at his discretion, proceed with the inquiry notwithstanding the absence of any such person (rule 10 (6)).

The Inspector is entitled, subject to disclosure thereof at the inquiry, to take into account any written representation or statement received by him before the inquiry from *any* person (rule 10 (7)).

The Inspector may, from time to time, adjourn the inquiry and if the date, time and place for the reopening of the inquiry are announced before its adjournment, then no further notice about the reopening of the inquiry need be given (rule 10 (8)).

(9) *Site inspection*

The Inspector may, either *before* or *during* the inquiry, and without giving notice of his intention to anybody, make an unaccompanied inspection of the land which is to be the subject of the inquiry (rule 11 (1)).

The Inspector *may*, and if so requested by the applicant (or appellant) or by the local planning authority *before* or *during* the inquiry, *must*, inspect the land *after the inquiry has closed*, and in any case where he decides to do this he must, during the course of the inquiry, announce both the date and the time at which he proposes to inspect the site (rule 11 (2)). At any inspection made after the close of the inquiry the applicant (or appellant), the local planning authority and the section 17 parties are all entitled to be present, but the Inspector is not bound to defer his inspection if any person entitled to be present does not attend at the time appointed (rule 11 (3)).

(10) *Procedure after inquiry*

When the inquiry is concluded the Inspector will prepare his report to the Secretary of State. The Planning Inquiries Rules 1969 require the Inspector to include his findings of fact and his recommendations, if he has any to make or, if he has no recommendations, then his reason for not making any (rule 12 (1)).

If the Secretary of State is disposed to disagree with any recommendation made by the Inspector because either:

(a) the Secretary of State differs from the Inspector on a finding of fact, *or*

(b) the Secretary of State, after the close of the inquiry, receives new evidence (and this includes expert opinion on a matter of fact) or takes into consideration any new issue of fact (not being a matter of government policy) which was not raised at the inquiry,

then the Secretary of State must not come to a decision which differs from any recommendation made by the Inspector without first notifying—

(1) the applicant (or appellant);

(2) the local planning authority; and

(3) any section 17 party *who appeared at the inquiry* of his (the Secretary of State's) disagreement and the reasons for it (rule 12 (2)). In any such case the Secretary of State must afford all the foregoing persons and parties an opportunity—

(1) of making representations to him in writing within 21 days; *or*

(2) of asking within 21 days (in a case where the Secretary of State has received new evidence or taken into consideration any new issue of fact not being a matter of government policy) for the reopening of the inquiry (*ibid.*).

It will be noted from the foregoing that if the Secretary of State is disposed to disagree with an Inspector's recommendation because he, the Secretary of State, *differs from the Inspector on a finding of fact,* then in any such case there is no question of the inquiry being reopened; all that has to happen in such a case is that the Secretary of State must notify the applicant (or appellant), the local planning authority and such of the section 17 parties *as appeared at the inquiry* of his disagreement and the reasons for it and allow them an opportunity to make representations in writing to him within 21 days. (How, or in what circumstances, the Secretary of State could differ from an Inspector on a finding of fact when the Inspector, unlike the Secretary of State, has been present throughout the whole of the inquiry is not clear.)

It is only in a case where the Secretary of State has:

(1) received *new evidence* (and this includes expert opinion in what may be termed appraising, assessing or interpreting any matter of fact) *or*

(2) has taken into consideration any *new issue* of fact (not being a matter of government policy) which was *not* raised at the inquiry,

that a call can be made, within 21 days, for the reopening of the inquiry, such call to be made by the applicant (or the appellant) or the local planning authority or any section 17 party *who appeared at the inquiry.* If a call to reopen the inquiry is made by any of these persons or parties the Secretary of State is *bound* to reopen the inquiry (rule 12 (3)).

Irrespective of the right of any of the foregoing persons or parties to call upon the Secretary of State to reopen the inquiry, the Secretary of State may, on his own volition in any case he thinks fit, cause the inquiry to be reopened (rule 12 (3)).

(11) *Notification of the Secretary of State's decision*

The last step in the appeal is, of course, the Secretary of State's decision. This must be given in writing, together with reasons supporting it, to the applicant (or the appellant),to the local planning authority, to all section 17 parties, and also to any person who, having appeared at the inquiry, has *asked to be notified* of the Secretary of State's decision (rule 13 (1)). Where a copy of the Inspector's report is not sent with the Secretary of State's notification of his decision, then the notification must be accompanied by a summary of the Inspector's conclusions and recommendations (*ibid.*).

If any person who is *entitled* to be notified of the Secretary of State's decision has not received a copy of the Inspector's report, then he must be supplied with a copy of the report on written application to the Secretary of State *made within one month from the date of the Secretary of State's decision* (rule 13 (2)).

In the foregoing context the reference to the Inspector's " report " does *not* include any documents, photographs or plans appended to the report (rule 13 (3)).

(12) *Private hearings in connection with applications or appeals*

The foregoing discussion on the Planning Inquiries Rules 1969 was dealt with on the basis that the Secretary of State, having decided to have a planning application referred to himself for decision, *or* having received notification of a planning appeal, has decided to hold a public local inquiry. But the Secretary of State is *not* obliged to hold such an inquiry and may content himself with offering to the applicant (or appellant) and to the local planning authority a private hearing (ss. 35 (5) and 36 (4)). If this is done, then the Rules—except those portions relating to the giving of public notice of the holding of a public local inquiry (rule 5 (2) and (3)) and rule 7 (1) (*g*) which entitles a person whom the Secretary of State has specifically required to be notified of a public inquiry to appear at such inquiry—are to apply to the private hearing in the same way as they apply to a public local inquiry (rule 15).

(13) *Appeals dealt with by written representations*

None of the Planning Inquiries Rules 1969 applies to any appeal which the appellant and the local planning authority agree shall be decided by written representations made to the Secretary of State.

4. The Town and Country Planning Appeals (Determination by Appointed Persons) (Inquiries Procedure) Rules 1968

The Lord Chancellor has made Rules—The Town and Country Planning Appeals (Determination by Appointed Persons) (Inquiries Procedure) Rules 1968 [10]—for the conduct of inquiries (and hearings) held by Inspectors of the Department of the Environment functioning under Schedule 9 to the 1971 Act.[11] These Rules make procedural provision in respect of *all those classes of appeal* which can now be transferred for determination by Inspectors under Schedule 9 to the 1971 Act.

The Inquiries Procedure Rules 1968 follow closely all corresponding provisions in the 1969 Rules and introduce no new principles into the procedure to be adopted at any inquiry held in connection with a town planning appeal. Accordingly, the discussion above on the 1969 Rules may be applied, *mutatis mutandis*, to any consideration of the 1968 Rules. The main point to remem-

[10] S.I. 1968 No. 1952.
[11] See Chap. 8, p. 122.

ber is that if a planning appeal is being determined, under Schedule 9 to the 1971 Act, by an Inspector instead of by the Secretary of State, and if a public local inquiry or a private hearing is held in connection with the appeal, then the Rules which will govern the procedure at any such inquiry or hearing will be the 1968 Rules and not the 1969 Rules. In short, these two sets of procedure Rules are mutually exclusive.

CHAPTER 16

COMPENSATION FOR PLANNING RESTRICTIONS

1. Summary

COMPENSATION may be payable under the Town and Country Planning Act 1971 in respect of planning restrictions which either:

(1) prevent or hamper the development of land; *or*

(2) cause loss or damage or depreciation in the value of land.

It is essential in connection with this matter of compensation for planning restrictions to draw a clear distinction, as does the 1971 Act, between

(1) compensation for planning restrictions on *new* development (Part VII of the Act); and

(2) compensation for planning restrictions on *other* development (Part VIII of the Act).

In this chapter compensation for restrictions on each of these two categories of development is examined in turn.

2. Compensation for Restrictions on " New Development " —Part VII of the 1971 Act

(1) *What is " new development "?*

Section 22 (1) to (4) of the 1971 Act gives a long definition of the meaning of " development " and this is discussed at length in Chapter 7. Having defined development as being (briefly) either:

(1) the carrying out of operations in, on, over or under land, or

(2) the making of a material change in the use of land,

section 22 (5) goes on to provide that " new development " means any development which does not fall within Schedule 8 to the Act. Schedule 8 to the Act gives various examples of development falling within the existing use of land and in respect of which special compensation rights attach (as discussed later in this chapter [1]). Thus new development is any development (as defined in section 22 (1) to (4) of the 1971 Act) which lies outside the bounds of Schedule 8 to the Act and thus may be said to go beyond the ambit

[1] See p. 231.

of the existing use of land.   When land is developed in the normal and ordinary way from one kind of state into another and different kind of state (either because, for example, it is subjected to building operations which go beyond the point of merely replacing what (if anything) was already there, or because the use of the land is changed from one kind of use to a materially different kind of use)—then it will be found, generally, that some " new development " of the land has occurred.

" New development " (like any other kind of development) cannot take place without planning permission being first obtained (s. 23) and, if planning permission is refused or is granted subject to conditions, compensation *may* become payable, under **Part VII** of the Act, by the Secretary of State (ss. 146, 157).

If a developer anticipates the imposition of a planning condition by voluntarily providing, in his application for planning permission, for the doing of whatever would be required under the condition, then compensation may become payable in the same way as if that which the developer had chosen to do voluntarily had been imposed upon him by means of a condition attached to the grant of planning permission (s. 150).

Where an application for planning permission is of no effect because it lacks an industrial development certificate,[2] but the local planning authority give a notice under section 72 of the 1971 Act declaring that, had the application been in order, they would nevertheless have refused it, such a notice is to be regarded (s. 151) as a refusal of planning permission for the purpose of making a claim for compensation under **Part VII** of the Act.

(2) *Unexpended balance of established development value*

It is a condition precedent to the getting of any compensation under Part VII of the Act for planning restrictions that there shall be an unexpended balance of established development value (ss. 135, 136, 139, 140) for the time being attaching to the land in question (s. 134 (2)).   Whether there is such a balance depends on whether a claim in respect of the land was duly made under the Town and Country Planning Act 1947, on the £300m. Fund set up under the 1947 Act and was formally accepted and established by the Central Land Board (s. 135).   If no such claim was ever made, or if it was

[2] See Chap. 12.

made and was accepted by the Central Land Board but was excluded from satisfaction by the *de minimis* provisions of section 63 of the 1947 Act, then no compensation for any planning restrictions on the land can ever be paid under Part VII of the 1971 Act.

Provision is made for the Secretary of State to issue to any person a certificate showing what is, for the time being, the unexpended balance (if any) of established development value attaching to any particular land (s. 145).

(3) *The amount of compensation*

The amount of the compensation (if any) will depend on how far the affected land is depreciated by the planning restriction (ss. 146, 152, 153, 156), but it will not exceed the amount of the unexpended balance of established development value for the time being attaching to the land (s. 152). Any compensation paid will go in reduction or complete extinguishment, as the case may be, of the unexpended balance attaching to the land (ss. 139, 140, 141, 143, 144).

It may be added that as the object of the 1971 Act is to compensate only for development value which, owing to planning restrictions, becomes incapable of being realised, the value of any " new development " taking place on or after July 1, 1948 (the date when the 1947 Act came into operation), and not made the subject of a development charge under the 1947 Act, will also go in reduction or extinguishment of the unexpended balance (s. 141), the value of any such " new development " being calculated in accordance with Schedule 8 to the 1971 Act (*ibid.*).

The calculation of value for the purposes of Part VII of the 1971 Act will be (s. 163) in accordance with Rules (2) to (4) of section 5 of the Land Compensation Act 1961.

The right to compensation vests in any person having an interest in the affected land, and whether or not he was the applicant for planning permission (ss. 146, 157), subject to certain exceptions (s. 149).

Where a planning restriction affects land only part of which has an unexpended balance attaching to it, or affects land in which there is an interest which comprises part only of the land, then the land is to be treated as divided into appropriate units for the purpose of assessing compensation (s. 152).

(4) *Exclusion of compensation*

The foregoing paragraphs set out the *general* position with respect to the payment of compensation under Part VII of the 1971 Act for planning restrictions on " new development." But it is necessary to bear in mind the many limitations in the Act on the payment of compensation in such circumstances. These fall under three main categories and are examined in succeeding paragraphs.

(i) **First category of exclusion—section 147.**   In the first category comes the effect of section 147 of the 1971 Act.   Under this section compensation is excluded in a variety of cases.

First there is no compensation payable on a refusal of planning permission for any development which *consists of or includes* the making of any material change in the use of land or buildings (s. 147 (1) (*a*)).   As most applications for planning permission in built-up areas are for change of use it follows that compensation will not often be payable in connection with such applications.

Secondly there is no compensation on refusal of planning permission for the display of advertisements or on the grant of such permission subject to conditions (s. 147 (1) (*b*)).

Thirdly, compensation is excluded where the reason (or one of the reasons) for the refusal of planning permission is because the application for permission is premature having regard to either one or both of the following matters, namely:
  (a) the order of priority, if any, indicated in the development plan for the area in which the land is situated for development in that area;
  (b) any existing deficiency in the provision of water supplies or sewerage services, and the period within which any such deficiency may reasonably be expected to be made good (s. 147 (4) (5)).

These two grounds are the only two on which prematureness of application can be used as a basis of refusal, and compensation, at the same time, be avoided.   The first ground may not always be available because development is not always staged (or programmed) in all parts of a development plan.   Moreover, a planning application cannot in any case be " stood down " on the ground of prematureness for more than seven years from the date when it was first refused on this ground (s. 147 (4)).

Fourthly, there is no compensation on a refusal of planning permission to develop land liable to flooding or subsidence (s. 147 (5)).

For the purposes of any of the four instances quoted above of *refusal* of planning permission, any grant of planning permission subject to a condition prohibiting development of a specified part of the land is to be regarded as a refusal of planning permission with respect to that part of the land (s. 147 (6)).

Fifthly, there is a wide exclusion under section 147 (2) of the 1971 Act of compensation in respect of planning permissions which are granted but which have conditions (some of them severe) attaching to them. These conditions relate to:

(a) the number or disposition of the buildings on the plot of land affected by the planning application—(thus if application is made for houses at ten to the acre but only three to the acre are permitted, no compensation will be payable);

(b) the dimensions, design, structure or external appearance of a building or the materials of which it may be constructed— (this gives a very wide power of control; under it stone may be required in place of brick, the number of floors in a building may be limited, the ratio of the size of the floor area to the size of the building plot may be reduced as the planning authority require, all of which things may or may not make a building an economic proposition in the eyes of the developer);

(c) the lay-out of land including provision of facilities for the parking, loading, unloading or fuelling of vehicles—(under this, basement car parks can be required in buildings without liability for compensation);

(d) the use of buildings or of land without buildings;

(e) the location or the design of a means of access to a highway or the materials of which it may be constructed;

(f) the winning and working of minerals.

(ii) Second category of exclusion—section 148. Section 147 of the 1971 Act is not the only section the function of which is to limit the liability for compensation for planning restrictions; section 148 must also be considered.

Under section 148 compensation is not to be paid (s. 148 (1)) on a refusal of planning permission " if, notwithstanding that refusal, there is available ... planning permission to which this section applies," and section 148 applies to (s. 148 (3)):

> " any development of a residential, commercial or industrial character, being development which consists wholly or mainly of the construction of houses, flats, shop or office premises, or industrial buildings (including warehouses), or any combination thereof."

This section is a re-enactment of section 20 of the Town and Country Planning Act 1954, the object of which (as explained in the House of Commons by the Minister of Housing and Local Government [3]) was to provide that: " ... compensation is not to be payable for refusal to allow one kind of development, let us say industrial, if another kind, let us say commercial or residential, is allowed. The principle is that, provided some reasonably remunerative development is allowed, the owner is not entitled to compensation because he is prevented from exploiting his land to the most remunerative development position."

(iii) **The third category of exclusion—sections 38 and 39.** The third category of limitation on the liability of the Secretary of State to pay compensation for planning restrictions is found in sections 38 and 39 of the 1971 Act, under which it is provided that whenever the planning decision of a local planning authority gives rise to a claim for compensation the Secretary of State may review the planning decision and, if he so desires, may give a direction (s. 38) varying it so as to avoid the payment, either in whole or in part (s. 155), of the compensation claimed.

Before the Secretary of State interferes in this way with the decision of a local planning authority he must give notice in writing of his proposed action to the authority and to the person whose proposed development will be affected by his decision and, if so required by either of them, must afford each of them an opportunity of appearing before, and being heard by, an Inspector appointed by the Secretary of State for the purpose (s. 39).

---

[3] *Hansard,* Vol. 525, col. 56.

Section 38, in giving the Secretary of State the final say on whether or not compensation is to be paid, is only reaffirming the power already given to him under the Minister of Town and Country Planning Act 1943 of having the last word on planning (whether or not matters of compensation are involved) by reason of his being charged under that Act of 1943 with the duty " of securing consistency and continuity in the framing and execution of a national policy with respect to the use and development of land throughout England and Wales."

As to the use of his powers under section 38, the Minister of Housing and Local Government said in the House of Commons [4] (in connection with section 23 of the Town and Country Planning Act 1954, now re-enacted in section 38 of the 1971 Act):

"There is a fear that the principle of 'pay as you go' [*i.e.* the payment of compensation as and when and not before the right to claim it arises] may mean that short term finance or even economy will dominate the planning. If I thought that, I should not have introduced the scheme. However, I must frankly admit that that is theoretically possible. Since the money has to be found as we go we have to pay as we go, and a Government could, if it wanted to, bring the whole thing to ruin by refusing to propose the necessary money supplies, or a House of Commons could do so by refusing to vote the money. . . .

"I admit that, theoretically, this is inherent in paying as we go. Nevertheless, I do not think that we need fear that any Government will fail to ask for it or that any House of Commons will refuse to vote the supplies needed to finance compensation, always provided that we stick to the principle of paying only on established claims and so maintain a strict hold over the money that will be needed. . . .

"The Government certainly have no intention whatever of subordinating the proper use of land to the need for budgetary economies."

(5) *Procedure for claiming compensation*

Claims for compensation under Part VII of the 1971 Act must be duly made (s. 154 (1)) within six months of the relevant decision

---

[4] *Hansard*, Vol. 525, col. 47.

(s. 154 (2)) but the Secretary of State may extend this period in a particular case (*ibid.*). A claim must be made (s. 154 (3)) in the form set out in Schedule 1 to the Town and Country Planning (Compensation and Certificates) Regulations 1963,[5] and must be sent to the local planning authority for transmission to the Secretary of State (s. 154 (4)).

If it appears to the Secretary of State that the claim is not in order he must notify the claimant accordingly and invite the withdrawal of the claim (s. 154 (5) (*a*)). If the claim is not withdrawn the Secretary of State must give notice of it to every other person (if any) who appears to the Secretary of State to have an interest in the land affected (s. 154 (5) (*b*)).

Details as to the action to be taken by a local authority on receiving a claim, the supporting material to be supplied by a claimant, the determination of the amount payable and the reference of a disputed amount for determination by the Lands Tribunal, are given in Part II of the aforementioned Regulations of 1963.

(6) *Apportionment, registration and repayment of compensation*

When an award of compensation exceeds £20 it will be apportioned among different parts of the relevant land in accordance with the manner in which such parts are affected by it (s. 158). The amounts charged to each part of the land will be registered by means of a " compensation notice " (s. 159 (1)) in the register of local land charges (s. 158) and will thereafter become a charge on the land to which they relate.

It is important for any purchaser of land on which compensation exceeding £20 has been paid to note that if, later, he wishes to carry out " new development " [6] on that land by—

(a) the construction of residential, commercial or industrial buildings (s. 159 (2) (*a*)); *or*

(b) the mining or working of minerals (s. 159 (2) (*b*)); *or*

(c) any other form of development which is in the Secretary of State's opinion of such value to warrant the requirement (s. 159 (2) (*c*)),

then he must first *pay back* the compensation or so much as is attributable to the area of land which he seeks to develop (ss. 159 (1),

[5] S.I. 1963 No. 798.
[6] See p. 86.

160). Any sum so repaid will be restored to the unexpended balance of established development value for the time being attaching to the land (s. 161).

The Secretary of State, however, has power to remit any such repayment in whole or in part in any case where proper development of the land is unlikely to be carried out if it is not remitted (s. 160 (2)).

(7) *Mortgages, rentcharges and trusts of a settlement*

The Town and Country Planning (Compensation and Certi- ficates) Regulations 1963 [7] relating to the application of payments and compensation made under section 162 of the 1971 Act must be considered in order to ascertain—

    (i) who shall exercise the right to apply for compensation under Part VII of the 1971 Act;

    (ii) who shall receive such compensation; and

    (iii) how such compensation shall be applied,

in any case in which the right to apply for compensation is exer- cisable by reference to an interest in land which is:

    (i) subject to a mortgage, or

    (ii) subject to a rentcharge, or

    (iii) subject to the trusts of a settlement.

3. Compensation for Restrictions on Other Development— Part VIII of the 1971 Act

Part VII of the 1971 Act having dealt with the matter of com- pensation (payable by the Secretary of State out of central funds) in respect of planning restrictions on " new development," Part VIII of the Act proceeds to deal with compensation (payable by local planning authorities out of their own funds) for *other* planning restrictions. These other restrictions fall into six separate cases and each is examined in turn in the later paragraphs of this chapter.[8]

It is to be noted that compensation payable under Part VIII of the 1971 Act in respect of *other* planning restrictions is not dependent upon the land in question having attached to it an unexpended balance of established development value as is the case with com-

---

[7] S.I. 1963 No. 798.

[8] As to special provisions relating to compensation where a purchase notice is served, see p. 237.

pensation payable under Part VII of the Act in respect of planning restrictions on *new* development.

Compensation under Part VIII of the 1971 Act for any depreciation in the value of land will be assessed (s. 178) in accordance with the rules set out in section 5 of the Land Compensation Act 1961, except in the case of compensation in respect of a tree preservation order (s. 178 (2)), in which case compensation will be payable in accordance with the provisions of the order itself in respect of damage or expenditure arising from the refusal of any consent required under the order or from the grant of any such consent subject to conditions (s. 174).

Questions of disputed compensation under Part VIII of the 1971 Act will be determined by the Lands Tribunal (s. 179) except in so far as a tree preservation order may otherwise provide (*ibid.*).

(1) *Compensation on revocation or modification of planning permission*

As has been shown,[9] a planning permission once granted can, in certain circumstances, be later revoked or modified under section 45 of the 1971 Act by an order made by the local planning authority and confirmed by the Secretary of State, in which case compensation may be payable by the local planning authority for abortive expenditure—including expenditure on plans [10] (s. 164 (2))—for loss or damage directly attributable to the revocation or modification (s. 164).

The above provision also applies (s. 165) when the planning permission which is revoked or modified is a permission granted, in the first instance not by a local planning authority acting under section 29 of the 1971 Act, but by a development order under section 24 of the Act.

Compensation on revocation or modification of planning permission must be claimed in writing from the local planning authority within six months of the revocation or modification (ss. 164 (1), 165 and the Town and Country Planning General Regulations 1969,[11] reg. 19).

The compensation on revocation or modification of a planning permission is payable by the local planning authority (s. 164 (1)); nevertheless that authority may receive from the Secretary of State

[9] See p. 128.
[10] *Holmes* v. *Bradfield R.D.C.* [1949] 2 K.B. 1 (D.C.).
[11] S.I. 1969 No. 286.

an Exchequer contribution equal to the amount which the Secretary of State would have had to pay (under Part VII of the 1971 Act) by way of compensation if the planning permission had been refused in the first place, or, as the case may be, had been granted in the form in which it was later modified (s. 167 and Part VI of the Town and Country Planning (Compensation and Certificates) Regulations 1963 [12]). As the Secretary of State is only liable to make this contribution if he would have been liable under Part VII of the 1971 Act to pay compensation, it follows that a contribution from the Secretary of State can be called for only if the land in question has attached to it an unexpended balance of development value.

Any compensation payable on the revocation or modification of a planning permission and exceeding £20 will, where it is practicable so to do, be apportioned among the various parts of the land affected (s. 166), will be registrable as a local land charge (s. 166 (5) applying s. 158 (4) to (6)) and will be recoverable by the Secretary of State on the subsequent carrying out (s. 168 applying ss. 159 and 160) of " new development " of a kind to which section 159 of the 1971 Act applies, that is to say, the kind of " new development " specified in section 159 (2) of the 1971 Act.[13] The Secretary of State may, however, remit the recovery of the compensation in whole or in part (s. 168 applying s. 160).

Any compensation recovered by the Secretary of State is payable by him to the local planning authority by whom the compensation was paid in the first place (s. 168 (2) (3)).

(2) *Compensation on the refusal of planning permission, or on the grant thereof subject to conditions, for development within Part II of Schedule 8*

Part II of Schedule 8 to the 1971 Act gives six cases of development which fall within the ambit of the existing use of land. If the Secretary of State refuses planning permission for this " existing-use development," or if he grants it subject to conditions, then compensation may be payable by the local planning authority if the value of the land is lessened by the refusal or the conditional grant (s. 169 (1) (2)).

The six cases referred to in Part II of Schedule 8 to the 1971 Act

[12] S.I. 1963 No. 798.
[13] See p. 228.

and which qualify for compensation under section 169 may be summarised as follows:

(i) the enlargement (Sched. 8, para. 11 (*a*)), improvement or other alteration as often as required of

    (a) any building in existence on the " appointed day " (s. 290 (1)), *i.e.* July 1, 1948, or

    (b) any building substituted for a building which was in existence before July 1, 1948, but which has been destroyed or demolished after January 7, 1937,

provided the cubic content, as ascertained by external measurement (Sched. 8, paras. 9 and 11 (*b*)), of the original building is not increased in the case of a dwelling-house by more than one-tenth or 1,750 cubic feet (whichever is the greater), and in any other case by more than one-tenth;

(ii) the carrying out of buildings or other operations for agricultural or forestry purposes (but not dwelling-houses or market garden or nursery buildings) on land which was agricultural or forestry land " at a material date " [14] (Sched. 8, para. 12);

(iii) the winning and working of minerals on land occupied along with agricultural land, provided such minerals are reasonably required for use on the agricultural land, *e.g.* for fertilisation or the repair of agricultural buildings;

(iv) where a building or land was used " at a material date " [14] for a purpose falling within any of the twenty-two general classes specified in the Town and Country Planning (Use Classes for Third Schedule Purposes) Order 1948 [15] or, if unoccupied at all times since July 1, 1948, was last used (otherwise than before January 7, 1937) for any such purpose, the use of that building for any other purpose falling within the same general class;

(v) where part of a building or land was, " at a material date," [14]

---

[14] The expression " at a material date " is defined (Sched. 8, para. 12) so as to mean at *either* of the following dates, that is to say—

    (a) the appointed day, *i.e.* July 1, 1948 (s. 290 (1)), *and*

    (b) the date by reference to which Schedule 8 to the 1971 Act falls to be applied in the particular case in question:

Provided that sub-para. (*b*) is not to apply in relation to any buildings, works, or use of land in respect of which, whether before or after the date mentioned in sub-para. (*b*), an enforcement notice served before that date has become, or does become, effective.

[15] S.I. 1948 No. 955. Schedule 3 has been repealed and replaced by Schedule 8 to the 1971 Act.

used for a particular purpose, the use for the same purpose of an additional part not exceeding one-tenth of the cubic content as ascertained by external measurement (Sched. 8, para. 9), of the first part;

(vi) where any land was, " at a material date," [16] comprised in a site being used for the deposit of waste materials or refuse in connection with the working of minerals, the use for the same purpose of any additional part of the site reasonably required in connection with the working of such minerals.

It is a condition precedent to the recovery of compensation in any of the cases above mentioned, that the applicant for planning permission shall challenge the decision of the local planning authority in refusing planning permission or in granting the same subject to conditions, by appealing against such decision to the Secretary of State under section 36 of the 1971 Act (s. 169 (1)).

Claims for compensation must be in writing and must be made within six months of the refusal of planning permission or, as the case may be, the grant thereof subject to conditions (Town and Country Planning General Regulations 1969,[17] reg. 19).

It will be noted that no compensation is payable in respect of a refusal of planning permission or the grant thereof subject to conditions, in respect of the two types of development falling within Part I of Schedule 8 to the 1971 Act, which part relates to (a) the replacement of war-damaged buildings, and (b) the use of a single dwelling-house for the purpose of two or more dwelling-houses, *e.g.* for the purpose of flats. The remedy of an aggrieved person in these cases is by way of a purchase notice served by him under section 180 of the Act whereby (if the Secretary of State confirms the notice) the local authority will be obliged to buy the land affected by the planning decision complained of.

(3) *Compensation for interference with authorised buildings or discontinuance of authorised uses*

Development plans are liable to alteration, and notions as to what constitutes the proper planning of an area change with the passing of the years. Accordingly, the proper planning of land may require from time to time the removal, or prohibition, of

---

[16] See note as to meaning of " at a material date " on p. 232.
[17] S.I. 1969 No. 286.

development originally undertaken with all due planning permission and a local planning authority may, by order made by the authority and confirmed by the Secretary of State, require the alteration or the removal of any authorised building or the discontinuance of any authorised use of land (s. 51). If this is done, compensation will be payable by the local planning authority to any person in respect of the depreciation in the value of his interest in the land or in respect of the disturbance of his enjoyment of the land (s. 170 (1) (2) (4)). Such a person may also claim compensation for expenses reasonably incurred by him in complying with the requirements of a local planning authority respecting authorised development (s. 170 (3)).

Claims for compensation must be in writing and made within six months of the taking effect of the order requiring the alteration or removal of any authorised building or, as the case may be, the discontinuance of any authorised use (Town and Country Planning General Regulations 1969,[18] reg. 19).

(4) *Compensation in connection with a Tree Preservation Order*

By means of a Tree Preservation Order,[19] a local planning authority may prevent the cutting down, topping, lopping or wilful destruction of trees and woodlands which, in the interests of amenity, the authority feels should be preserved (s. 60).

Compensation may become payable by the local planning authority subject to such exceptions and conditions as may be specified in the order, to any person in respect of damage or expenditure caused or incurred by reason of the fact that any consent required by the order to be obtained from the local planning authority is either refused by the authority or is granted subject to conditions (s. 174).

(5) *Compensation for expenditure on removal of certain advertisements*

The control of advertisements is dealt with in sections 63 and 64 of the 1971 Act and the Town and Country Planning (Control of Advertisements) Regulations 1969.[20] The expression " advertisement " is given wide definition by section 290 (1) of the 1971 Act and regulation 2 of the aforementioned Regulations.

---

[18] S.I. 1969 No. 286.
[19] See Chap. 13, p. 174.
[20] S.I. 1969 No. 1532; see Chap. 9.

Any person who is required to remove an advertisement which was being displayed when the first Advertisements Regulations came into force on August 1, 1948, or who is required to discontinue the use for the display of advertisements of any site which was being used for that purpose on August 1, 1948, may claim compensation from the local planning authority with respect to any expenses reasonably incurred by him in carrying out works necessary in order to comply with such requirements (s. 176).   The claim must be submitted in writing to the local planning authority within six months of the completion of any such works (Advertisements Regulations 1969, reg. 30 (1)).

(6) *Contributions by Ministers towards compensation paid by local authorities*

It will be noted that compensation in respect of restrictions on " new development " is payable by the Secretary of State,[21] whilst compensation in respect of restrictions on " other development " is payable by the local planning authority.[22]   Provision is made whereby a local authority may be repaid, in whole or in part by the Exchequer, any compensation which they have been called upon to pay following a decision or order made under Parts III or IV of the 1971 Act when the decision or order was in respect of action taken, wholly or partly, in the interests of a service provided by a Government department (s. 254).

---

[21] See pp. 227 and 228.
[22] See pp. 229 and 230.

CHAPTER 17

PURCHASE NOTICES AND PLANNING BLIGHT

1. Purchase Notices for Interests Affected by Planning Decisions or Orders

(1) *Service of a purchase notice*

On a refusal either by a local planning authority or by the Secretary of State of planning permission for development of land, or on a grant of planning permission subject to conditions, an aggrieved applicant, provided he is an " owner " as defined in section 290 (1) of the 1971 Act (and a freeholder who has let his land for less than a rack-rent is excluded by the definition [1]), may, *in certain cases*, require his interest in the land affected by the planning decision to be purchased by the council of the county borough or county district (*i.e.* not necessarily the local planning authority) for the area where the land is situated (s. 186). The requirement must be by a notice in writing called a " purchase notice " (s. 180 (7)) given within twelve months of the planning decision on which the service of the notice is founded (s. 180 (1) and Town and Country Planning General Regulations 1969,[2] reg. 19).

A purchase notice cannot be founded on a " deemed " refusal of planning permission operating under section 37 of the 1971 Act. In such a case an owner (provided he was the applicant for planning permission) must first appeal to the Secretary of State under section 37 and get a confirmation by the Secretary of State of the " deemed " refusal of permission, after which he will be able to serve a purchase notice under section 180 of the Act.

(2) *Action by the Secretary of State*

Except when the council on whom a purchase notice is served are, of their own accord, willing to comply with it or can get some other local authority or statutory undertaker to comply with it (s. 181 (1) (*a*) (*b*)) and buy the interest referred to in it (s. 181 (2)), a

[1] *London Corporation* v. *Cusack-Smith* [1955] A.C. 337 (H.L.).
[2] S.I. 1969 No. 286.

236

purchase notice needs confirmation by the Secretary of State before it can become effective (s. 181 (1) (c), (3)).

Before confirming a purchase notice (ss. 182 (1) and 183 (1)) or taking any other action open to him in lieu of confirming the notice—such as granting planning permission for development as sought by the applicant (s. 183 (2)), or directing a grant of planning permission for some other kind of development on an application therefor being made (s. 183 (3)), the Secretary of State must give notice of his proposed action to the person who served the notice, to the local authority on whom it was served, to the local planning authority and to any other local authority who might be substituted for the authority on whom the notice was served (s. 182 (2)). The Secretary of State must afford any of these persons or authorities which **require** it an opportunity of being heard by his Inspector before he takes action in the matter ³ (s. 182 (3)). However, where the Secretary of State has given notice of his proposed action and his Inspector has heard interested parties, the Secretary of State is *not* precluded from taking a different line of action if it appears to him to be expedient so to do (s. 182 (4)).

(3) *Special provisions as to compensation*

Where the Secretary of State, in lieu of confirming a purchase notice, takes one of the alternative courses open to him under section 183 and directs (under section 183 (3)) that there shall be granted planning permission, not for the development sought by the owner, but for some other kind of development, compensation will become payable by the local planning authority (s. 187 (2)) if the permitted development value of the owner's interest is thereby shown to be less than its existing use value (s. 187 (2) (5)). The " permitted development value " of the owner's interest is the value attaching to it having regard to the amount of development which would be permitted under the Secretary of State's direction (s. 187 (5)), whilst the " existing use value " of that interest means the value attaching to it for its existing use and as if all the development regarded as falling within the ambit of the existing use of land and referred to in Schedule 8 to the 1971 Act were permitted (*ibid.*).

The claim for compensation must be made to the local planning

---

³ *Ealing Corporation* v. *Minister of Housing and Local Government* [1952] Ch. 856.

authority within six months of the decision on which the claim is based (Town and Country Planning General Regulations 1969, reg. 19).

(4) *Challenging Secretary of State's decision*

The decision of the Secretary of State either to confirm or not to confirm a purchase notice, or to grant planning permission in lieu of confirming a purchase notice, may be challenged within six weeks on a point of law by application in the High Court (ss. 242 (1) (*e*), (3) (*i*) (*j*) and 245). Where upon any such challenge the Secretary of State's decision is quashed, the purchase notice is to be treated as cancelled, but this is without prejudice to the right of the owner to serve a further purchase notice (s. 186 (4) (5)).

(5) *Grounds for confirming a purchase notice*

Before confirming a purchase notice the Secretary of State must be satisfied (ss. 183 (1) and 180 (1)):

(a) that the land to which it relates has become incapable of reasonably beneficial use in its existing state; *and*

(b) in a case where permission to develop the land has been granted subject to conditions, that the land cannot be rendered capable of reasonably beneficial use if the development is undertaken in accordance with those conditions; *and*

(c) in any case, that the land cannot be rendered capable of reasonably beneficial use by the carrying out of any other development for which permission

     (i) has been granted, *or*

     (ii) has been undertaken to be granted by the local planning authority or by the Secretary of State.

It will be noted that section 180 of the 1971 Act requires it to be shown that " the land has become incapable of reasonably beneficial use in its existing state." The words " in its existing state " are of importance both to the landowner and to the local authority because they narrow down the cases in which the landowner can " unload " his land onto the local authority.

The prime need for section 19 of the Town and Country Planning Act 1947 (the predecessor of s. 180 of the 1971 Act) was to meet the case of a war-damaged plot of land (often near a city or town centre) the redevelopment of which was prevented by planning restrictions imposed because the blitzed area which incorporated the particular plot of land was to be relaid out and redeveloped as a whole consequent upon general war damage in the district.   In such a case the war-damaged plot in its existing state (it was probably a heap of rubble or a hole in the ground) was clearly incapable of any beneficial use and therefore, under section 19 of the 1947 Act, was liable to have to be purchased by the local authority.

The question is, and always has been, to what kind of development was it appropriate and lawful to pay regard when deciding whether land was incapable of beneficial use in its existing state. There was a tendency, particularly where planning permission was refused for the development of green belt land which, being situated on the fringe of a town, could be said to be ripe for development, to pay attention to the possibility of the land's potential development into, for example, a residential suburb.   But the law, as now contained in section 180 of the 1971 Act, requires that the owner who serves a purchase notice must make his case on one ground only—the uselessness of his land in its existing state.   He must be able to show that his land, *quite apart from any potential value for development which it may have*, has become incapable of reasonably beneficial use in its existing state (s. 180 (2)).

The Secretary of State may refuse to confirm a purchase notice where the land has a restricted use by virtue of a previous planning permission (s. 184). This would occur in the following circumstances.

If land in respect of which a purchase notice has been served has *a restricted use* by reason of the fact that some previous planning permission has required that the land shall be used only for a restricted purpose (the reason for this being that the land in question is part of a larger area for which planning permission for development was previously granted subject to the condition that the land in respect of which the purchase notice was later served should not be developed at all or should be developed only in some restricted fashion) then, if the land is restricted in this fashion, the Secretary of State can decline to confirm the purchase notice if it appears to him that the land in question ought, in accordance with the previous planning permission, to remain undeveloped or restricted as to the manner of its development.   This is the position notwithstanding the fact that, by virtue of the previous planning decision, the land in question has become incapable of reasonably beneficial use in its existing state (s. 184 (3)). The effect of section 184 of the 1971 Act is to nullify the decision in *Adams and Wade Ltd.* v. *Ministry of Housing and Local Government and Wokingham R.D.C.* (1965) 18 P. & C.R. 60.

(6) *Effect of Secretary of State's action*

When the Secretary of State confirms a purchase notice the local authority affected by the notice are deemed to be authorised to acquire compulsorily the interest of the " owner " who served the notice and to have served a notice to treat to acquire that interest (s. 186 (1)). Such a constructive notice to treat may not be withdrawn (s. 208).

If the Secretary of State, within nine months of the service of the purchase notice or within six months of the transmission of a copy of the notice to the Secretary of State (whichever is the shorter period—(s. 186 (3))), has, on the one hand, neither confirmed the notice (nor taken alternative action in lieu of confirmation) nor, on the other hand, notified the " owner " who served the notice that he, the Secretary of State, does not intend to confirm it, then in such case the notice is deemed to have been confirmed at the end of the period above mentioned and the local authority on whom the notice was served are deemed to be authorised to acquire compulsorily the interest of the " owner " and to have served a notice to treat (which, again, is incapable of being withdrawn (s. 208)) to acquire that interest (s. 186 (2)).

(7) *Purchase notices in other cases*

A purchase notice may be served not only when there is a planning decision refusing planning permission for development or granting permission subject to conditions but also when an order is made under section 45 of the 1971 Act revoking or modifying an existing grant of planning permission (s. 188 and Town and Country Planning General Regulations 1969, reg. 19).

Similarly, a purchase notice may follow the making of an order under section 51 of the 1971 Act requiring the discontinuance of an existing use of land or the alteration or removal of existing buildings or works on land (s. 189 and Town and Country Planning General Regulations 1969, reg. 19).

The provisions of sections 180 to 183, 186 and 187 of the 1971 Act relating to purchase notices, together with regulation 19 of the

Town and Country Planning General Regulations 1969, are also applied in the case of a Tree Preservation Order [4] (s. 60 (1) (c) referring to ss. 60 (2) (b) and 191 (1)), and to the control of advertisements [5] (s. 63 (2) (c) referring to ss. 60 (2) (b) and 191 (1)).

Again, where an application for planning permission for industrial development is of no effect because it lacks an industrial development certificate issued by the Secretary of State [6] (s. 67), the local planning authority must consider whether, if the application had been in order, they would have refused it and, if satisfied that they would have done so, they must certify accordingly (s. 72), whereupon the provisions of sections 180 to 183, 186 and 187 of the 1971 Act relating to purchase notices are to apply as if the application for planning permission had been effective and as if planning permission had been refused (s. 191 (2)).

2. Owner-occupiers Adversely Affected by Planning Proposals —Planning Blight

(1) *When planning blight arises*

The making and coming into effect under the Town and Country Planning Act 1971 of a development plan can have dramatic effects on the value of land.   Whilst the development plan does not itself grant any permission for development, it does show the kind of thing for which permission may well be granted if it is sought. Thus a development plan may, merely by coming into operation, drain away development value from land or, conversely, may attract development value, to land.

The draining away of development value has been referred to, somewhat inelegantly, as " planning blight " and so important has this matter come to be regarded that the 1971 Act makes special provision to deal with it.   There is good reason for this for a small symbol on a development plan may mean a great deal to the owner of the land to which the symbol is attached.   If, for example, the symbol shows a new highway is to be constructed across a man's land, then he may find it impossible either to sell his land or to get planning permission to develop it himself, assuming he wants to do so.   But whilst the development plan may show a proposed road,

[4] See Chap. 13, p. 174.
[5] See Chap. 9.
[6] See Chap. 12, p. 171.

it will not necessarily show the particular year in which the road is to be constructed and, even if it does, it may yet turn out to be the case that, for one reason or another, the authority who are responsible for constructing the road are not able to get on with the work at the date contemplated by the development plan. In the meantime, what is to happen to the landowner whose land is blighted in this fashion? Sections 192 to 208 of the 1971 Act make provision for this by means of a procedure which may be termed " compulsory purchase in reverse."

While these sections are wide enough to catch more things than provisions in development plans which have the effect of depressing land values, their ambit is not by any means as wide as some hoped and their restrictive terms need to be watched closely. Accordingly it is proposed first to examine those *cases* where planning blight comes within the ambit of sections 192 to 208 of the 1971 Act, and, secondly, to examine what *persons* can, in those cases, make a claim for compensation arising from planning blight.

By way of warning it should be mentioned that sections 192 to 208 of the 1971 Act are intricate in the extreme, containing a good deal of legislation in one section by reference to the contents of another section. Many expressions used in these seventeen sections are given specialised definition, for which reference should be made to sections 203, 205, 206 and 207 of the 1971 Act. Special provisions as to hereditaments or agricultural units occupied by a partnership firm are contained in section 204 of the Act.

Turning then to the cases which fall within the ambit of sections 192 to 208 of the 1971 Act, it may be stated that there are ten classes of proposal (not all of them associated with development plans) in respect of which a claim arising from planning blight can be made. The ten classes are, briefly, where land is:

(1) indicated in a structure plan in force for the district in which the land is situated either as land which may be required for the purposes of any functions of a Government department, local authority or statutory undertakers, or of the National Coal Board, or as land which may be included in an action area (s. 192 (1) (*a*));

(2) land allocated for the purposes of any such functions by a local plan in force for the district in which it is situated, or land defined in such a plan as the site of proposed

development for the purposes of any such functions (s. 192 (1) (*b*));

(3) land indicated in a development plan as land on which a highway is to be constructed, improved or altered (s. 192 (1) (*c*));

(4) land on or adjacent to the line of a highway indicated in an order or scheme made under Part II of the Highways Act 1959 or under section 1 of the Highways Act 1971, being land in relation to which compulsory acquisition may be exercisable under Part X of the Highways Act 1959 or Part III of the Highways Act 1971 (s. 192 (1) (*d*));

(5) land shown on plans approved by a resolution of a local highway authority as land comprised in a highway proposed to be constructed, approved or altered (s. 192 (1) (*e*));

(6) land on which the Secretary of State proposes to provide a trunk road or a special road and has given to the local planning authority written notice of his intention together with maps and plans (s. 192 (1) (*f*));

(7) land in respect of which a compulsory purchase order made by a highway authority is in force and in respect of which the authority have power to serve, but have not served, notice to treat (s. 192 (1) (*g*));

(8) land indicated under section 31 of the Housing Act 1969 as land proposed to be acquired under Part II of that Act as a general improvement area (s. 192 (1) (*h*));

(9) land authorised by a special Act of Parliament to be compulsorily acquired (s. 192 (1) (*i*));

(10) land in respect of which a compulsory purchase order is in force but no notice to treat has been served (s. 192 (1) (*j*)).

On the point of land (item (5), above) shown on a plan approved by resolution of a local highway authority, it should be noted that the Secretary of State, in the Annex to Ministry Circular No. 48/59 dated August 11, 1959, declared (in paragraph 57) that

" the attention of local highway authorities is drawn to paragraph (*f*) of [section 39 (1) of the 1959 Act—now section 192 (1) (*e*) of the 1971 Act] which refers to ' land shown on plans approved by a resolution of a local highway authority.' The Minister understands that decisions to carry out road schemes are sometimes taken without the formal approval of plans by resolution. He suggests that, where necessary, local highway authorities should review their procedures so as to ensure that owner-occupiers whose property is blighted by road schemes will not be deprived of the remedy offered by the [1962] Act."

The list of ten classes set out above shows those examples of planning blight in respect of which something may be done under the 1971 Act. If the blight of which complaint is made does not fall fairly and squarely within one or other of the classes set out above, then the Act has no application to it.

It will be noticed that a basic feature of all the foregoing cases of blight is that there is suggested somewhere *the prospect of compulsory purchase*. It is the prospect of compulsory purchase which is to be exercised at some time, perhaps unspecified, in the future which causes the depression in the value of the affected land to occur. In short, it is blight caused *solely by the tentative prospect of compulsory purchase* and not by any other prospect which causes a case to fall within the ambit of the 1971 Act. Thus if land is blighted not by the prospect of itself being compulsorily acquired but by the prospect (not uncommon) of adjacent or neighbouring land being compulsorily acquired, this sort of blight sustained by the land first mentioned is *not* catered for by the Act.

(2) *Owner-occupiers who are entitled to claim*

Once the narrowly defined cases of blight which are capable of being dealt with under the 1971 Act have been appreciated, the next question to determine is what sort of persons can take action. Such persons are, generally speaking, *owners* of one kind or another and they fall into three categories as follows:

(1) the " resident owner-occupier " (see s. 203 (3)) of a " hereditament " (see s. 207 (1)) wholly or partly contained in the blighted land which includes a private dwelling-house occupied by him (s. 192 (3) (4) (*b*));

(2) the non-resident " owner-occupier " (see s. 203 (1)) of a hereditament (see s. 207 (1))—other than a private dwelling-house as, for example, a hereditament used for business purposes—not exceeding the prescribed limit of annual value, namely, £750, which hereditament is wholly or partly contained in the blighted land (s. 192 (3) (4) (*a*) and Town

and Country Planning (Limit of Annual Value) Order 1963 [7]);

(3) the " owner-occupier " (see s. 203 (2)) of an " agricultural unit " (see s. 207 (1))—as, for example, a farm, grazing land, market garden, etc. (see definition of " agriculture " in section 290 (1))—wholly or partly contained in the blighted land (s. 192 (3) (5)).

For the foregoing purposes an owner-occupier includes not only a freeholder but also a tenant having a tenancy granted (or extended) for a term of years certain of which at least three years remain unexpired (s. 203 (4)).

Before qualifying to make a claim an owner-occupier of a hereditament must have occupied the hereditament either *in whole or in part* for a period of at least six months immediately prior to making his claim, *or* for a period of at least six months before leaving the premises unoccupied for a period of not longer than twelve months immediately prior to making his claim (s. 203 (1)). If the occupation is of *part only* of a hereditament it must, nevertheless, be occupation of a *substantial part* (*ibid.*).

An owner who stopped living in his house some ten years ago but continued to store goods in three sheds in the garden of the house and in the garage is not such an owner-occupier of the house as brings him within the ambit of the blight provisions of the 1971 Act.[8]

A Nonconformist chapel, not being liable as a place of worship to be assessed for rates (Rating and Valuation (Miscellaneous Provisions) Act 1955, s. 7) was entered, in accordance with rule 22 of the Valuation Lists Rules 1955,[9] in the local valuation list as " exempt." In other words, the annual value of the chapel was not entered as " nil." It was given, as the opinion of the court, that since no value was shown in the valuation list, and the premises were entered as " exempt," it could not be said that their value was either greater or less than a specified sum, and hereditaments of that kind did not qualify for protection from blight.[10]

In the case of a claim by the owner-occupier of an agricultural

[7] S.I. 1963 No. 606.
[8] *Ministry of Transport* v. *Holland* (1962) 14 P. & C.R. 259.
[9] S.I. 1955 No. 1680.
[10] *Essex C.C.* v. *Essex Incorporated Congregational Church Union* [1963] A.C. 808 (H.L.).

unit, the owner-occupier must show that he has occupied *the whole* of the agricultural unit either for a period of at least six months immediately prior to making his claim; *or* for a period of at least six months ending not more than six months before the making of the claim (s. 203 (2)).

Apart from " owners " it is to be noted that a mortgagee is also given specific power (s. 201) to take advantage of sections 192 to 207 of the 1971 Act relating to the obligatory purchase of land by a local authority on the ground of planning blight.

(3) *Service of purchase notice relating to blight*

If qualified as above mentioned the owner-occupier of a hereditament can require the whole of the hereditament to be taken off his hands whilst the owner-occupier of an agricultural unit can require action to be taken in respect of that part of the agricultural unit which falls within the area of blight (s. 196).

Provided a person is the owner-occupier (as detailed above) of land blighted (as detailed above) by planning proposals, then the 1971 Act authorises him to serve a blight notice (in accordance with the Town and Country Planning General Regulations 1969,[11] reg. 24 and Sched. 2) requiring the acquisition of his interest in the blighted land by the appropriate authority (s. 205), *i.e.* the authority which would, at some later date in the future, have come to acquire that interest compulsorily in accordance with the planning proposals which have currently brought about the blight (s. 193 (1)).   In serving such a notice the owner-occupier must show that:

(1) he has made reasonable efforts to sell his interest in the blighted land, and

(2) that he could not have sold it except at a price substantially lower than that for which it might reasonably have been expected to sell if no part of the land had been affected by the blight (*ibid.*).

These efforts on the part of the owner-occupier must all have occurred since " the relevant date," that is to say, the date on which the blighting proposals took effect, which, in the case of proposals contained in a structure plan or local plan, would be the date when the plan, or the amendment thereto bringing about blight, came into operation (s. 193 (3) (*a*)).   In the case of *other* planning proposals

[11] S.I. 1969 No. 286.

causing blight, section 193 (3) sets out in each instance the date which is to be regarded as " the relevant date " when serving a blight notice.

A blight notice served by an owner-occupier may be withdrawn by him at any time before compensation for the acquisition of his land has been determined by the Lands Tribunal *or* within a period of six weeks after any such determination (s. 198 (1)), but there can be no such withdrawal if the acquiring authority have entered on the land in pursuance of the notice to treat deemed to have been served in connection with the purchase notice (s. 198 (2)). No compensation is payable in connection with the withdrawal of the notice to treat deemed to be withdrawn on the withdrawal by the owner-occupier of the purchase notice (s. 198 (3)).

If an owner-occupier dies after serving a blight notice his personal representatives take over his powers and responsibilities in the matter (s. 200).

(4) *Service of counter-notice by appropriate authority*

The question of whether the price which the owner-occupier could have got for his land in the open market is a price " substantially lower " than its price in the open market if it had not been affected by blight is, of course, a matter of valuation and opinion. Accordingly, provision is made for any blight notice served by an owner-occupier calling for the purchase of his land to be challenged or objected to within two months by the appropriate authority on whom the notice was served (s. 194). Both the service of a blight notice by an owner-occupier upon the appropriate authority and the service by the appropriate authority of a counter-notice upon the owner-occupier, are referred to in the Town and Country Planning General Regulations 1969,[12] reg. 24 and Sched. 2.

A counter-notice may be served by the appropriate authority on one or more of the following grounds (s. 194 (2)), namely:

(1) that no part of the hereditament or agricultural unit required to be purchased is comprised in land directly affected by blight as specified above (see s. 192 (1) (*a*)–(*j*));

(2) that the appropriate authority do not propose to acquire compulsorily any part of the hereditament or, in the case

[12] S.I. 1969 No. 286.

of an agricultural unit, any part of the area of that unit which is directly affected by the blight;

(3) that, in the case of an agricultural unit, whilst the appropriate authority do propose to acquire compulsorily part of the affected area specified in the counter-notice, the authority do not propose to acquire any other part of that area;

(4) that, in the case of land falling under items (1) or (3) but not (4), (5) or (6) as detailed above (see pages 242 and 243), the appropriate authority do *not* propose to acquire any part of the hereditament, or (in the case of an agricultural unit) any part of the affected area, during a period of fifteen years from the date of the counter-notice, or during such longer period from that date as may be specified in the counter-notice;

(5) that on the date of the service of the blight notice by the owner-occupier upon the appropriate authority the owner-occupier had no interest in the hereditament or agricultural unit;

(6) that the owner-occupier is not a freeholder or a tenant with a term of at least three years yet to run;

(7) that the owner-occupier, making reasonable endeavours, could have sold his interest in the blighted land at a price which was not substantially lower than it would have been if no part of the land had been comprised in land affected by the blight.

The matter of the fifteen years referred to under item (4) is an important one because it allows the appropriate authority to neutralise the effect of a blight notice by declaring their intention to postpone action on the planning proposals which have caused blight to occur.

Where a counter-notice has been served, then the owner-occupier may, within a period of two months from the date of the service of the counter-notice, require the matter to be referred for decision by the Lands Tribunal (s. 195 (1)).

Any counter-notice served by the appropriate authority will set out the ground or grounds on which the blight notice by the owner-occupier is challenged (s. 194 (5)).

Except in a case where the appropriate authority denies that they have any intention to acquire any part of the blighted land

(s. 195 (3)) any ground of objection set out in the appropriate authority's counter-notice *must* be upheld on appeal to the Lands Tribunal unless it is shown, to the satisfaction of the Tribunal, that the objection is *not* " well founded " (s. 195 (2)). In other words, the onus is on the owner-occupier to show that any ground of objection set out in the appropriate authority's counter-notice is not well founded, *except* in a case where the authority denies any intention to acquire the blighted land compulsorily in which case the onus is on the authority to show that their objection *is* " well founded " (s. 195 (3)). Thus any argument about whether or not a blight notice can be countered on the fifteen-year principle above quoted is a matter which can be referred for arbitration to the Lands Tribunal and the fifteen-year basis of objection is not to be upheld unless the Tribunal is satisfied that it is " well founded " (*ibid.*).

(5) *Effect of valid blight notice*

If the Lands Tribunal determine not to uphold the counter-notice they must declare that the notice served by the owner-occupier is valid (s. 195 (4)) and the appropriate authority are then deemed to be authorised to acquire compulsorily the interest of the owner-occupier and to have served a notice to treat so to do (s. 196 (1)), the notice to treat being dated as specified in directions to be given by the Tribunal (ss. 195 (6), 196 (2) (*a*)).

Similarly, where no counter-notice is served by an appropriate authority, then the authority will be deemed to have served a notice to treat (s. 196 (1)) on a date which will be two months after the date on which the blight notice was served by the owner-occupier (s. 196 (2) (*b*)). A constructive notice to treat (*i.e.* one which, in the foregoing circumstances, is *deemed* to have been served) may not be withdrawn (s. 208) though where the blight notice requiring purchase is itself withdrawn (s. 198), any notice to treat deemed to have been served in consequence of that notice is deemed to have been withdrawn (s. 198 (1)) and no compensation is payable in respect of any such withdrawal (s. 198 (3)).

(6) *Compensation*

The price to be paid for the blighted land on compulsory acquisition pursuant to a blight notice served by an owner-occupier

will, of course, be the " unblighted " price of the land in the open
market (Land Compensation Act 1961, s. 9) that is to say, the value
of the land *not* (as was previously the case) at the date of the deemed
notice to treat but (since the House of Lords decision in *Birmingham
Corporation* v. *West Midland Baptist* (*Trust*) *Association* (*Inc.*)) [13]
at the date when compensation is agreed or assessed, or the date
(if earlier) when possession is taken.

Compensation for severance and disturbance in connection with
planning blight was formerly excluded by section 143 of the Town
and Country Planning Act 1962, which section was repealed by the
Town and Country Planning Act 1968.   Thus, compensation under
these two heads may now be claimed.

[13] [1970] A.C. 874.

CHAPTER 18

TOWN PLANNING AND COMPULSORY PURCHASE OF LAND

1. Powers as to Compulsory Purchase of Land

THE statutory grounds on which a local authority or the Secretary of State for the Environment can acquire land compulsorily for the purposes of town and country planning are set out in sections 112 and 113 of the 1971 Act.

Section 112 confers compulsory purchase powers on the councils of counties, county boroughs, London boroughs and non-county boroughs, urban district councils, rural district councils and the Greater London Council (s. 112 (5)). The Secretary of State may, under the 1971 Act (s. 112 (1)), authorise any of the foregoing local authorities to acquire compulsorily any land in their area if he is satisfied:

(a) that the land is required in order to secure or assist the treatment as a whole, by development, redevelopment or improvement or partly by one and partly by another method, of the land or of any area in which the land is situated; *or*

(b) that it is expedient in the public interest that the land should be held together with land so required; *or*

(c) that the land is required for development or redevelopment, or both, as a whole for the purpose of providing for the relocation of population or industry or the replacement of open space in the course of the redevelopment or improvement, or both, of another area as a whole; *or*

(d) that it is expedient to acquire the land immediately for a purpose which it is necessary to achieve in the interests of the proper planning of an area in which the land is situated.

The Secretary of State may authorise a local authority if satisfied, as aforesaid, to acquire land which is within the area of another local authority (s. 112 (2)), but before doing this he must consult with the local authority for the area where the land is situated (s. 112 (3)).

The actual procedure for acquisition will be by means of a compulsory purchase order made (s. 112 (4)) in accordance with the procedure set out in the Acquisition of Land (Authorisation Procedure) Act 1946.

Section 113 of the 1971 Act confers power upon the Secretary of State to acquire compulsorily any land necessary for the public service (s. 113 (1)). The expression "the public service" is nowhere defined in the Act and it would appear to be a far-reaching expression.

Compulsory acquisition under section 113 includes power to acquire an easement or other right over land (s. 113 (2)).

Any public inquiry or private hearing in connection with the compulsory purchase of land by a local authority will have to be conducted in accordance with the Compulsory Purchase by Local Authorities (Inquiries Procedure) Rules 1962.[1] These Rules follow generally the lines of the Town and Country Planning (Inquiries Procedure) Rules 1969 [2] discussed in Chapter 15, to which reference may be made.

2. Acquisition of Land by General Vesting Declaration

Under section 30 of the Town and Country Planning Act 1968 (not repealed by the 1971 Act) an acquiring authority, whether the Secretary of State or a local authority, having obtained a compulsory purchase order (but not before), will be able to obtain actual ownership of the land covered by the compulsory purchase order by the method of making a general vesting declaration (1968 Act, s. 30 and Sched. 3).

Under this procedure, details as to:

(1) the form and execution of general vesting declarations;
(2) the effect of such a declaration when it has been executed;
(3) the recovery by the acquiring authority of compensation overpaid; and
(4) the penalties recoverable for giving false information in claiming compensation

—all these matters are dealt with in Schedule 3 to the 1968 Act and in the Compulsory Purchase of Land (General Vesting Declaration) Regulations 1969.[3]

---

[1] S.I. 1962 No. 1424.
[2] S.I. 1969 No. 1092.
[3] S.I. 1969 No. 425.

3. Compulsory Acquisition of Land for Highways

The Secretary of State or a local highway authority may be authorised to acquire land compulsorily (s. 218 (1)) for providing or improving any highway which is to be provided or improved in pursuance of an order made under section 209, 211 or 212 of the 1971 Act (relating to the stopping up and diversion of highways and the conversion of a highway into a footpath or bridleway), or for any other purpose for which land is required in connection with such an order or for the purpose of providing any public right of way in lieu of a right of way extinguished under section 214 (1) (*a*) of the 1971 Act (s. 218 (1)).   Compulsory acquisition is by means of a compulsory purchase order made (s. 218 (2)) in accordance with the procedure under section 1 of the Acquisition of Land (Authorisation Procedure) Act 1946.

Proceedings required in connection with the acquisition of land under section 218 of the 1971 Act may be taken concurrently with any stopping up or diversion proceedings required to be taken under a stopping up or a diversion order made under section 209 of the Act (s. 219 and the Stopping Up of Highways (Concurrent Proceedings) Regulations 1948 [4]).

4. Extinguishment of Rights over Land Compulsorily Acquired [5]

Upon the completion of any compulsory purchase of land under the 1971 Act, all private rights of way and rights of laying down, erecting, continuing or maintaining any apparatus on, under or over the land will be extinguished and any such apparatus will vest in the acquiring authority (s. 118 (1)).   But this will not apply to rights and apparatus belonging to a statutory undertaker (s. 118 (2)) nor to other rights or apparatus in respect of which other arrangements are made by the acquiring authority (s. 118 (3)).   Any person suffering loss by the extinguishment of a right or the vesting of apparatus as above mentioned is entitled to compensation from the acquiring authority (s. 118 (4)), the compensation being determined (s. 118 (5)) in accordance with the Land Compensation Act 1961.

[4] S.I. 1948 No. 1348.
[5] As to other powers of a local authority over land acquired for planning purposes, see Chap. 20.

5. Acquisition by Agreement of Land Required by Local Authorities for Planning Purposes

Any local authority may acquire by agreement any land which they require for any purpose for which a local authority may be authorised to acquire land compulsorily under section 112 of the 1971 Act, that is to say, for comprehensive development or redevelopment (s. 119 (1)).

The foregoing power to acquire land by agreement may not be exercised by a local authority without the consent of the Secretary of State unless the land is immediately required by the acquiring authority for the purpose for which it is being bought or, if the land is not so required, unless the land is situated within the area of the acquiring authority (s. 119 (2)).

6. Acquisition of Land for Purposes of Exchange

It is provided specifically (s. 120) that the power of a local authority under the 1971 Act to acquire land whether compulsorily or by agreement shall include power to acquire land required for giving in exchange for: (1) land appropriated for planning purposes,[6] or (2) for Green Belt land within the meaning of the Green Belt (London and Home Counties) Act 1938 appropriated for any purpose specified in a development plan.

7. Compulsory Purchase or Appropriation of Open Spaces

A change in the law relating to the compulsory acquisition or appropriation of open space land is contained in section 31 of the Town and Country Planning Act 1968 (not repealed by the 1971 Act). Hitherto, under the Acquisition of Land (Authorisation Procedure) Act 1946, when open space land has been acquired or appropriated for other purposes, the acquiring authority had to submit the appropriate order to Special Parliamentary Procedure *unless* the Minister gave a certificate certifying either that equally advantageous land would be provided in exchange or that the land was needed for road improvements and no alternative land was necessary. Under section 31 of the 1968 Act the Secretary of State can give his certificate without the need for " exchange land,"

---

[6] See Chap. 20.

provided the open space land which is being taken does not exceed 250 square yards in extent.

8. Joint Body to Hold Land Acquired for Planning Purposes

If the Secretary of State, after consultation with the local authorities concerned, thinks it expedient, he may by order constitute a joint body to hold land which has already been acquired for planning purposes by those local authorities (s. 131). The order will provide for the transfer of the land from the local authorities to the joint body (s. 131 (1)) and may confer upon the joint body all or any of the powers of a local authority under the 1971 Act with respect to land acquired by such an authority for planning purposes (s. 131 (2)).

9. Effect of Acquisition on Unexpended Balance of Established Development Value

Where land is purchased compulsorily, or by agreement under threat of compulsion, any unexpended balance of established development value [7] attaching to the land will be extinguished unless all the interests in the land are *not* required, in which event the balance must be apportioned and will be reduced in value by the amount which is attributable to those interests which are in fact acquired (s. 142).

[7] See Chap. 16, p. 222.

CHAPTER 19

COMPENSATION PAYABLE ON COMPULSORY PURCHASE OF LAND

1. Summary

THE Acquisition of Land (Assessment of Compensation) Act 1919 laid down the principle of market value compensation as that which should be payable on a compulsory purchase of land. This basic principle was subsequently subjected by statute to three artificial distortions.

Part II of the Town and Country Planning Act 1944 introduced " the 1939 ceiling " value on compulsory purchase. This was followed by Part V of the Town and Country Planning Act 1947 which repealed " the 1939 ceiling " and enacted the principle of existing use value compensation on a compulsory purchase under a notice to treat served after July 1, 1948. Part III of the Town and Country Planning Act 1954 supplemented Part V of the 1947 Act by enacting that on a compulsory purchase under a notice to treat served on or after January 1, 1955, compensation should be the existing use value of the land (in accordance with Part V of the 1947 Act) *plus* the 1947 development value of the land (in accordance with Part III of the 1954 Act).

After some fifteen years of these artificial arrangements, Part I of the Town and Country Planning Act 1959 brought them to an end by enacting that on a compulsory purchase under a notice to treat served after October 29, 1958, compensation should once again be the market value of the land (in accordance with the Acquisition of Land (Assessment of Compensation) Act 1919) but subject to modifications contained in the 1959 Act.

Thus, as time passes and notices to treat served before October 30, 1958, fulfil their purpose and compulsory purchases based upon them are completed, it will become less and less necessary to consider the provisions of the 1947 and 1954 Acts relating to compensation on the compulsory purchase of land. When all compulsory purchases based on such notices to treat have been completed (or the notices themselves have by agreement been withdrawn), Part V of the 1947 Act and Part III of the 1954 Act

256

will become dead letters. Accordingly, Part III of the 1954 Act and most of Part V of the 1947 Act were formally repealed by section 58 (5) of, and Schedule VIII to, the Town and Country Planning Act 1959 in respect of notices to treat served after October 29, 1958.

2. Compensation at Market Value

The whole of the Acquisition of Land (Assessment of Compensation) Act 1919, together with Part I of the Town and Country Planning Act 1959 (in so far as it relates to compensation on compulsory purchase of land), was repealed by the Land Compensation Act 1961, but their joint effect is re-enacted in the 1961 Act which came into operation on August 1, 1961. The 1961 Act (including the repeals made by it) does not affect any compulsory purchase of land under a notice to treat served before August 1, 1961 (1961 Act, s. 41).

Thus the statutory foundation for the amount of compensation to be paid on a compulsory purchase of land is now to be found in the Land Compensation Act 1961 which, to put the matter briefly, provides that such compensation shall be the market value [1] of the land (1961 Act, s. 5) subject to the modifications contained in the Act and to the intricate provisions of the Act relating to assumptions concerning planning permission (1961 Act, ss. 14, 15 and 16) and to the certification of appropriate alternative development (Part III of the 1961 Act).

3. The Four Modifications of the Market Value Principle

To the general provision that compensation shall be the market value of the land—" the amount which the land if sold in the open market by a willing seller might be expected to realise " (1961 Act, s. 5 (2))—there are now four statutory modifications. Not all of these are new, some of them, indeed, being based on what has hitherto been customary.

The first and most important modification on the market value principle is to the effect that an acquiring authority shall not pay any increase in the value of the acquired land if the increase may be said to have been brought about by the scheme of development

---

[1] Since the House of Lords decision in *Birmingham Corporation* v. *West Midland Baptist (Trust) Association (Inc.)* [1970] A.C. 874, the date by reference to which the land is to be valued is the date when compensation is agreed or assessed, or the date (if earlier) when possession of the land is taken.

which gives rise to the need for the compulsory purchase (1961 Act, s. 6). The important point here is to define what, in any particular case, may be said to be the *scheme of development*, and the effect of the 1961 Act is to widen the customary concept of this in three important instances.

The scheme of development is now to be regarded (1961 Act, s. 6 (1) and Sched. 1, Part I) as covering, for example, any development carried out in any part of an action area for which a local plan is in force (1961 Act as adapted by the Town and Country Planning Act 1971, s. 291 (1) and Sched. 23, Part I) *or* in any part of an area delineated as the site of a new town (under the New Towns Act 1965) *or* in any part of an area delineated in a development plan as an area of town development (under the Town Development Act 1952).

The second modification secures that if on a compulsory purchase of land the scheme of development causes an increase in value of other " contiguous or adjacent " land belonging to the same owner, such increase shall be set off against the price paid for the land compulsorily acquired (1961 Act, s. 7).

The third modification operates in favour of the vendor whose land has been taken compulsorily and ensures that any diminution in the value of the land caused by the threat of compulsory purchase shall be ignored (1961 Act, s. 9). This provision is important in connection with the contents of Part IX of the Town and Country Planning Act 1971, under which certain property which has become unsaleable due to the provisions of a development plan (that is to say, property suffering from " planning blight "[1a]) can be required by the owner to be purchased by a local authority but at an " unblighted price."

Finally the fourth modification makes general what is already lawful under certain Acts, namely, the payment on any compulsory purchase of land to which the 1961 Act applies of discretionary allowances to cover costs of removal and trade losses, sustained as a result of the compulsory purchase, by the " little man " whose interest in the land acquired is not such as to entitle him to receive a notice to treat (1961 Act, s. 30). These allowances, which cannot be claimed as of right, are without prejudice to any other payments claimed by law (1961 Act, s. 30 (3)).

[1a] See Chap. 17.

4. Special Cases

The return to market value compensation on compulsory purchase has necessitated special provisions in the 1961 Act relating to the acquisition of slum property (1961 Act, s. 10), to the acquisition of land of statutory undertakers (1961 Act, s. 11), to the acquisition of land in relation to which there is already outstanding a right to compensation for refusal of planning permission (1961 Act, s. 12) and to the acquisition of war-damaged land (1961 Act, s. 13).

So far as the owner-occupier of a slum house is concerned, the 1961 Act secures (1961 Act, s. 10 and Sched. 2) that, though the house may be acquired under the Housing Act 1957 at its site value, the minimum payment by way of compensation on compulsory purchase shall at least be equal to the gross value of the house for rating purposes. There is thus established a " compensation floor " (as distinct from a " compensation ceiling ") for owner-occupiers of private dwellings found to be unfit for human habitation under the provisions of the Housing Act 1957.

5. How to Calculate Market Value in an Era of Town Planning Control

In the comparatively simple days of 1919 the assessment of market value was little affected by the incidence of town planning control, for the simple reason that there was hardly any such control at all. But after the dramatic strokes of the Town and Country Planning Act 1947 (now re-enacted in the 1971 Act), which require planning permission to be obtained before any development of land, including material change of use, can take place, town planning control plays an important, perhaps the most important, part in establishing what a particular piece of land will fetch in the open market when sold for development.

Nowadays, under the current system of regulatory town planning control backed by legal sanctions, the whole question of the market value of land depends largely upon what sort of planning permission would be granted for the development of the land if an application for planning permission were to be made. It is because of a desire to help in the solution of this question that many of the complexities of the Land Compensation Act 1961 have arisen.

The 1961 Act provides that on assessing compensation for the compulsory purchase of land certain assumptions as to planning permission *shall* be made (1961 Act, s. 14). There are seven of these assumptions; three are general and four are special.

6. The Three General Planning Assumptions

Taking the three general planning assumptions first, these require that upon any compulsory purchase it will be assumed that:

(1) planning permission will be granted for the development which brings about the need for the compulsory purchase (1961 Act, s. 15 (1) (2));

(2) planning permission will be granted for all development falling within the ambit of the " existing use of land " (1961 Act, s. 15 (3))—as to which reference should be made to the provisions of Schedule 8 to the 1971 Act—but not, of course, if the existing use value of the land has already been realised by the payment to the landowner of compensation (1961 Act, s. 15 (4)); and

(3) planning permission will be granted for " certificated development," that is to say, development in respect of which a certificate is issued under Part III of the 1961 Act [2] (1961 Act, s. 15 (5)).

7. The Four Special Planning Assumptions

Turning now to the four special planning assumptions (1961 Act, s. 16) these, it may be said, all arise from insufficiencies in the development plan for the area where the compulsorily acquired land is situated. Attention is to be paid to the state in which the development plan exists at the date of the notice to treat, any amendment to the plan subsequent to that date being irrelevant.

The four special planning assumptions require it to be assumed that:

(1) where the development plan defines the land as a site for specified development—that planning permission will be given for that development (1961 Act, s. 16 (1) and (6));

(2) where the development plan allocates the land for some

[2] See p. 261.

" primary use "—that planning permission will be granted for any development falling within the scope of that " primary use," *provided* it is development for which planning permission might reasonably be expected to be granted (1961 Act, s. 16 (2) (6) (7) and (8));

(3) where the development plan allocates the land for a range of two or more " primary uses "—that planning permission will be granted for any development falling within the scope of that range of uses, *provided* it is development for which planning permission might reasonably be expected to be granted (1961 Act, s. 16 (3) (6) (7) and (8)); and

(4) where the land is in an action area for which a local plan is in force (1961 Act as adapted by the Town and Country Planning Act 1971, s. 291 (1) and Sched. 23, Part I)—that, irrespective of the proposed layout of the area, planning permission will be given for any development falling within the range of uses allowed in the action area, *provided* it is development for which planning permission might reasonably be expected to be granted (1961 Act, s. 16 (4) (5) (6) (7) and (8)).

It is to be noted that the first three of these four special assumptions do *not* apply to land in an action area, such land being catered for under the fourth special assumption.

It is further to be noted that while the 1961 Act requires the making of the foregoing planning assumptions (or such of them as are relevant to the matter in hand) the Act does not exclude the taking into account of other types of development to which the market in land might conceivably have regard (1961 Act, s. 14 (3)).

8. Certification of Development

Notwithstanding the making of the foregoing assumptions, there may still remain, under the current system of planning control, some difficulty in computing what would be the market value of land which is being compulsorily acquired. The relevant development plan may be unhelpful on the point if, for example, the acquired land happens to be in an area in respect of which the development plan has refrained from committing itself, that is to say, in an area sometimes referred to as " white land." Again, a development plan may provide that an area shall be zoned as a green belt. Although this usually means that no development in that area will be allowed at all, it is well known that, on occasion, certain kinds of development are permitted even in a green belt.

To deal with cases of this kind the 1961 Act makes further provision (1961 Act, Part III, and the Land Compensation Development Order 1963 [3]) whereby either the landowner or the authority seeking the compulsory purchase may apply (1961 Act, s. 17) to the local planning authority to issue a certificate stating what, in all the circumstances, would be the kind of development for which planning permission might reasonably be expected to be granted if the land were not being compulsorily acquired by the acquiring authority and an application for planning permission for development were lodged in respect of the land.

The applicant for such a certificate must himself specify one or more classes of development which appear to him appropriate for the land in question (1961 Act, s. 17 (3)).

The local planning authority must issue a certificate (1961 Act, s. 17 (4)) declaring either the nature of the development which might have been permitted had it been applied for, or declaring that no development (other than that—if any—proposed by the acquiring authority) would have been permitted.

Any person aggrieved by any such certificate has a right of appeal to the Secretary of State (1961 Act, s. 18) who, before determining the appeal must afford the landowner and the acquiring authority and also the local planning authority whose certificate is being appealed against an opportunity of being heard by a person appointed by the Secretary of State.

In an appeal against a certificate, where the Secretary of State does not accept the reasons given by the local planning authority, he may nevertheless confirm the certificate and give his own reasons; the essential matter of such a certificate is its conclusion, and the Secretary of State may well agree with the conclusion (for reasons of his own) even though he does not accept the reasons of the local planning authority because, for example, he finds them to contain inaccuracies of fact.[4]

It is to be noted that the procedure with respect to the certification of development does *not* apply if the land which is being

---

[3] S.I. 1963 No. 749.
[4] *Parrish* v. *Minister of Housing and Local Government* (1961) 13 P. & C.R. 32.

compulsorily acquired is land in an action area *or* is in an area allocated primarily for residential, commercial or industrial purposes (1961 Act, s. 17 (1) as adapted by the Town and Country Planning Act 1971, s. 291 (1) and Sched. 23, Part I).

It may also be noted that a certificate can be given only by the local planning authority and this does not include the council of any county district to whom a local planning authority have delegated their functions under section 3 of the Town and Country Planning Act 1971. The 1961 Act makes no provision whereby a local planning authority can delegate its responsibility for issuing certificates under the Act.

9. Ministerial Comment on Certification

Some interesting comments on the working of the certificate system are to be found in paragraphs 2 to 7 of the Annexe to Ministry of Housing and Local Government Circular 48/59 dated August 11, 1959.

The Minister " thinks it important that the certificate system should be worked on broad common sense lines " and draws attention to the fact that a certificate can be at variance with the use shown by a development plan for the particular land in question. The Minister remarks that " a certificate is not a planning permission but a statement to be used in ascertaining the fair market value of land," its purpose being to state what, if any, other forms of development would have been allowed under town planning control had the land not been compulsorily acquired. In this connection the Minister comments that he " would expect the local planning authority to determine this question in the light of the character of the development in the surrounding area and the general policy of the development plan " and he quotes, by way of example, the case where the land which is being compulsorily acquired is surrounded almost entirely by residential development, and observes that in such an instance a certificate of residential use would normally be appropriate.

There is no doubt that all sorts of difficult questions can be propounded in connection with the working of the certificate system but the clue to its successful working appears to be to let common sense have full play and to avoid nice, legalistic refinements.

CHAPTER 20

LOCAL AUTHORITIES' POWERS WITH RESPECT TO APPROPRIATION, DEVELOPMENT, DISPOSAL, OF LAND FOR PLANNING PURPOSES

1. Appropriation for Planning Purposes of Open Spaces

ANY local authority may, by Order confirmed by the Secretary of State, appropriate, for any purpose for which they can be authorised to acquire land, any land already held by them for other purposes and forming part of a common, open space (including a disused burial ground (s. 290 (1)), or fuel or field garden allotment (including any such land which is specially regulated by any public, local or private enactment), provided it is not Green Belt land under the Green Belt (London and Home Counties) Act 1938 (1971 Act, s. 121).

The order appropriating any such open space land will be subject, by virtue of the provisions of section 121 (2) of the 1971 Act applying paragraph 11 of Schedule 1 to the Acquisition of Land (Authorisation Procedure) Act 1946, to " special parliamentary procedure," as dealt with in the Statutory Orders (Special Procedure Act 1945, before it can come into operation *unless* the Secretary of State certifies that such Special Procedure is not necessary. The Secretary of State cannot give this certificate unless he is satisfied (and certifies accordingly) that for the land appropriated equivalent open space land will be given in exchange *or*, in the case of open space land taken for road widening, that no such exchange is necessary (*ibid.*). However, the Secretary of State, acting under section 31 of the Town and Country Planning Act 1968 (which is not repealed by the 1971 Act) can now give his certificate without the need for " exchange land " if the open space land which is being appropriated does not exceed 250 square yards in extent.

2. Appropriation for Other Purposes of Land Held for Planning Purposes

When a local authority have either acquired or appropriated land for planning purposes and are currently holding it for such

264

purposes, they may appropriate it for *other* purposes for which they are entitled to acquire land by any enactment other than the 1971 Act (s. 122). The consent of the Secretary of State is in certain circumstances (s. 122 (2)) required to any such appropriation.

Thus land which, either by acquisition or appropriation, has once been brought under the " control " of the 1971 Act, may be " appropriated out " of that control and used for purposes other than the planning purposes for which it was originally acquired or appropriated.

On appropriating planning land to other purposes a local authority must have regard (s. 125) to the desirability of preserving features of special architectural or historic interest including in particular any " listed building " (s. 54 (9)).

3. Development of Land by Local Authorities

Prior to the Town and Country Planning Act 1944 a local authority, whilst they could make a planning scheme and so control the development of land by other parties, could not, generally speaking, undertake development themselves. In other words, planning control was negative and a local authority could not implement the provisions of their own planning scheme by carrying out positive development of land in accordance with their scheme. The 1944 Act, however, introduced an entirely new and important principle by conferring on local authorities power to carry out development of land themselves.

This power is now found in the 1971 Act which provides that a local authority shall, on any land which was acquired or appropriated and is for the time being held for planning purposes, have power to erect, construct or carry out any building or work not being a building or work in respect of which statutory authority exists otherwise (s. 124). The consent of the Secretary of State is required before a local authority can avail themselves of the foregoing power and embark upon any scheme of positive development (s. 124 (3) (4)).

Once a local authority have, with the Secretary of State's consent, completed a building or work under the foregoing powers, they are authorised to repair, maintain and insure it and generally to deal with it in a proper course of management (s. 124 (5)).

Instead of carrying out positive development themselves the

local authority may, with the Secretary of State's consent, enter into arrangements with an authorised association for such development to be carried out by the association (s. 124 (6)).

When carrying out positive development a local authority must have special regard to the need to preserve features and buildings of architectural or historic interest (s. 125).

4. Miscellaneous Powers Relating to Land Acquired, Appropriated or Developed by Local Authorities

In connection with the acquisition, appropriation or development of land under the 1971 Act by a local authority, the Act makes provision with respect to a number of consequential matters so as to facilitate such acquisition, appropriation or development. These consequential provisions relate, briefly, to:

(a) power to override easements and other rights (s. 127);

(b) extinction of public rights of way (s. 214);

(c) extinction of private rights of way and rights as to apparatus (s. 118);

(d) extinction of rights of way and rights as to apparatus vested in statutory undertakers (ss. 230 and 231);

(e) extension or modification of functions of statutory undertakers (ss. 233, 234 and 236);

(f) relief of statutory undertakers from obligations rendered impracticable (ss. 235 and 236);

(g) use and development of consecrated land and burial grounds notwithstanding restrictions (s. 128);

(h) use and development of commons, open spaces, etc., notwithstanding restrictions (s. 129);

(i) displacement of persons from land and the obtaining of possession of occupied dwelling-houses and other buildings (s. 130);

(j) stopping up and diversion of highways [1]; conversion of highways into footpaths and bridleways; extinguishment of rights of way, etc. (ss. 209 to 221);

(k) alteration of telegraphic lines (s. 220).

---

[1] See *Harlow* v. *Ministry of Transport and Others* [1951] 2 K.B. 98 (C.A.); reversing [1950] 2 K.B. 175.   See further as to highways, p. 130.

5. Disposal of Land by Local Authorities

Where a local authority have acquired or appropriated land for planning purposes and are for the time being holding the land for these purposes—in other words, where a local authority are possessed of " planning land "—they may, instead of developing it themselves, dispose of it to such person, in such manner and subject to such conditions as may appear expedient in order that the land may be developed by that person (s. 123 (1)). The consent of the Secretary of State to any such disposal of planning land is required in a number of instances (s. 123 (2)) and particularly in the case of land (s. 123 (2) (b)) acquired or appropriated for planning purposes for a reason mentioned in section 112 (1) (a) to (c) of the 1971 Act.[2]

Thus land may be made available by a local authority to a private individual lacking compulsory purchase powers but wishful to carry out the development of land. Much land in war-damaged areas has been made available in this way for development by private individuals. Indeed, the Secretary of State may require a local authority holding planning land to make it available in this way to a specified individual (s. 123 (4)), but the authority cannot be required to dispose of the land for a figure which is less than the best that is reasonably obtainable (s. 123 (5) and (6)).

Where the planning land which is being disposed of is land acquired or appropriated for planning purposes for a reason mentioned in section 112 (1) (a) to (c) of the 1971 Act,[2] the power of disposal of such land must be exercised so as to secure, so far as may be practicable, that persons formerly living or carrying on business on such land before the local authority acquired it may be able to get reaccommodation on the land suitable for their reasonable requirements and at a price settled with due regard to the price at which such land was acquired from them (s. 123 (7)).

6. Former Restrictions on Right of Disposal Removed

Formerly, under section 19 (5) of the Town and Country Planning Act 1944, the Secretary of State was precluded from consenting to a disposal of planning land by a sale of the freehold

[2] See p. 251.

or by a lease for more than ninety-nine years unless he was satisfied that there were " exceptional circumstances which render the disposal of the land in that manner expedient . . . in order to secure the best use of that or other land and any buildings or works which have been, or are to be, erected . . . thereon . . . or to secure the erection . . . thereon of any buildings . . . needed for the proper planning of the area of the [local] authority."

Section 19 (5) of the 1944 Act was, however, repealed by the Town Development Act 1952, s. 18, with the result that whilst the mode of disposal of land held by a local authority for the purposes of the 1971 Act is still, in certain instances, at the discretion of the Secretary of State, he is no longer under any obligation to find exceptional circumstances before consenting to a sale of the freehold or a lease for more than ninety-nine years.

7. The Uthwatt Report

The principle formerly embodied in section 19 (5) of the 1944 Act whereby the freehold of land, once it had been acquired by a local authority, is not thereafter to be disposed of, derives from a recommendation of the Expert Committee on Compensation and Betterment (the Uthwatt Committee), who, in paragraph 147 of their Final Report of September 1942,[3] stated:

" It may be possible for much of the work of rebuilding in the replanned area to be carried out by private enterprise and land should be made available to developers for approved development in accordance with the plan. In our view it is essential to secure that the land should not again be divided up among owners of small freeholds. We recommend, therefore, that once any interest in land has passed into public ownership it should be disposed of by way of lease only and not by way of sale, and that the authority should have the power to impose such covenants in the lease as planning requirements make desirable, breach of such covenants to be enforceable by re-entry.

" Although this recommendation is made primarily in

[3] Cmd. 6386.

connection with Reconstruction Areas, we intend it to be of general application to any interest in land disposed of by a public authority."

8. The New Towns Report

The foregoing recommendation of the Uthwatt Committee was repeated by the New Towns Committee in paragraph 15 of their Second Interim Report of April 1946,[4] with the result that a development corporation operating under the New Towns Act 1946 was formerly subject to the same restriction (s. 5 of New Towns Act 1946) on the disposal of the freehold in, or the grant of a lease for more than ninety-nine years of, any land which it held, as was a local authority operating under the 1944 Act. This restriction was likewise removed by the Town Development Act 1952, s. 18.

9. The Central Advisory Committee Report

As to the length of leases to be granted by a local authority, it is stated in paragraph 71 of the Report of the Central Advisory Committee on Estate Development and Management in War Damaged Areas (a report made to the Secretary of State in 1947) that " the time when the general run of buildings in a central area will become obsolete will almost certainly be reached considerably before the end of ninety-nine years," and in paragraph 72 it is recommended " that in the interest of good estate management, the general practice in regard to commercial and industrial buildings in central areas should be to grant ground leases for an average term of seventy-five years."

The foregoing extracts from the Reports of the Uthwatt Committee, the New Towns Committee and the Central Advisory Committee indicate the kind of thing which may have to be met by those who seek to prevail upon the Secretary of State to authorise a local authority (as he now, at his discretion, may authorise them) to sell the freehold of any land which the authority have acquired for planning purposes or to grant a lease for more than ninety-nine years of such land.

[4] Cmd. 6794.

10. Restriction on Sale of " Council Houses "

Finally, it needs to be mentioned that some local authorities are addicted to the selling of council houses. Their wings are now clipped by section 39 of the Town and Country Planning Act 1968 (not repealed by the 1971 Act) which precludes any such disposal without the consent of the Secretary of State.

CHAPTER 21

NEW INQUIRY PROCEDURE—PLANNING INQUIRY COMMISSIONS

1. Why Have a New Procedure?

THREE sections of the Town and Country Planning Act 1971, namely, sections 47, 48 and 49, contain important provisions whereby the Secretary of State is empowered to set up Planning Inquiry Commissions to inquire into any matters referred to them. The motivating factor behind the reference of anything to a Planning Inquiry Commission is that the development which is the subject of the inquiry is development which raises considerations of national or regional importance or presents unfamiliar, technical or scientific aspects which merit a special inquiry.

The responsibility of setting up any particular Planning Inquiry Commission rests with the Secretary of State (s. 47 (1)). The customary single Inspector, so well known at public inquiries held in connection with planning matters, will now be replaced, where a Planning Inquiry Commission is set up, by a team of investigators consisting of a chairman and not less than two nor more than four other members (s. 47 (2)), thus making a minimum of three members and a maximum of five.

Once set up, the Commission will not be confined simply to the hearing of objections or representations. It will have something more in the nature of a roving commission to undertake a full examination of all problems associated with the matter which is laid before it.

2. Matters Capable of Treatment by the New Procedure

The 1971 Act specifies those particular matters which the Secretary of State may refer for investigation to a Planning Inquiry Commission. These matters are four in number as follows (s. 48 (1)), namely,

(a) any application for planning permission which has been called in for decision by the Secretary of State himself under section 35 of the 1971 Act;

(b) any planning appeal to the Secretary of State against a planning decision under section 36 of the 1971 Act;

(c) any proposal that a government department should direct, under section 40 of the 1971 Act, that planning permission should be deemed to be granted for development by a local authority or by a statutory undertaker; and

(d) any proposal that development should be carried out by a government department.

Any two or more of the foregoing four matters may be referred at the same time to a Planning Inquiry Commission if they appear to relate to proposals to carry out development for similar purposes on different sites (s. 48 (3)).

A Planning Inquiry Commission may, with the approval of the Secretary of State (s. 48 (7)) and at his expense, arrange for the carrying out of research of any kind which appears to them to be relevant to the matter referred to them for inquiry and report (*ibid.*).

The foregoing are the four matters (and the only four matters) which can be referred by the Secretary of State for investigation by a Planning Inquiry Commission.

3. When is the New Procedure Applicable and Who Decides?

The next question is: When should the Secretary of State decide that a Planning Inquiry Commission should investigate any of the foregoing matters rather than that they should be dealt with under the other procedures of the 1971 Act? Whether or not any one of the foregoing matters should be referred to a Planning Inquiry Commission is to be decided by either the " responsible Minister or Ministers " (s. 48 (2)). Schedule 10 to the 1971 Act gives details as to who in any particular circumstances will be " the responsible Minister " (s. 48 (8)).

What are to be the considerations to be borne in mind before it is decided to refer a matter to a Planning Inquiry Commission? The answer to this question is found in section 48 (2) of the 1971 Act. Before a reference can be made the Minister concerned must come to the conclusion that it is expedient for the reference to be made so as to ensure that the matter in hand becomes the subject of a special inquiry on either one or both of the following two grounds, that is to say,

(1) that there are considerations of national or regional impor-

tance which require evaluating but that a proper evaluation cannot be made *unless there is a special inquiry for the purpose*; and

(2) that the technical or scientific aspects of the proposed development are of so unfamiliar a character—so new, so strange—as to prejudice a proper determination of the question of whether or not the development should be permitted *unless there is a special inquiry for the purpose* (s. 48 (2)).

The 1971 Act caters specifically for the question of whether an alternative site for any proposed development should be considered, by providing that whenever a proposal to carry out development on a particular site is referred to a Planning Inquiry Commission, the Commission can also consider the question of whether such development should be carried out instead on some alternative site (s. 48 (4)).

The Minister referring a matter for inquiry to a Planning Inquiry Commission must state in the reference the reasons why he does so and may draw the attention of the Commission to any point which seems to him to need investigation (s. 48 (5)).

4. What a Planning Inquiry Commission Must Do

When a Planning Inquiry Commission have a matter before them, their duty appears to fall under three headings, as follows (s. 48 (6)).

Their first duty is to *identify* those considerations or those technical or scientific aspects of the matter which are relevant to the question of whether or not the proposed development should be permitted and then *assess* the importance to be attached to such considerations or aspects (s. 48 (6) (*a*)).

When the foregoing is done their next duty is to afford to the applicant for planning permission and to the local planning authority and to other interested parties an opportunity of appearing before or being heard by one or more members of the Commission if any of these persons or parties desire to be heard (s. 48 (6) (*b*)). If a desire to be heard is expressed by the applicant for planning permission or by the local planning authority or by any other interested party, then the Planning Inquiry Commission *must* hold a local inquiry (s. 49 (3)) but they may, in any case and at their own discretion, hold such an inquiry if they think it necessary for the proper discharge of their functions (*ibid.*). Any local inquiry held as aforesaid by a Planning Inquiry Commission will come (s. 49 (5)) within the ambit of the Tribunals and Inquiries Act 1971 and the provisions of the Local Government Act 1933 relating to evidence and costs will apply (s. 49 (6)).

Thirdly and lastly the Planning Inquiry Commission must make a report on the matter referred to them to the Minister who initiated the reference (s. 48 (6) (*c*)).

When a Planning Inquiry Commission hold a local inquiry (s. 49 (3)) they may do so concurrently with some other ministerial inquiry into any cognate matter (s. 49 (4)), or, alternatively, the two inquiries may be combined (*ibid.*).

5. Notices about, and Timing for, a Reference to a Planning Inquiry Commission

Whenever a reference to a Planning Inquiry Commission is made, notice of the making of the reference is to be published in the *London Gazette* and in at least one newspaper circulating in the locality of the proposed development (s. 49 (2) and the Town and Country Planning (Planning Inquiry Commissions) Regulations 1968).[1] A copy of the notice is to be served on the local planning authority for the area in which the proposed development is to be carried out (*ibid.*). Notice of the reference is also to be served on other interested parties as, for example, the applicant for planning permission or any person who has made representations relating to the matter (*ibid.*).

A reference relating to development by a government department can be made to a Planning Inquiry Commission at any time (s. 49 (1)). References of any other matter can be made before *but not after*, the relevant application for planning permission or the relevant appeal or the relevant direction has been determined or given (*ibid.*). It is worthy of special note that any such reference may be made (*ibid.*) notwithstanding that there has already been held one of the conventional local inquiries or private hearings provided for under the 1971 Act.

The question of whether the conventional and familiar procedures

[1] S.I. 1968 No. 1911.

of inquiry under the 1971 Act shall be followed, or whether the procedure by way of a Planning Inquiry Commission shall be brought into operation, is a matter *not* for the applicant for planning permission but for " the responsible Minister or Ministers."

Attention may again be drawn to the fact that a reference to a Planning Inquiry Commission can still be made notwithstanding that the conventional private hearing or public inquiry into the matter has already been held under the 1971 Act (s. 49 (1)). No such reference can, however, take place *if a decision has been given* following the holding of the aforementioned conventional hearing or public inquiry under the 1971 Act (*ibid.*).

6. How Will it all Work Out in Practice?—What the Minister Said

Developers will be interested to learn just how the procedure by way of a Planning Inquiry Commission is going to be handled in practice. Accordingly, it will be useful to conclude this chapter by quoting a statement made by the Minister of State, Ministry of Housing and Local Government, when the Bill for the Town and Country Planning Act 1968 was in Committee (Hansard, Standing Committee G.—April 2, 1968, col. 903 *et seq.*):

" We definitely envisage the work of these Commissions falling into two distinct parts. The first part is modelled on the procedures of a Royal Commission or a Departmental committee that is set up to investigate some particular problem. The second part is modelled on the public inquiry procedure with which we are all familiar through planning applications.

" As I explained a few moments ago, one of the reasons for our putting forward this procedure is that we feel that the kind of problems that we want to refer are such that the existing procedure is inadequate because the inspector at the inquiry often is not qualified to probe and investigate some of the issues involved. And the procedure of a public inquiry, which is a public inquiry to receive, hear and inquire into objections to the proposal, does not enable the kind of highly technically qualified investigation in depth of the issues to be made which is needed in this type of case.

" We have had very much in mind, of course, the point about how to keep down the time that is going to be spent on these investigations, so that they do not produce intolerable delays in the planning procedure. Therefore, we envisage the first stage as what I shall call the stage of investigation by the Commission. . . .

" The way in which we envisage the commissions will work is that at this stage they will begin by receiving written memoranda from the applicant, from Government Departments which are concerned and affected, from outside bodies which have an interest; they may have to commission some research to investigate some aspect on which they have not adequate information, and receive a report from a research body.

" Having studied those memoranda, the Commission may wish them to hear oral evidence from the persons who have submitted memoranda, as, for example, a Royal Commission does. We envisage that the Commission will itself conduct the investigation, and will be qualified to do it. It will do the questioning; there will not be examination and cross-examination by legal representatives at this stage. This is a commission set up by the Government to investigate a problem in depth for itself, and it will be qualified to do it.

" Evidence will be taken at both stages, but in a different way, with a different procedure. . . .

" May I add a word here about alternative sites? It is at this stage that we envisage the Commission really being able to introduce helpfully a new element in the procedure. Let us suppose that, at the end of this stage, it forms the view that the development could equally well—perhaps better—be done at some site other than the one the applicant has applied for. It might well say to the applicant, ' We shall be greatly assisted if you would make an application in respect of this alternative site. We know it is not your first choice, but we are impressed by the objections against your site, and this looks to us to be one we would like to be able to consider and report on. We could, perhaps, have a public inquiry into that site as well as the one for which you have already applied.' The applicant is then confronted with this situation: if he refuses to take the hint, or accept the invitation, and he says, ' No; it is all or nothing on the site I have asked for,' he is in serious danger of having a recommendation against him, and he will fail to get his permission. On the other hand, if he is prepared, as second best but perhaps under protest, to put in an alternative application, he has a chance of getting finality then and, at the end of the day, getting a decision in his favour either for site A or for site B.

" So much for the moment for the first stage. Then comes the second stage of the public inquiries. In our anxiety to cut short time, we wondered whether the first stage would be enough and one could avoid, as it were, the second stage. But I think people have come so much to accept the public local inquiry as a necessary and proper part of the machinery for investigating these controversial cases that we thought we must retain it. But we want to avoid, if we can, too much duplication between the two stages and having to go over all the same evidence again. So what we propose ... is that all the evidence which has been collected, both the written evidence and the oral evidence at the first stage, will be made available to the parties at the public inquiry at the second stage. Then it will be up to the inspector who is conducting the inquiry, and to legal representatives, counsel and others who are involved in the second stage, to avoid time-wasting repetition of evidence which is all there on the record. But, of course, there may be matters in that evidence which they want to investigate and probe further, cross-examine on at the second stage, and they will be free to do so. They will not be prevented from doing so. It is at this stage that people who wish to be legally represented and be able to cross-examine and probe the evidence in that way would be able to do so. That is, broadly speaking, how we envisage the two stages."

APPENDIX

The following provisions of the Local Government Act 1972 will come into operation on April 1st, 1974 (Local Government Act 1972, s. 273 (1) (3)). These provisions have an important effect, as from April 1, 1974, on the functioning of the Town and Country Planning Act 1972 and, accordingly, are here set out *in extenso.*

Provisions relating to Town and Country Planning extracted from the Local Government Act 1972

PART VI

101.—(1) Subject to any express provision contained in this Act or any Act passed after this Act, a local authority may arrange for the discharge of any of their functions—

    (*a*) by a committee, a sub-committee or an officer of the authority; or

    (*b*) by any other local authority.

(2) Where by virtue of this section any functions of a local authority may be discharged by a committee of theirs, then, unless the local authority otherwise direct, the committee may arrange for the discharge of any of those functions by a sub-committee or an officer of the authority and where by virtue of this section any functions of a local authority may be discharged by a sub-committee of the authority, then, unless the local authority or the committee otherwise direct, the sub-committee may arrange for the discharge of any of those functions by an officer of the authority.

(3) Where arrangements are in force under this section for the discharge of any functions of a local authority by another local authority, then, subject to the terms of the arrangements, that other authority may arrange for the discharge of those functions by a committee, sub-committee or officer of theirs and subsection (2) above shall apply in relation to those functions as it applies in relation to the functions of that other authority.

(4) Any arrangements made by a local authority or committee under this section for the discharge of any functions by a committee, sub-committee, officer or local authority shall not prevent the authority or committee by whom the arrangements are made from exercising those functions.

(5) Two or more local authorities may discharge any of their functions jointly and, where arrangements are in force for them to do so,—

    (*a*) they may also arrange for the discharge of those functions by a joint committee of theirs or by an officer of one of them and subsection (2) above shall apply in relation to those functions as it applies in relation to the functions of the individual authorities; and

(b) any enactment relating to those functions or the authorities by whom or the areas in respect of which they are to be discharged shall have effect subject to all necessary modifications in its application in relation to those functions and the authorities by whom and the areas in respect of which (whether in pursuance of the arrangements or otherwise) they are to be discharged.

(6) A local authority's functions with respect to levying, or issuing a precept for, a rate or borrowing money shall be discharged only by the authority.

(7) A local authority shall not make arrangements under this section for the discharge of any of their functions under the Diseases of Animals Act 1950 by any other local authority.

(8) Any enactment, except one mentioned in subsection (9) below, which contains any provision—

(a) which empowers or requires local authorities or any class of local authorities to establish committees (including joint committees) for any purpose or enables a Minister to make an instrument establishing committees of local authorities for any purpose or empowering or requiring a local authority or any class of local authorities to establish committees for any purpose; or

(b) which empowers or requires local authorities or any class of local authorities to arrange or to join with other authorities in arranging for the exercise by committees so established or by officers of theirs of any of their functions, or provides that any specified functions of theirs shall be discharged by such committees or officers, or enables any Minister to make an instrument conferring such a power, imposing such a requirement or containing such a provision;

shall, to the extent that it makes any such provision, cease to have effect.

(9) The following enactments, that is to say—

(a) paragraphs 1 and 3 to 11 of Part II of Schedule 1 to the Education Act 1944 (education committees of local education authorities);

(b) section 30 (2) of the 1963 Act (special education committee of the Greater London Council);

(c) sections 2 and 3 of the Police Act 1964 (police committees);

(d) section 1 of the Sea Fisheries Regulation Act 1966;

(e) section 35 (3) of the Children and Young Persons Act 1969 (children's regional planning committees);

(f) section 2 of the Local Authority Social Services Act 1970 (social services committees);

(g) section 7 of the Superannuation Act 1972 (superannuation of persons employed in local government service, etc.); and

(h) Part I of Schedule 17 to this Act;

are exempted from subsection (8) above.

(10) This section shall not authorise a local authority to arrange for the discharge by any committee, sub-committee or local authority of any functions which by any enactment mentioned in subsection (9) above are required or authorised to be discharged by a specified committee, but the foregoing provision shall not prevent a local authority who are required by or under any such enactment to establish, or delegate functions to, a committee established by or under any such enactment from arranging under this section for the discharge of their functions by an officer of the local authority or committee, as the case may be.

(11) It is hereby declared that this section authorises the Greater London Council to arrange for the discharge of any of their functions by the Inner London Education Authority or any education committee established by that Authority under Part II of Schedule 1 to the Education Act 1944.

(12) References in this section and section 102 below to the discharge of any of the functions of a local authority include references to the doing of anything which is calculated to facilitate, or is conducive or incidental to, the discharge of any of those functions.

(13) In this Part of this Act " local authority " includes the Common Council, the Sub-Treasurer of the Inner Temple, the Under Treasurer of the Middle Temple, a joint board on which a local authority within the meaning of this Act or any of the foregoing authorities are represented and, without prejudice to the foregoing, any port health authority.

(14) Nothing in this section affects the operation of section 5 of the 1963 Act or the Local Authorities (Goods and Services) Act 1970.

102.—(1) For the purpose of discharging any functions in pursuance of arrangements made under section 101 above—

(a) a local authority may appoint a committee of the authority; or

(b) two or more local authorities may appoint a joint committee of those authorities; or

(c) any such committee may appoint one or more sub-committees.

(2) Subject to the provisions of this section, the number of members of a committee appointed under subsection (1) above, their term of office, and the area (if restricted) within which the committee are to exercise their authority shall be fixed by the appointing authority or authorities or, in the case of a sub-committee, by the appointing committee.

(3) A committee appointed under subsection (1) above, other than a committee for regulating and controlling the finance of the local authority or of their area, may, subject to section 104 below, include persons who are not members of the appointing authority or authorities or, in the case of a sub-committee, the authority or authorities of whom they are a sub-committee, but at least two-thirds of the members appointed to any such committee (other than a sub-committee) shall be members of that authority or those authorities, as the case may be.

(4) A local authority may appoint a committee, and two or more local authorities may join in appointing a committee, to advise the appointing authority or authorities on any matter relating to the discharge of their functions, and any such committee—

(a) may consist of such persons (whether members of the appointing authority or authorities or not) appointed for such term as may be determined by the appointing authority or authorities; and

(b) may appoint one or more sub-committees to advise the committee with respect to any such matter.

(5) Every member of a committee appointed under this section who at the time of his appointment was a member of the appointing authority or one of the appointing authorities shall upon ceasing to be a member of that authority also cease to be a member of the committee; but for the purposes of this section a member of a local authority shall not be deemed to have ceased to be a member of the authority by reason of retirement if he has been re-elected a member thereof not later than the day of his retirement.

103. The expenses incurred by a joint committee of two or more local authorities whether appointed or established under this Part of this Act or any other enactment shall be defrayed by those authorities in such proportions as they may agree or in case of disagreement as may be determined—

(a) in any case in which those authorities are the councils of parishes or communities or groups of parishes or communities situated in the same district by the district council; and

(b) in any other case, by a single arbitrator agreed on by the appointing authorities or, in default of agreement appointed by the Secretary of State.

182.—(1) For section 1 (1) and (2) of the Town and Country Planning Act 1971 (local planning authorities for England, elsewhere than Greater London and the Isles of Scilly, and for Wales) there shall be substituted the following subsections—

" (1) Subject to the provisions of this section, the council of a county is the county planning authority for the county and the council of a district is the district planning authority for the district.

(2) If it appears to the Secretary of State that it is expedient that a joint board should be established as the county planning authority for the areas or parts of the areas of any two or more county councils or as the district planning authority for the areas or parts of the areas of any two or more district councils, he may by order constitute those areas or parts as a united district for the purposes of this Act, and constitute a joint board (in this Act referred to as a "joint planning board") as the county planning authority or the district planning authority, as the case may be, for that united district:

Provided that the Secretary of State shall not make such an order except after holding a local inquiry unless all the councils concerned have consented to the making of the order.

(2A) References in this Act to a local planning authority shall, except as respects Greater London and the National Parks, be construed as references to a county planning authority and a district planning authority, and the foregoing provision shall have effect subject to section 183 of and Part I of Schedule 16 to the Local Government Act 1972."

(2) In England (exclusive of Greater London and the Isles of Scilly) and in Wales all functions conferred on local planning authorities by or under the Town and Country Planning Act 1971 shall, subject to subsection (4) and section 183 below and to Part I of Schedule 16 to this Act, be exercisable both by county planning authorities and by district planning authorities.

(3) In that Schedule—

(a) Part I shall have effect with respect to the exercise by such authorities of functions under that Act and for making minor amendments and modifications of that Act;

(b) Part II shall have effect with respect to the exercise by such authorities of functions under other enactments relating to town and country planning and for making minor amendments and modifications of such other enactments; and

(c) Part III shall have effect with respect to arrangements for obtaining advice in connection with certain of those functions.

(4) As respects an area in a National Park all functions conferred by or under the Town and Country Planning Act 1971 on a local planning authority or district planning authority shall, subject to the provisions of subsections (5) and (6) below, be functions of the county planning authority and no other authority, and references in that Act, in its application to a National Park, to a local planning authority or district planning authority shall be construed accordingly.

(5) The functions conferred on a local planning authority by the

following provisions of that Act, that is to say, sections 60, 61, 62 and 103 (tree preservation and replacement), and section 65 (waste land) shall, as respects any part of a National Park, be exercisable concurrently with the county planning authority by the district planning authority whose area includes that part of the Park.

(6) Where an order is made under section 7 of the National Parks and Access to the Countryside Act 1949 designating, or extending the area of, a National Park, the functions exercisable by a local planning authority immediately before the coming into force of the order for any area which under the order becomes part of the Park shall continue to be exercisable by that authority as respects that area unless and until a joint planning board is constituted under section 1 of the Town and Country Planning Act 1971 or a National Park Committee is appointed under Part I of Schedule 17 to this Act for an area co-terminous with or including that area or, as the case may be, is authorised to exercise those functions.

183.—(1) The functions of a local planning authority under sections 6 to 10 of the Town and Country Planning Act 1971 (surveys and structure plans) shall be exercisable by the county planning authority and references in those sections to a local planning authority shall be construed accordingly.

(2) Immediately before section 11 of that Act there shall be inserted the following section

" *Development plan schemes*

10C.—(1) The functions of a local planning authority of preparing local plans under section 11 of this Act shall, subject to the following provisions of this section, be exercisable by the district planning authority.

(2) Subject to regulations under this section, it shall be the duty of the county planning authority in consultation with the district planning authorities to make, and thereafter to keep under review and amend, if they think fit, a scheme (to be known as a development plan scheme) for the preparation of local plans for those areas in the county in which sections 11 to 15 of this Act are in force, except any part of the county included in a National Park, and—

(a) the scheme shall designate the local planning authority or authorities (whether county or district) by whom local plans are to be prepared for any such area and provide for the exercise of all functions of a local planning authority under those sections in relation to any such plan exclusively by the authority designated in relation to that plan; and

(b) references in those sections to a local planning authority shall be construed accordingly.

(3) A development plan scheme may include such incidental, consequential, transitional or supplementary provision as

may appear to the county planning authority to be necessary or proper for the purposes or in consequence of the provisions of the scheme and for giving full effect thereto, and, without prejudice to the foregoing provision, shall—

(a) specify the title and nature of each local plan for the area in question and the part or parts of the area to which it is to apply and give an indication of its scope;

(b) set out a programme for the preparation of the several local plans for that area; and

(c) where appropriate indicate the relationship between the several local plans for that area, specifying those which should be prepared concurrently with the structure plan for that area.

(4) As soon as practicable after making or amending a development plan scheme the county planning authority shall send a copy of the scheme or the scheme as amended, as the case may be, to the Secretary of State.

(5) A structure plan prepared by a county planning authority may provide, to the extent that provision to the contrary is not made by a development plan scheme, for the preparation of local plans exclusively by the county planning authority and, where it so provides, shall also provide for the exercise exclusively by that authority of all other functions of a local planning authority under sections 11 to 15 of this Act, and any provision included in a structure plan by virtue of this subsection shall be treated for the purposes of the other provisions of this section as if it were contained in a development plan scheme.

(6) The Secretary of State may direct a county planning authority after consultation with the district planning authorities—

(a) to prepare a development plan scheme before a date specified in the direction; and

(b) where it appears to the Secretary of State that any such scheme should be amended, to amend it in terms so specified before a date so specified.

(7) Where a district planning authority make representations to the Secretary of State that they are dissatisfied with the proposals of the county planning authority for a development plan scheme, or a county planning authority fail to comply with a direction under subsection (6) of this section to make or amend such a scheme, the Secretary of State may himself make or, as the case may be, amend the scheme; and any scheme or amendment so made shall have effect as if made by the county planning authority.

(8) The Secretary of State may make regulations—

(a) providing for the content of such schemes;

(b) requiring or authorising county planning authorities

to take prescribed procedural steps in connection with the preparation of such schemes."

(3) A county planning authority may exercise their power under section 10C of the Town and Country Planning Act 1971 of making a development plan scheme before 1st April 1974 and shall do so if so directed by the Secretary of State under subsection (6) of that section, and accordingly he may before that date exercise his power of giving directions under subsection (6), and of making regulations under subsection (8), of that section, but any scheme made before that date by virtue of this subsection shall not come into operation until that date.

SCHEDULE 16

FUNCTIONS UNDER, AND AMENDMENT AND MODIFICATION OF, ENACTMENTS RELATING TO TOWN AND COUNTRY PLANNING

PART I

TOWN AND COUNTRY PLANNING ACT 1971

Structure and local plans

1.—(1) For section 11 (1) and (2) there shall be substituted the following subsections—

" (1) Where a county planning authority are in course of preparing a structure plan for their area, or have prepared for their area a structure plan which has not been approved or rejected by the Secretary of State, the local planning authority to whom it falls to prepare a local plan for any part of that area may, if they think it desirable, prepare a local plan for all or any of that part of the area.

(2) Where a structure plan for the area of a county planning authority has been approved by the Secretary of State, the local planning authority to whom it falls to prepare a local plan for any part of that area shall as soon as practicable consider, and thereafter keep under review, the desirability of preparing and, if they consider it desirable and they have not already done so, shall prepare one or more local plans for all or any of that part of the area."

(2) In section 11 (3) (*a*), after the words " such detail as the " there shall be inserted the words " local planning."

(3) In section 11, after subsection (9) there shall be inserted the following subsection:—

" (9A) For the purpose of discharging their functions under this section a district planning authority may in so far as it appears to them necessary to do so having regard to the survey made by the county planning authority under section 6 of this Act, examine the matters mentioned in subsections (1) and (3) of that section so far as relevant to their area."

2.—(1) For section 12 (1) (*a*) there shall be substituted the following paragraph:—

" (*a*) that adequate publicity is given in the area in question to any relevant matter arising out of a survey carried out under section 6 or 11 of this Act and to the matters proposed to be included in the plan."

(2) In section 12, after subsection (1), there shall be inserted the following subsection:—

" (1A) A county or district planning authority to whom it falls to prepare a local plan for any part of their area shall—

(*a*) consult the district planning authority or the county planning authority, as the case may be, with respect to the contents of the plan;

(*b*) afford the latter authority a reasonable opportunity to express their views;

(*c*) take those views into consideration."

(3) For section 12 (2) there shall be substituted the following subsection:—

" (2) When a local planning authority have prepared a local plan and the Secretary of State has approved the structure plan so far as it applies to the area of that local plan and, in a case where the local planning authority are required to obtain a certificate under section 14 of this Act, they have obtained that certificate, they shall before adopting the local plan or submitting it for approval under that section make copies of it available for inspection at their office and at such other places as may be prescribed and send a copy to the Secretary of State and to the district or county planning authority, as the case may require; and each copy made available for inspection shall be accompanied by a statement of the time within which objections to the local plan may be made to the local planning authority."

3.—(1) In section 14 (2), after the word " conforms ", there shall be inserted the words " and, in the case of a local plan prepared by a district planning authority, a certificate is issued under subsection (5) or (7) of this section that it conforms ".

(2) In section 14, at the end there shall be added the following subsections:—

" (5) Where a district planning authority have prepared a local plan for any part of their area the structure plan for which has been approved by the Secretary of State, they shall request the county planning authority to certify that the local plan conforms generally to the structure plan and, subject to subsection (6) below, the county planning authority shall, within the period of one month from their receipt of the request or such longer period as may be agreed between them and the district planning authority, consider the matter and, if satisfied that the local plan does so conform, issue a certificate to that effect; and if it appears to the county planning authority that the local plan does not so conform in any respect, they shall, during or as soon as practicable after the end of that period, refer the question whether it so conforms in that respect to the Secretary of State to be determined by him.

(6) The Secretary of State may in any case by direction to a county planning authority reserve for his own determination the question whether a local plan conforms generally to a structure plan.

(7) Where on determining a question referred to or reserved for him under subsection (5) or (6) of this section the Secretary of State is of opinion that a local plan conforms generally to the relevant structure plan in the relevant respect or, as the case may be, all respects he may issue, or direct the county planning authority to issue, a certificate to that effect, and where he is of the contrary opinion, he may direct the district planning authority to revise the local plan in such respects as he thinks appropriate so as to secure that it will so conform and thereupon those subsections and the preceding provisions of this subsection shall apply to the revised plan. "

4. In section 17 (1) (*a*), after the words " that the " there shall be inserted the word " relevant ".

5. In section 18 (1) (*d*) after the words " notified the " there shall be inserted the word " relevant. "

6. In Part I of Schedule 5 in its application outside Greater London for references to the local planning authority there shall be substituted references to the county planning authority.

7. The local planning authority who are to be treated by paragraph 4 of Schedule 7 as having adopted any street authorisation map mentioned in that paragraph shall be the county planning authority.

Joint plans

8.—(1) The following provisions of this paragraph shall have effect where two or more county planning authorities prepare a structure plan jointly.

(2) The county planning authorities shall take such steps as will in their opinion secure—

(*a*) that persons who may be expected to desire an opportunity of making representations to any of the authorities are made aware that they are entitled to an opportunity of doing so;

(*b*) that such persons are given an adequate opportunity of making such representations.

(3) Section 8 (1) (*b*) and (*c*) shall not apply in relation to a joint structure plan and references in section 8 to subsection (1) of that section and the purposes of paragraphs (*a*) to (*c*) thereof shall include references respectively to sub-paragraph (2) above and the purposes of paragraphs (*a*) and (*b*) thereof.

(4) Each of the county planning authorities by whom a joint structure plan has been prepared shall have the duty imposed by section 8 (2) of making copies of the plan available for inspection.

9.—(1) Where a structure plan has been prepared jointly, the power of making proposals under section 10 (1) for the alteration, repeal or replacement of the plan may be exercised as respects their respective areas by any of the authorities by whom it was prepared and the Secretary of State may under that section direct any of them to submit such proposals as respects their respective areas.

(2) In relation to the joint submission of such proposals, the reference in section 10 (2) to section 8 shall include a reference to paragraph 8 above.

10.—(1) The following provisions of this paragraph shall have effect where two or more local planning authorities prepare a local plan jointly.

(2) The local planning authorities shall take such steps as will in their opinion secure—

(a) that persons who may be expected to desire an opportunity of making representations to any of the authorities are made aware that they are entitled to an opportunity of doing so; and

(b) that such persons are given an adequate opportunity of making such representations.

(3) Section 12 (1) (b) and (c) shall not apply in relation to joint local plans and references in section 12 to subsection (1) of that section and the purposes of paragraphs (a) to (c) thereof shall include references respectively to sub-paragraph (2) above and the purposes of paragraphs (a) and (b) thereof.

(4) Each of the local planning authorities by whom a joint local plan has been prepared shall have the duty imposed by section 12 (2) of making copies of the plan available for inspection, and objections to the plan may be made to any of those authorities and the statement required by section 12 (2) to accompany copies of the plan made available for inspection shall state that objections may be so made.

11.—(1) It shall fall to each of the local planning authorities by whom a joint local plan was prepared to adopt the plan under section 14 (1) and they may do so as respects any part of their area to which the plan relates, but any modifications subject to which it is adopted must be agreed between all those authorities.

(2) Where a structure plan has been jointly prepared by two or more county planning authorities or a local plan has been jointly prepared by two or more district planning authorities, a request for a certificate under section 14 (5) that the local plan conforms generally to the structure plan shall be made by each district planning authority to the county planning authority for the area comprising the district planning authority's area and it shall fall to that county planning authority to deal with the request.

12.—(1) Where a local plan has been prepared jointly, the power of submitting proposals under section 15 (1) for the alteration, repeal or replacement of the plan may be exercised as respects their respective areas by any of the authorities by whom it was prepared and the Secretary of State may under that subsection direct any of them to submit such proposals as respects their respective areas.

(2) In relation to the joint submission of such proposals the reference in section 15 (3) (as it has effect outside Greater London) to section 12 shall include a reference to paragraph 10 above.

13. The date appointed under section 18 (4) for the coming into operation of a local plan prepared jointly by two or more local planning authorities or for the alteration, repeal or replacement of a local plan in pursuance of proposals so prepared shall be one jointly agreed by those authorities and be specified in their respective resolutions adopting the plan.

14.—(1) Paragraph 10 (3) and (4) above shall not, and the following provisions of this paragraph shall, apply in Greater London.

(2) Notwithstanding anything in paragraph 8 (3) of Schedule 4, the Greater London Council may prepare a local plan for the whole or part of a G.L.C. action area (within the meaning of that paragraph) jointly with a London borough council or the Common Council.

(3) Sub-paragraph (1) (b) and (c) of paragraph 12 of that Schedule shall not apply in relation to joint local plans and the reference in sub-paragraph (3) of that paragraph to sub-paragraph (1) of that paragraph, and the reference in paragraph 14 (2) to sub-paragraph (1) (a) to (c) of the said paragraph 12, shall both include a reference to paragraph 10 (2) above.

(4) Where the Greater London Council is one of the local planning authorities by whom a joint local plan has been prepared, that Council shall not be required to take any steps under the said sub-paragraph (2) which can in their opinion be taken, and are taken, by any other local planning authority whose area comprises any part of the area to which the plan relates.

(5) Each of the local planning authorities by whom a joint local plan has been prepared for any part of Greater London shall have the duty imposed by sub-paragraph (2) of the said paragraph 12 of making copies of the plan available for inspection, and objections to the plan may be made to any of those authorities and the statement required by sub-paragraph (3) of that paragraph to accompany copies of the plan made available for inspection shall state that objections may be so made.

(6) In relation to the joint submission of proposals under section 15 (1) for the alteration, repeal or replacement of a local plan the reference in section 15 (3) (as it has effect in Greater London) to the said paragraph 12 shall include a reference to paragraph 10 above and the foregoing provisions of this paragraph.

Planning and special control

15.—(1) The functions of a local planning authority of determining—

(*a*) applications for planning permission under Part III;

(*b*) applications for determining under section 53 whether an application for such permission is required;

(*c*) applications for an established use certificate under section 94;

shall, subject to sub-paragraph (2) below be exercised by the district planning authority.

(2) The functions of a local planning authority of determining any such application as aforesaid which appears to the district planning authority to relate to a county matter shall be exercised by the county planning authority unless the application relates to a county matter mentioned in paragraph 32 (*d*) below and the district planning authority propose—

(*a*) to refuse planning permission;

(*b*) to determine that an application for planning permission is required; or

(*c*) to refuse an application for an established use certificate as respects the whole of the land to which the application relates.

(3) Every application mentioned in sub-paragraph (1) above shall be made to the district planning authority, and in the case of an application for planning permission that authority shall send a copy of the application as soon as may be after they have received it to the county planning authority and also to the local highway authority, if not a local planning authority, except in any case or class of case with respect to which the county planning authority or the local highway authority, as the case may be, otherwise direct.

(4) The foregoing provisions of this paragraph shall not apply to applications relating to land in a National Park, but paragraph 16 below shall apply to such applications instead.

16.—(1) Each of the following applications under the Town and Country Planning Act 1971, that is to say—

(*a*) applications for planning permission;

(*b*) applications for determining under section 53 whether an application for such permission is required;

(*c*) applications for listed building consent under section 55;

(*d*) applications for consent to the display of advertisements under section 63; and

(*e*) applications for an established use certificate under section 94;

shall, if relating to land in a National Park, be made to the district planning authority who shall, unless it falls to be determined by them, send it on to the county planning authority and, in the case of an application for planning permission, shall send a copy to the local highway authority, except where the local highway authority are a local planning authority and except in any case or class of case with respect to which the local highway authority otherwise direct.

(2) Where any such application relating to land in a National Park or an application so relating for approval of a matter reserved under an outline planning permission within the meaning of section 42 falls to be determined by a county planning authority, that authority shall before determining it consult with the district planning authority for the area in which the land to which the application relates is situated.

17. The Secretary of State shall include in a development order under section 24 provision enabling a local highway authority to impose restrictions on the grant by the local planning authority of planning permission for the following descriptions of development relating to land in the area of the local highway authority, that is to say—

(a) the formation, laying out or alteration of any means of access to a road classified under section 27 of the Local Government Act 1966 or to a proposed road the route of which has been adopted by resolution of the local highway authority and notified as such to the local planning authority;

(b) any other operations or use of land which appear to the local highway authority to be likely to result in a material increase in the volume of traffic entering or leaving such a classified or proposed road, to prejudice the improvement or construction of such a road or to result in a material change in the character of traffic entering, leaving or using such a road.

18. The provisions which may be contained in any such order shall include provision—

(a) requiring a county planning authority who are determining any application mentioned in paragraph 15 above and relating to a county matter, or an application for approval of a matter reserved under an outline planning permission within the meaning of section 42 and so relating, to afford the district planning authority for the area in which the land to which the application relates is situated an opportunity to make recommendations to the county planning authority as to the manner in which the application shall be determined, and to take into account any such recommendations;

(b) requiring a county or district planning authority who have received any application so mentioned or any application for such approval (including any such application relating to land in a National Park) to notify the district or county planning authority, as the case may be, of the terms of their decision, or, where the application is referred to the Secretary of State, the date when it was so referred and, when notified to them, the terms of his decision.

19. Except in the case of any description of operations or use of land specified in an order made by the Secretary of State, the county planning authority for any area may give directions to the district planning authority for any part of that area as to how the district planning authority are to determine any application under the Town and Country Planning Act 1971 in any case where it appears to the county planning authority that any proposals in the application would substantially and adversely affect their interests as local planning authority.

20.—(1) Where a district planning authority have been notified in writing by the council of a parish or community wholly or partly situated in the area of that authority that the council wish to be informed of every application for planning permission relating to land in the parish or community or of every application so relating for approval of a matter reserved under an outline planning permission within the meaning of section 42, or of any description of such applications, and receive any such application or, as the case may be, an application of any such description, they shall inform the council in writing of the application, indicating the nature of the development to which the application relates and identifying the land to which it relates.

(2) The provisions which may be contained in a development order under section 24 shall include provision requiring—

(a) a local planning authority, who are determining any application of which the council of a parish or community are entitled to be informed, to afford that council an opportunity to make representations to the local planning authority as to the manner in which the application should be determined and to take into account any such representations;

(b) the district planning authority to notify that council of the terms of their or the county planning authority's decision on any such application or, where the application is referred to the Secretary of State, the date when it was so referred and, when notified to them, the terms of his decision.

21.—(1) In section 28 (2) (publicity for applications affecting conservation areas), for the words " The local planning authority " there shall be substituted the words " In Greater London the local planning authority, in a National Park the county planning authority and elswhere the district planning authority. "

(2) Where it is the duty of the district planning authority to take the steps required by section 28 (2) in relation to an application which falls to be determined by the county planning authority, the district planning authority shall as soon as may be after taking those steps notify the county planning authority of the steps which they have taken and the date on which they took them.

22. In section 3 (1) (directions as to method of dealing with

applications for planning permission), for paragraph (c) there shall
be substituted the following paragraph—

> " (c) for requiring that, before planning permission for any
> development is granted or refused, local planning authorities
> prescribed by the order or by directions given by the Secre-
> tary of State thereunder shall consult with such authorities
> or persons as may be so prescribed. "

23. Elsewhere than in a National Park the functions of a local
planning authority under section 44 (completion notices) shall be
exercisable by the district planning authority, except that where
the relevant planning permission was granted by the county planning
authority, those functions, so far as relating to that permission, shall
be exercisable by the county planning authority and also by the
district planning authority after consulting the county planning
authority.

24.—(1) The functions of a local planning authority of—

> (a) making orders under section 45 revoking or modifying
> planning permission, or under section 51 requiring
> discontinuance of use, or imposing conditions on
> continuance of use, or requiring the alteration or removal
> of buildings or works, or
>
> (b) serving enforcement notices under section 87 or stop
> notices under section 90,

shall, subject to sub-paragraph (2) below, be exercisable by the
district planning authority.

(2) In a case where it appears to the district planning authority
that the functions mentioned in sub-paragraph (1) above relate to
county matters they shall not exercise those functions without first
consulting the county planning authority.

(3) Those functions shall also be exercisable by a county planning authority in a case where it appears to that authority that they
relate to a matter which should properly be considered a county
matter.

25.—(1) Subject to sub-paragraph (2) below, the functions of a
local planning authority under sections 34 (registers of applications
and decisions), sections 55, 56, 96, 99 and Schedule 11 (listed buildings) and sections 63 and 109 (control of advertisements) shall be
exercised by the district planning authority.

(2) The power of defining areas of special control for the purposes
of regulations under section 63 by orders approved by the Secretary
of State under section 63 (4) shall be exercisable both by county
planning authorities and by district planning authorities.

26.—(1) Sections 48 and 49 (planning inquiry commissions) shall
be amended in accordance with sub-paragraphs (2) and (3) below.

(2) The copy of the notice required to be served by section 49 (2)
on a local planning authority shall, in the case of a proposal that
a government department should give a direction under section 40
or that development should be carried out by or on behalf of a

government department, be served on the local planning authority who in the opinion of the Secretary of State, would have been, responsible for dealing with an application for planning permission for the development in question if such an application had fallen to be made.

(3) References in sections 48 (6) (b) and 49 (3) to the local planning authority shall be construed as references to the local planning authority on whom the said copy is required to be served.

27. Where a county planning authority or district planning authority have made a tree preservation order under section 60 or the Secretary of State has made such an order by virtue of section 276 (default powers), the power of varying and revoking the order and the powers of dispensing with section 62, or serving, or appearing on an appeal relating to, a notice under section 103 (enforcement of duties as to replacement of trees) shall be exercisable only by the authority who made the order or, in the case of an order made by the Secretary of State, the authority named in the order.

28.—(1) In section 54 (4) (lists of buildings of special architectural or historic interest), for all the words after " deposited with " there shall be substituted the words " the proper officer of the borough or district council and, outside Greater London, with the proper officer of the county planning authority whose area or any part of whose area includes the district, or any part of it, and where the district council are not the district planning authority, the proper officer of that authority ".

(2) In section 54 (11) for the words after " consult with " there shall be substituted the words—

" (a) in Greater London, the local planning authority;

(b) in a National Park, the county planning authority;

(c) elsewhere the district planning authority; and

(d) in any case the owner and the occupier of the building."

29. In sections 91 (1) and 93 (4) (b) (enforcement notices) and section 108 (2) (enforcement of orders under s. 51 requiring discontinuance of use, etc.) any reference to the local planning authority shall be construed as a reference to the authority who served the notice or made the order in question or, in the case of a notice served or an order made by the Secretary of State, the authority named in the notice or order.

30. The local planning authority who may appeal to the Crown Court under section 106 (further appeals in connection with notice as to waste land) shall be the authority who served the notice in question under section 65 or, if the notice was served by the Secretary of State, the authority named in the notice.

31. The powers of local authorities under sections 114, 115 and 126 (compulsory acquisition and management of listed buildings) and 119 (acquisition of land by agreement) shall be exercisable by joint planning boards as well as by the local authorities mentioned in those sections.

32. In the foregoing provisions of this Schedule " county matter " means in relation to any application, order or notice—

(a) the winning and working of minerals in, on or under land (whether by surface or underground working) or the erection of any building, plant or machinery—

    (i) which it is proposed to use in connection with the winning and working of minerals or with their treatment or disposal in or on land adjoining the site of the working; or

    (ii) which a person engaged in mining operations proposes to use in connection with the grading, washing, grinding or crushing of minerals;

(b) the carrying out of searches and tests of mineral deposits or the erection of any building, plant or machinery which it is proposed to use in connection therewith;

(c) the disposal of mineral waste;

(d) the carrying out of operations or a use of land which, in either case—

    (i) would conflict with, or prejudice the implementation of, fundamental provisions of the structure plan for the area in question or fundamental proposals for such a plan or for alterations to such a plan to which publicity has been given in pursuance of section 8;

    (ii) would conflict with, or prejudice the implementation of, fundamental provisions of a development plan approved under Part I of Schedule 5, or any enactments replaced by that Part, so far as in force in the area in question or with proposals submitted to the Secretary of State for alterations or additions to such a plan;

    (iii) would be inconsistent in any respect with the provisions of a local plan for the area in question prepared by the county planning authority or proposals for such a plan or for alterations to such a plan to which publicity has been given in pursuance of section 12; or

    (iv) would be inconsistent in any respect with any statement of planning policy adopted by the county planning authority or with any proposals of theirs for development which in either case have been notified by them to the district planning authority;

(e) the carrying out of operations in, on, over or under land, or any use of land, which is situated partly in and partly outside a National Park;

(f) the carrying out of any operation which is, as respects the area in question, a prescribed operation or an operation of a prescribed class or any use which is, as respects that area, a prescribed use or use of a prescribed class.

33. In section 134 (4) (interpretation of Part VII), for the words after " interest therein " there shall be substituted the words " and ' local planning authority,' in relation to a planning decison, means the authority who made the decision."

Compensation

34.—(1) Claims for payment of compensation under the following provisions, that is to say, section 164 (compensation where planning permission is revoked or modified), including that section as applied by section 165, and sections 169, 170, 171, 172, 173, 176 and 177 (compensation in connection with other restrictions) shall, subject to sub-paragraph (3) below, be made to and paid by the local planning authority who took the action by virtue of which the claim arose or, where that action was taken by the Secretary of State, the local planning authority from whom the appeal was made to him or who referred the matter to him, or, in the case of an order made or notice served by him by virtue of section 276 (default powers) the appropriate authority, and references in those sections to a local planning authority shall be construed accordingly.

(2) In this paragraph " appropriate authority " means—

 (a) in the case of a claim for compensation under section 164, 165 or 172, the local planning authority who granted, or are to be treated for the purposes of section 164 as having granted, the planning permission or listed building consent the revocation or modification of which gave rise to the claim;

 (b) in the case of a claim for compensation under section 173 or 176, the district planning authority;

 (c) in the case of a claim for compensation under section 170 or 177, the local planning authority named in the relevant order or stop notice of the Secretary of State.

(3) The Secretary of State may after consultation with all the authorities concerned direct that where a local planning authority is liable to pay compensation under any of the provisions mentioned in sub-paragraph (1) above in any particular case or class of case they shall be entitled to be reimbursed the whole of the compensation or such proportion of it as he may direct from one or more authorities specified in the direction.

35. Claims for payment of compensation under a tree preservation order by virtue of section 174, and claims for payment of compensation under section 175 by virtue of directions given in pursuance of such an order, shall be made to and paid by the local planning authority who made the order or, in the case of an order made by the Secretary of State, the authority named in the order.

36. The local planning authority by whom compensation is to be paid under section 237 (1) (a) to statutory undertakers shall be the authority who referred the application for planning permission to

the Secretary of State and the appropriate Minister, or from whose decision the appeal was made to them or who served the enforcement notice appealed against, as the case may be.

Purchase notices

37. The duty of the Secretary of State to give a notice under section 182 (2) (c) (procedure on purchase notices) to the local planning authority shall be a duty to give it—
  (a) to the county planning authority and also, where that authority is a joint planning board, to the county council; and
  (b) to the district council on whom the purchase notice in question was served and also, where that council is a constituent member of a joint planning board, to that board.
38. The local planning authority by whom compensation is to be paid and on whom a claim for compensation is to be served under section 187 (2) (compensation where purchase notice served) shall be the district planning authority.

Stopping up and diversion of highways

39. In section 209 (stopping up and diversion of highways), in subsection (2) (b), for the words from " any local " to " order " there shall be substituted the words " any county council or London borough council specified in the order or, if it is so specified, the Greater London Council or the Common Council of the City of London."
40. The following subsection shall be substituted for section 210 (4) (stopping up and diversion of footpaths and bridleways):—
  " (4) In this section ' competent authority ' means, in the case of development authorised by a planning permission, the local planning authority who granted the permission or, in the case of a permission granted by the Secretary of State, who would have had power to grant it and in the case of development carried out by a government department, the local planning authority who would have had power to grant planning permission on an application in respect of the development in question if such an application had fallen to be made. "

Conversion of highway into footpath or bridleway

41.—(1) Section 212 (changing highways for vehicles into footpaths or bridleways) shall be amended in accordance with the following provisions of this paragraph.
  (2) In subsection (2) for the words from " made " to " different) " there shall be substituted the words " by a local planning authority who have so resolved made after consultation with the highway

authority (if different) and any other authority who are a local
planning authority for the area in question."

(3) In subsection (3) after " consultation with " there shall be inserted the words " every authority who are a local planning authority
for the area in question and ".

(4) In subsections (5) and (6) after the words " local planning
authority " there shall be inserted the words " on whose application
the order was made ".

(5) In subsection (8) for the words from " made " to " different) "
there shall be substituted the words " by any authority who are a
local planning authority for the area in question made after consultation with the highway authority (if different) and any other authority
who are a local planning authority for that area ".

42. In section 213 (5) (requirement for competent authority to
obtain consent from certain other authorities before carrying out and
maintaining amenity works on highways reserved to pedestrians) for
the words from " have " to the end of the subsection there shall be
substituted the words " consulted the highway authority (if different)
and any authority (other than themselves) who are a local planning
authority for the area in question ".

Miscellaneous

43. In section 1 (local planning authorities)—
   (*a*) in subsection (4) (*b*) for the words " county borough ",
      in both places where they occur, there shall be substituted
      the word " district " and for the words " that district "
      there shall be substituted the words " the united district ",
      and
   (*b*) in subsection (6) for the words from " section 8 " onwards
      there shall be substituted the words " Part I of Schedule
      17 to the Local Government Act 1972 ".

44. Section 3 (delegation of functions to district councils) shall
cease to have effect.

45. In section 192 (1) (scope of blight provisions), the reference
in paragraph (*f*) to the local planning authority shall be construed,
in relation to land in a National Park, as a reference to the county
planning authority and, in relation to land elsewhere, as a reference
to the district planning authority.

46. In section 245 (7) (proceedings for questioning the validity of
certain orders, etc.) for the words from " and any reference " onwards
there shall be substituted the words " and any reference to the
authority directly concerned with any order or action to which this
section applies—
   (*a*) in relation to any such decision as is mentioned in section
      242 (3) (*i*) or (*j*) of this Act, is a reference to the council on
      whom the notice in question was served and, in a case where

the Secretary of State has modified such a notice wholly or in part by substituting another local authority or statutory undertakers for that council, includes a reference to that local authority or statutory undertakers;

(b) in any other case in Greater London, is a reference to the local planning authority; and

(c) in any other case outside Greater London, is a reference to the local planning authority who made the order in question or made the decision or served the notice to which the proceedings in question relate, or who referred the matter to the Secretary of State, or, where the order or notice in question was made or served by him, the authority named in the order or notice."

47.—(1) The local planning authority to whom the Secretary of State may give directions under section 276 (1) (default powers) and whom he is required to consult under that subsection or serve with a notice of his proposals under section 276 (4) shall be the county planning authority or the district planning authority, as he thinks appropriate, and references in those subsections to the local planning authority shall be construed accordingly.

(2) In section 276 (5) any reference to the local planning authority shall be construed—

(a) in relation to a listed building enforcement notice, as a reference to the district planning authority; and

(b) in any other case, as a reference to the county planning authority or the district planning authority, as the Secretary of State thinks appropriate.

48. The duty imposed by section 277 on local planning authorities of determining which areas shall be conservation areas and of designating them shall be the duty of district planning authorities but county planning authorities, shall have the power to make determinations under that section and to designate such areas, and—

(a) references in that section to a local planning authority shall be construed accordingly; and

(b) in subsection (3) of that section for the words from " and a local " to the end there shall be substituted the words " a district planning authority outside Greater London shall consult with the council or councils of the county or counties in which the area of the authority is comprised and a county planning authority shall before making any such determination consult with the council or councils of the district or districts of which any part is included in the area to which the proposed determination relates."

49. In Schedule 1, for the words " Schedule 2 to this Act " there shall be substituted the words " sections 102 and 103 of the Local Government Act 1972 ".

50. In paragraph 7 of Schedule 4, as set out in Schedule 1 to the Town and Country Planning (Amendment) Act 1972, for the words

" 11 and 12 " there shall be substituted the words " 10C, 11, 12 and 14 (5) to (7) ".

51.—(1) The validity of any permission, determination or certificate granted, made or issued or purporting to have been granted, made or issued by a local planning authority in respect of an application mentioned in paragraph 15 or 16 above shall not be called in question in any legal proceedings, or in any proceedings under the Town and Country Planning Act 1971 which are not legal proceedings, on the ground that the permission, determination or certificate should have been granted, made or given by some other local planning authority.

(2) The validity of any order or notice mentioned in paragraph 24 above and purporting to have been made or served by a local planning authority shall not be called in question in any such proceedings on the ground—

(a) in the case of an order or notice purporting to have been made or served by a district planning authority, that they failed to comply with paragraph 24 (2) above;

(b) in the case of an order or notice purporting to have been made or served by a county planning authority, that they had no power to make or serve it because it did not relate to a county matter.

52. The foregoing provisions of this Schedule, except paragraphs 10 to 14, 21, 22, 28, 33, 39, 40, 43, 46, 50 and 51, shall not apply to Greater London.

53. In this Part of this Schedule a reference made to any enactment without specifying the Act in which it is contained shall be construed as a reference to a provision of the Town and Country Planning Act 1971.

INDEX

Acquisition of land,
  agreement by, 254
  exchange, for, 254
  general vesting declaration, by, 252
  local authorities, by, 254
Action areas, 40–43
  certificate of development, 262–263
  Greater London, 66, 67
  local plans, 52, 55
  planning assumptions, 261
Advertisements,
  advice, 142
  appeals, 139, 140
  applications for consent, 138
  areas of special control, 135–136
  building,
    forming part of fabric, of, 134
    within, 134, 141
  business premises, 137
  compensation, 140–141, 224, 234–235
  consent to display,
    challenge procedure, 139, 140
    deemed, 136–138
    express, 136, 138–139
    permission of owner of land required, 140
    revocation or modification, 139
  control of, 133–142, 205–206
  decisions relating to, 141–142
  defined, 78–79, 134
  discontinuance notice, 137–138
  display constituting development, 70, 72, 78
  elections, 137
  enclosed land, on, 134
  enforcement of control, 205–206
  existing, 140
  fairs, 141
  fine, 133, 140
  flags, 137
  fly-posting, 140
  forecourt, 134, 137
  functional, 136
  Independent Tribunal,
    appeal to, 140
  inquiries, 208
  local planning authorities, displayed by, 137, 141
  London, application for consent, 138
  permission of owner of land required, 140
  planning permission deemed to be granted, 72
  purchase notice, 241

Advertisements—*cont.*
  register of applications for express consent, 139
  Regulations, 133
    contravention, 133, 140
  Secretary of State,
    appeal to, 139
  temporary, 136
  traffic signs, 137
  travelling circuses, 141
  vehicle, on or inside, 134
Agreements,
  development restricting or regulating, 130
Agricultural buildings,
  permitted development, 91–92
Agricultural land,
  caravan site, 151
  defined, 92
Agricultural purposes,
  planning permission for, 104
Agricultural tenants,
  planning application, notification, 98–99
Agricultural unit,
  defined, 92
  planning blight, 245–246, 248
Agriculture,
  defined, 82
  use of land, not development, 70, 81
Ancient monuments, 182
  compulsory purchase, 184
Apparatus,
  rights extinguished, 253, 266
Appeals,
  advertisements, 139
  buildings of special architectural or historic interest, 182, 185
  bulletins of selected, 121
  caravan site licence conditions, 149
  certificate of development, 262
  development, determination of what constitutes, 86
  enforcement notices, against, 167, 190, 192–195
  established use certificate, 200
  Independent Tribunal, to, 121, 140
  inquiries, procedure, 207–220
  Inspector, determined by, 121–126
  offices, enforcement notice, 167
  planning decision against, 119–126
  planning permission, 233
    application, 103
    time limits, 109, 110